HOW THE PEACE WAS LOST

John Van Antwerp MacMurray

HOW THE PEACE WAS LOST

The 1935 Memorandum

Developments Affecting American Policy in the Far East

Prepared for the State Department by
John Van Antwerp MacMurray

Edited, and with Introduction and Notes by
ARTHUR WALDRON

HOOVER INSTITUTION PRESS
Stanford University • Stanford, California

Hoover Press Publication 407

First printing, 1992

98   97   96   95   94   93   92   9   8   7   6   5   4   3   2   1

Simultaneous first paperback printing, 1992

98   97   96   95   94   93   92   9   8   7   6   5   4   3   2   1

Manufactured in the United States of America
Printed on acid-free paper

Library of Congress Cataloging in Publication Data

MacMurray, John Van Antwerp, 1881–1960.
    How the peace was lost : the 1935 memorandum, Developments
affecting American policy in the Far East / prepared for the State
Department by John Van Antwerp MacMurray ; edited, and with
introduction and notes by Arthur Waldron.
          p.   cm. — (Hoover archival documentaries)
    Includes bibliographical references and index.
    ISBN 0-8179-9151-4
    ISBN 0-8179-9152-2 (paper)
    1. East Asia—Foreign relations—United States.   2. United
States—Foreign relations—East Asia.   I. Waldron, Arthur.
II. Title.   III. Title: Developments affecting American policy in the
Far East.   IV. Series.
DS518.M2   1992
327.7305—dc20

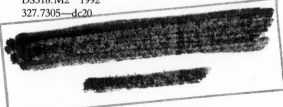

91-25737
CIP

For
Fritz Mote

Contents

Preface

PREPARING A CONSPECTUS OF THE EVENTS IN CHINA AND THE WORLD THAT
had brought Asia from the seeming new peace established by the Washington Conference to the brink of full-scale war a decade later was no easy task
when John Van Antwerp MacMurray undertook it in 1935 in the memorandum published here. Presenting the memorandum to today's audience is in
its own way comparably challenging. MacMurray's text is distinguished
both by its concision and by the acuity of its analysis. The original author
could assume that the colleagues in the Department of State for whom the
memorandum was written would be intimately familiar with the many
complex diplomatic and legal issues to which it alludes. More than fifty
years later, the same assumption cannot be made. No reader today will
share that factual background. Modern scholarship on the period, furthermore, will be of little use in providing it. Many events that MacMurray
considers crucial are scarcely mentioned by current writers. Furthermore,
concepts that today frame discussion—"nationalism" and "revolution" in
particular—were fifty years ago only beginning to be current, and are
scarcely used by MacMurray. Their arrival gradually displaced the style of
analysis that came naturally to MacMurray and his colleagues, which was
broadly realist, and layed stress on power balances and treaty law. An editor
today must attempt not only to supply explanations for now-obscure
allusions, but also to provide a sense of the larger intellectual and political
context in which the memorandum was initially produced and read.

No editor can hope to perform these tasks completely. Here I have sought to allow the memorandum to speak for itself. The Introduction presents the author, describes how he wrote the memorandum and how it was first received, and evaluates it critically in the light of modern scholarship. The notes give basic information and further references about the many persons and historical incidents to which MacMurray refers. A selective chronology and bibliography are also provided. In every case the purpose is simply to illuminate the memorandum and its arguments; to deal comprehensively with the period it treats would require writing a shelf of books.

I owe many debts of gratitude to those who have helped with this project. The memorandum was originally brought to my attention by colleagues during my time as assistant professor at Princeton, and I should thank Richard Challener, Frederick Mote, Denis Twitchett, and Marius Jansen in particular for their interest and suggestions. During his two-year visit to Princeton, Professor Shin'ichi Kitaoka, of Rikkyo University, took special interest in the project. Professor Noel Pugach, of the University of New Mexico, read and criticized an earlier manuscript, as did Zhitian Luo of Sichuan University, and Nicholas Cull of the University of Leeds. Robert Hessen, general editor of the Hoover Archival Documentaries, Ramon Myers, curator of the East Asian Collection and a senior fellow at the Hoover Intitution, and E. Ann Wood of the Hoover Institution Press made many helpful suggestions. Others to whom I owe thanks include Dorothy Borg, Nicholas Clifford, Waldo Heinrichs, Michael Hunt, Gary Hess, Akira Iriye, Charles R. Lilley, Marlene Mayo, James Megginson, Thomas Metzger, Richard Neu, and E. Adger Williams. I would also like to thank the staffs of the various libraries and archives where I have worked, in particular those of the Hoover Institution at Stanford University, the Houghton Library at Harvard University, the East Asian Library at Columbia University, the Firestone, Gest, and Seeley Mudd Libraries at Princeton University, the Franklin D. Roosevelt Library in Hyde Park, N.Y., the U.S. Naval War College Library in Newport, R.I., and the National Archives in Washington. Special thanks are owed to George Kennan for numerous helpful comments and to members of the MacMurray family for their continuing interest in the project. This research was supported by a grant from the Henry Luce Foundation.

ARTHUR WALDRON
Lawrenceville, N.J.
February 1991

Introduction
The Making of the Memorandum

JOHN VAN ANTWERP MACMURRAY COMPOSED THE MEMORANDUM PUBLISHED here in the autumn of 1935, amid great tension in Asia and uncertainty about American policy. The framework for peace in the Pacific established by the Washington treaties of 1922 had been shattered by Japan's military conquest of Manchuria in 1931, and her brief seizure of Shanghai early in the following year. Although no broader conflict had yet begun, Japan's action seemed such a clear violation of international law that many feared it would lead, sooner or later, to a general war between China and Japan, into which other Powers, including the United States, might well be drawn. How Washington should respond to these ominous developments—what was then called the Far Eastern Crisis—was a matter of heated debate, both inside and outside government. Some argued that the United States should move to contain Japan, a course that threatened conflict, while others saw accommodation as the wisest course. MacMurray was a senior career diplomat who had spent twenty years dealing with Asia, most recently as U.S. minister to China from 1925 to 1929, as well as an expert on international law who had been a key member of the U.S. delegation at the Washington Conference. He was, in short, the sort of man to whom others turned both for technical expertise and diplomatic wisdom. It made sense, then, in the summer of 1935, for Stanley Hornbeck, Assistant Secretary of State for Far Eastern Affairs, to commission him to write an overview of the situation in Asia. This became the document presented here, intended originally for the highest officers of government, for whom it would provide an authoritative survey of the origins of the crisis and recommendations about response by the United States.

As it turned out, MacMurray's analysis profoundly challenged much conventional wisdom of the time. Most people in the United States then believed that Japan was the villain of the drama that was plunging Asia into war, but MacMurray disagreed. He contended that Japan's newly assertive policies of the 1930s, far from being examples of unprovoked aggression or of the effects of the virus of militarism, were in fact direct consequences of the actions of other countries, including the United States, in the preceding period. He maintained that the Washington Conference had established a potentially workable framework for cooperation in Asia, but that during the 1920s, while Japan adhered strictly to the letter and spirit of the treaties, other parties to the agreements, notably China and the United States, had repeatedly undermined or refused to enforce their provisions. Thus, abetted by the United States, China had systematically flouted the legal framework that alone guaranteed her international position, and by so doing invited Japan's wrath. MacMurray argued that Japanese adherence to the Washington treaties had been difficult to obtain, and should therefore have been valued. When it was not, and Japan saw its interests threatened by the breakdown of the entire international system in which it had willingly participated, Tokyo began to rely on its "own strong arm to vindicate its rightful position in eastern Asia." By the mid-1930s MacMurray believed the situation had become grave, and predicted that if the United States continued to refuse to acknowledge Japanese grievances and instead tilt to China, the result almost certainly would be "war with Japan." Many of his diplomatic colleagues disagreed. When that war came six years later, MacMurray appeared prescient (see memorandum, pp. 66, 68).

In 1935 MacMurray's analysis displeased the man who had commissioned it, Stanley Hornbeck (1883–1966), who believed the United States could support China diplomatically without in fact risking war with Japan. When the memorandum was first submitted, he seems to have shown it to no one, and instead simply filed it away. Nevertheless, it became known, was ever more widely read, and eventually recognized as a classic.

Its success has several sources, which reflect the changing concerns of U.S. policy over the decades since it was completed. The diplomats who read it in the 1930s were impressed primarily by the powerful analytical light it cast on the origins of the Pacific war, a product of MacMurray's intimate familiarity with Asia and in particular with the complex international legal disputes among Japan, China, and the Powers. Readers in government in the early cold war period of the 1950s, by contrast, were struck by what MacMurray had to say about the future role of the Soviet

Union in Asia—by its author's sure grasp of *realpolitik,* and the clear-eyed way in which he assessed how Japan's defeat would disrupt the balance of power and create a power vacuum in Korea and other areas previously controlled by Tokyo. By the 1960s diplomatic historians were beginning to wrestle with the origins of the Pacific War and the origins of Chinese–United States estrangement, and they too started to draw on the memorandum. Some strongly criticized it; others adopted major portions of its analysis. Even today, an informed reader will be impressed by the way issues MacMurray discusses in the memorandum seem to have reappeared, albeit in different guises and with different names. For those fond of historical might-have-beens, the memorandum has proved a rich source, for if war with Japan had been avoided, the consequences could have been substantial for the entire world. Few diplomatic documents, unpublished at that, can boast such a record of influence and perennial relevance, which testifies to the memorandum's basic nature. It is above all a work of analysis, an argument based not only on the specifics of the previous twenty years in Asia, but also on principles of international law and balance of power having potentially general applicability. As a result, it still has intellectual life well over half a century after its composition.

MacMurray almost certainly hoped that his friend Franklin D. Roosevelt (whose administration had been searching since 1933 for a way out of the Far Eastern Crisis) would be among the first to see the memorandum.[1] But the first important reader (other than Hornbeck) appears in fact to have been another friend, Joseph C. Grew (1886–1965), ambassador to Japan, who records in his diary how MacMurray mentioned his memorandum during a visit to Tokyo in late November 1937. By that time the situation in Asia had become grim: The full-scale invasion of China had begun four months earlier, Nanking had already fallen, the Chinese mainland was blockaded from Ch'in-huang-tao to Canton, and bitter fighting was continuing inland. As he left, MacMurray lent Grew a copy of his appraisal of the situation. Grew records:

> I brought it back after seeing him off on the PRESIDENT COOLIDGE and although rather tired I sat down to read a few pages. It is a masterly work

---

[1]MacMurray told Dorothy Borg in a letter of November 1954 that "his memorandum was not written with reference to any of the specific policies of the Roosevelt administration." Dorothy Borg, *The United States and the Far Eastern Crisis of 1933–1938* (Cambridge, Mass.: Harvard University Press, 1964), p. 590, n. 112. For more diplomatic background, see Norman A. Graebner, "Hoover, Roosevelt, and the Japanese," in *Pearl Harbor as History: Japanese–American Relations, 1931–1941,* ed. Dorothy Borg and Shumpei Okamoto with Dale K. Finlayson (New York: Columbia University Press, 1973) pp. 25–52.

and I only wish that every officer, from the President down, who has anything to do with our Far Eastern Policy could read and study it, for it gives both sides of the Sino-Japanese picture accurately and objectively, and would serve to relieve many of our fellow countrymen of the generally accepted theory that Japan has always been the big bully and China the downtrodden innocent. It bears out completely the soundness of the policy which we in Tokyo have been recommending ever since the present hostilities began. [Its] summing up of . . . "The Present Situation"—and this was written more than a year and a half before the current hostilities began—is admirably and soundly presented.[2]

On November 22 Grew wired the author aboard ship, urging him to have Secretary of State Cordell Hull (1871–1955) read the memorandum, and two days later he [Grew] sent him [MacMurray] an appreciative letter.[3]

Neither the memorandum's approach nor the one "which we in Tokyo have been recommending" carried the day in Washington. In formulating policy, Hull followed closely the initial U.S. response laid down by Hoover's secretary of state, Henry L. Stimson (1867–1950), who, while foreswearing the use of force, had immediately identified Japan as the unprovoked aggressor and sought to rally world public opinion against it. Japan, however, had been unimpressed by what Stimson called "non-recognition"; indeed, if anything, its attitude had hardened. Hull's approach was similarly definite yet ineffective. In his view, Japan was an Asian version of Germany, confronting the United States not with "regional wars or isolated conflicts," but with "an organized, ruthless, and implacable movement of steadily expanding conquest. We are in the presence [Hull wrote] of forces which are not restrained by considerations of law or principles of morality, which have no limits for their program of conquest."[4] Hull believed that if the aggressor could be eradicated, peace would be assured. Yet no one explained how this could be accomplished without strong sanctions and even possibly war with Japan. Grew, by contrast, took the possibility of war seriously, and appeared willing to contemplate very large concessions to Japan in order to avoid it.[5]

[2]Grew Diary, p. 3574. Papers of Joseph C. Grew, Houghton Library, Harvard University.

[3]Grew Correspondence, 1937, vol. 2, Papers of Joseph C. Grew.

[4]Cordell Hull, January 15, 1941, quoted in Stanley K. Hornbeck, *The United States and the Far East: Certain Fundamentals of Policy* (Boston: World Peace Foundation, 1942), pp. 28–29.

[5]On Grew, see Waldo Heinrichs, *American Ambassador: Joseph C. Grew and the Development of the United States Diplomatic Tradition* (Boston: Little, Brown, 1966); also Edward M. Bennett, "Joseph C. Grew: The Diplomacy of Pacification," in *Diplomats in Crisis,* ed. Richard Dean Burns and Edward M. Bennett (Santa Barbara: Clio Books, 1974), pp. 65–90.

The second "rediscovery" of MacMurray's memorandum came more than a decade later, at a time when quite different Asian wars were preoccupying policy planners: first the Chinese Civil War, and then Korea. It was not its analysis of diplomacy prior to World War II, but instead its uncannily accurate prediction of the consequences war would have, that caught the attention of its readers. Stimson, Hull, Hornbeck, and others had believed to greater or lesser degrees that Japan was the source of Asia's problems. Control Japan, they thought, and the area would be pacified. MacMurray's memorandum took quite a different approach. Rather than focusing on the rights and wrongs of conflict, or the needs or interests of a single state, it looked at the balance of power, and in particular what the defeat of Japan would mean for it. MacMurray predicted that the very achievement for which U.S. policy had single-mindedly striven throughout the Pacific war would turn out to solve no problems:

> Utter defeat of Japan would be no blessing to the Far East or to the world. It would merely create a new set of stresses, and substitute for Japan the USSR as the successor to Imperial Russia—as a contestant (and at least an equally unscrupulous and dangerous one) for the mastery of the East. Nobody except perhaps Russia would gain from our victory in such a war.[6]

It is not hard to imagine how farsighted those words must have seemed to planners in the State Department charged with formulating postwar policies. The war against Japan had begun with the United States allied with China and the Soviet Union, but had come to an unexpected conclusion. The United States and the USSR had quickly become estranged, the seemingly pro-Soviet Communist party had come to power in China, and in 1950 Washington found itself involved in a war in Korea with its two erstwhile allies.

The memorandum was apparently rediscovered in August 1949 by Max W. Bishop (b. 1908), later Eisenhower's ambassador to Thailand, who brought it to the attention of Philip C. Jessup (1897–1986). Secretary of State Dean Acheson (1893–1971) had entrusted Jessup with the preparation of the China White Paper, an attempt to justify American policy there to a public opinion thunderstruck by the Communist victory and extension of

---

[6]See memorandum, p. 129; also quoted in George F. Kennan, *American Diplomacy, 1900–1950* (Chicago: University of Chicago Press, 1951), pp. 51–52.

Soviet influence in Asia.[7] A few days later, Philip Sprouse (1906–1977), a career officer who had accompanied Secretary of State George C. Marshall (1880–1959) on his China mission, also mentioned the memo to Jessup. He felt that its analysis was "so basic and timeless that I think it well worth your attention and that of the consultants."[8] In February 1950 Sprouse sent a copy to the deputy assistant secretary of State for Far Eastern Affairs, Livingston Merchant (1903–1976) with the comment, "I consider it a definite must on the list of things required for an understanding of China and its place in the area." On the chit returning it, Merchant wrote, "Thank you. Wonderful!"[9]

It was George F. Kennan (b. 1904) who brought the memorandum to the attention of a larger public. Kennan had taken part in preparing the China White Paper as a member of the Policy Planning Staff of the State Department and probably first encountered it at that time. He was clearly impressed. In 1950 he wrote MacMurray:

> I would like to tell you that I know of no document on record in our government with respect to foreign policy which is more penetrating and thoughtful and prescient than this one. It was an extraordinary work of analysis and of insight into the future; and it is a disturbing reflection on the ways of our government that it failed to leave a deeper mark than it did on the minds of those to whom it was presented and who had access to it at that time. It has done a great deal to clarify my own thinking on Far Eastern problems.[10]

Indeed, when he left Washington for the Institute for Advanced Study in Princeton, Kennan had taken a copy of the memorandum with him, "as an indispensable aid for some of the studies I hope to do here."[11]

One product of Kennan's studies was his Walgreen Foundation lectures

---

[7]Bishop to Jessup, August 16, 1949, State Department Files, National Archives, 050.014; for the White Paper and its origins, see Lyman P. Van Slyke, ed., *The China White Paper, August 1949* (Stanford, Calif.: Stanford University Press, 1967); also Robert M. Blum, *Drawing the Line: The Origin of the American Containment Policy in East Asia* (New York, London: W. W. Norton, 1982), pp. 87–95.

[8]Sprouse to Jessup, August 19, 1949, State Department Files, 050.014; Blum, *Drawing the Line,* pp. 14–15; also Warren I. Cohen, "Ambassador Philip D. Sprouse on the Question of Recognition of the People's Republic of China in 1949 and 1950," *Diplomatic History* 2 (1978), pp. 213–17.

[9]Sprouse to Merchant, February 21, 1950, State Department Files, 050.014.

[10]Kennan to MacMurray, September 19, 1950, Starkey Archives, Brookline, Mass.

[11]Ibid.

given at the University of Chicago in the spring of 1951, and later published as *American Diplomacy*. These had a powerful effect. Americans had seen World War II in moral terms and, at the time the lectures were presented, were having difficulty coming to grips with the end of the wartime alliance with the Soviet Union, and the outbreak of cold war in Europe and active war in Korea. To such an audience Kennan's lectures presented an alternative approach to diplomacy, one that stressed balance of power rather than ideology, and proved immediately influential. Treating East Asia, Kennan cited in particular the passage from MacMurray quoted above, which foresaw how, if Japan were utterly defeated, the Soviet Union would fill the resulting power vacuum. Just exactly this seemed to be happening in Korea. Once again MacMurray seemed prescient; indeed, Kennan called him "prophetic."[12]

Not everyone, of course, agreed. The U.S. habit of applying moral criteria to foreign policy, and thus thinking more about individual nations than international systems, was justified to some extent, and deeply rooted in culture. In 1951 Kennan had sent MacMurray a copy of the published version of the Chicago lectures, to which MacMurray had replied that it was "apparent . . . we share a number of very unpopular beliefs and disbeliefs."[13]

These were the views of the "realist" school, which in writings about China policy went back at least to A. Whitney Griswold's *The Far Eastern Policy of the United States*[14] and were then variously espoused by "George Kennan, Robert Osgood, Hans Morgenthau, and Tang Tsou." Their common, prevailing theme was "the need for greater realism in American policy. Notes, reliance on principles like the open door, and moral suasion were of little avail. The American people had to appreciate the role of power in world affairs."[15] Among scholars, this view, once dominant, has been widely challenged in Asian studies since the 1940s. Some scholars, notably Akira Iriye in his influential study, *After Imperialism,* have closely paralleled MacMurray's arguments.[16] For other scholars, criticism of MacMurray and

---

[12]Kennan, *American Diplomacy,* p. 52.

[13]MacMurray to Kennan, October 28, 1951, Papers of George F. Kennan, Seeley Mudd Library, Princeton University.

[14]New York: Harcourt, Brace and Co., 1938; reprinted, New Haven: Yale University Press, 1962.

[15]Warren I. Cohen, ed., *New Frontiers in American–East Asian Relations: Essays Presented to Dorothy Borg* (New York: Columbia University Press, 1983), p. xvii.

[16]Akira Iriye, *After Imperialism: The Search for a New Order in the Far East, 1921–1931* (Cambridge, Mass.: Harvard University Press, 1965).

those who agreed with him has served as an avenue of attack on a whole school of thought.[17] The memorandum stands, however, as a classic enunciation of the "realist" position on interwar Asian policy, and some mention of it has become almost obligatory when the twists and turns of the road to the Pacific war are being catalogued.

At the same time, however, the memorandum reflects the passionate belief in international law that MacMurray acquired from two of his mentors, Woodrow Wilson and Charles Evans Hughes (1862–1948), a belief that was widespread among serious students of international politics in the interwar period. MacMurray had made his diplomatic reputation as an expert on international law as applied to Asia, and he devoted much of his memorandum to the finer points of legal and diplomatic questions that even in 1935 were scarcely common knowledge: Who, even then, for example, remembered the fact, let alone the technicalities, of the negotiations beginning in 1926 over the Sino-Belgian treaty of 1865? Yet it was by analyzing such details, and showing how departures from the Washington principles in a host of seemingly minor cases had in the end undermined a whole general system of security that MacMurray interpreted the origins of the Far Eastern Crisis.

To justify the departures from the letter of the law that MacMurray condemned, Chinese diplomats and their foreign supporters regularly invoked nationalism. MacMurray sympathized with genuine nationalism, but nevertheless claimed primacy for international law, insisting that any changes in it should follow legally prescribed procedures. As will be seen, this view was unpopular with some of MacMurray's superiors, who were more concerned to get on the side of nationalism. Against them MacMurray argued for the importance of the world balance of power and the legal framework that regulates it, as well as the interests of other countries, Japan in particular, and stressed the risks to regional stability that developments in China could pose. This clash between MacMurray's advocacy of international legality and others' willingness to bend the law to suit a more assertive China, thoroughly explored in the memorandum, has relevance to more than China policy alone. It is an instance of a perennial and controversial problem in U.S. foreign policy generally.

The memorandum, then, is a rigorously analytical piece, and one that provides almost classic statement of a whole series of abiding issues in international affairs. It is also a document informed by the controlled passion of one who tried, without success, to keep U.S. policy on the

---

[17]Warren I. Cohen provides a useful summary of the main lines of debate in his "Introduction" to *New Frontiers in American–East Asian Relations,* especially pp. xiii–xxii.

internationalist course during the crucial years leading to World War II. It reflects deep convictions, derived from the career, experience, and disappointments, of its author.

The Author

The writer of the memorandum was a shy, scholarly man, overtaken by bitter controversy just as he reached what should have been the pinnacle of his career. When he was appointed minister to China in 1925, John Van Antwerp MacMurray (1881–1960) was one of the rising stars of the first professional generation of U.S. diplomats and widely regarded, in President Coolidge's words, as "our top China expert."[18] His service in Peking, however, was scarcely the triumph that might have been expected. No sooner had he arrived in the Chinese capital than he found himself caught up in chronic disagreement with his Washington superiors over policy toward the emergent Chinese Nationalist party (the Kuomintang) and its demands for immediate revision or repudiation of the treaty system that had regulated foreign relations with China for more than two generations. Finding himself at an impasse in 1929, MacMurray not only resigned as minister to China, but he also left the foreign service (only temporarily, it turned out) to take up an academic post at Johns Hopkins University. These events, which form part of the background to the memorandum, must have seemed a disappointing denouement to what had been a very promising career.

MacMurray was born in Schenectady, New York, in 1881. His father, Junius Wilson MacMurray (1844–1898), was a career soldier who, in the Civil War, had "defied his family, who owned slaves on their Mississippi plantation, by enlisting in the Union Army." His mother, Henrietta Wiswall Van Antwerp (1847–1929), was daughter of the first president of the Bank of Albany (now Fleet-Norstar).[19] At age eleven, MacMurray was sent to Captain Wilson's boarding school, near Princeton, and then to Lawrenceville School. He received a deep emotional blow at age sixteen, with the death of his father. To his mother he remained devoted for the rest of

---

[18]Quoted in Howard H. Quint and Robert H. Ferrell, eds., *The Talkative President: Calvin Coolidge* (Amherst: University of Massachusetts Press, 1964), pp. 257–58.

[19]Lois MacMurray Starkey, "J.V.A. MacMurray: Diplomat and Photographer in China, 1913–1929" (Master's thesis, Harvard University, 1990), pp. 5–6. Mrs. Starkey's work sheds important light on MacMurray's personality, and provides a sampling of the superb photographs of China, indicative of his aesthetic sense, to which he devoted painstaking care.

his life, writing to her faithfully from his various foreign postings, and bitterly resenting the State Department's refusal of leave to visit her as she was dying in 1929. After Lawrenceville MacMurray attended Princeton, graduating in 1902. There, as at school, MacMurray showed himself independent-minded—"rationalist" was his word—refusing (as he had at Lawrenceville) to attend chapel, or to join an eating club. He also manifested a sensitivity for language and literature that led Princeton's president, Woodrow Wilson, whom he greatly admired, to urge him to pursue an academic career. MacMurray decided otherwise, however, entering Columbia University Law School, graduating a year ahead of Franklin D. Roosevelt, and passing the bar in 1906. A letter from Wilson helped open the door to examination for the then–unreformed U.S. foreign service, and while he waited for the results, MacMurray earned a Master's degree in literature from Princeton, writing on the influence of the Italian renaissance on Elizabethan literature. In 1907 he took up his first posting, as second secretary at the mission in Bangkok.

By the time he wrote the memorandum, MacMurray was a senior statesman. His daughter remembers him as a handsome but taciturn man of refined tastes. "Said to look like the Hollywood movie actor Robert Montgomery, he was slight [120 lbs., 5'9½"], and immaculately groomed, with the coiled alertness of a jockey." His suits were from Poole's in Savile Row; his shoes, from Church's of London. Witty, if short on small-talk, he moved with ease in the highest circles of society around the world.[20]

Few traces, by contrast, are left from his time in Bangkok. In light of the issues in which he later became involved, it is worth noting that like China, Thailand (then called Siam) had been forced, in the reign of King Mongkut (1851–1868), to accept "unequal" treaties. As Thailand reformed and modernized itself under King Chulalongkorn (1868–1910) and after, these treaties were revised and abolished, a process that began during MacMurray's posting there and culminated just as he was taking up similar questions as minister in China.[21]

From 1909 to 1911, MacMurray served as second secretary in St. Petersburg. The ambassador (1909–1911) was William Woodville Rockhill (1854–1914), a larger-than-life figure—an accomplished Asian linguist and a pioneering explorer of Mongolia and Tibet, as well as a career diplomat who played a key role in setting the long-term course of U.S. China

[20]Starkey, "MacMurray," p. 12.
[21]MacMurray Diary, February 10, 1910, mentions work for the Department on "the proposed revision of the treaties with Siam." Papers of John Van Antwerp MacMurray, Seeley Mudd Library, Princeton University.

policy.[22] China in the late nineteenth century was weak, and "some of the world's statesmen viewed the disintegration of the Manchu empire with indifference if not outright glee." Rockhill, however, understood "that the breakup of China would be a disaster." He was convinced that "a sovereign China, able to preserve order within its own boundaries, was essential to the balance of power in Asia." Confronted by the scramble for foreign concessions in China at the close of the nineteenth century, Secretary of State John Hay (1838–1905) had turned to Rockhill for advice, and the result was the "open door," a cornerstone policy designed to prevent China's partition.[23]

Rockhill's internationalism clearly reinforced in MacMurray a viewpoint he had already imbibed from Woodrow Wilson and his mentor at Columbia, Frank J. Goodnow (1859–1939), professor of international law. Service in St. Petersburg, however, would have supplemented all of this with a series of object lessons. From the Russian capital he would have been able to observe the interplay of the Eurasian powers—the Ottoman, Russian, Ch'ing, and Japanese empires—all relatively mysterious to most professional diplomats of the time. The Russian Empire, at the time MacMurray served, was chastened by defeat at the hands of Japan and by the outbreak of street violence in 1905, which had led to far-reaching constitutional change, but it was also an increasingly mighty military and economic power.

A traveler to Russia cannot help but be impressed by the vast size and immense, if graceless, might of the place. Both were increasing in the late nineteenth and early twentieth centuries. The conquests of the Central Asian khanates had taken place over the nineteenth century: Kokand, last to fall, was conquered in 1875–76, a little more than a hundred years after it had recognized Ch'ing sovereignty. Vladivostok ("Lord of the East") had been founded in 1860; Port Arthur had become Russian, and would remain so until the Russo-Japanese war. In the first decade of the twentieth century, Russia's economy boomed. Those interested in the fate of Asia, even before the abdication of the Manchu dynasty in 1912 and the destruction of much of Europe's accumulated military and economic superiority in World War I, would have been bound to wonder whether it would be Russia or Japan that would end up as the supreme power.

Even more specifically, MacMurray's service in St. Petersburg coin-

---

[22]See Paul A. Varg, *Open Door Diplomat: The Life of W. W. Rockhill* (Urbana: University of Illinois Press, 1952).

[23]Warren I. Cohen, *America's Response to China: An Interpretative History of Sino-American Relations,* 2d ed. (New York: Knopf, 1980), pp. 47–48; also Varg, *Open Door Diplomat.*

cided with an abortive effort by the U.S. secretary of state, Philander C. Knox (1853–1921), to neutralize what was already a cockpit of rivalry among powers—Manchuria. In 1909 Knox had proposed a scheme for the internationalization of the Manchurian railroads that would have kept Russian and Japanese influence from becoming paramount there. On January 21, 1910, "the event of the day" at the embassy "was the receipt of the Russian *aide-mémoire* rejecting the American proposal to neutralize present and future railway enterprises in Manchuria." This cleared the way for the division of the territory into Russian and Japanese spheres of influence.[24]

After returning to Washington, MacMurray served briefly as assistant chief of the Division of Information, and then as assistant chief and finally chief of the Division of Near Eastern Affairs. In August 1913, he was appointed first secretary of the Peking Legation. Possibly at the behest of President Woodrow Wilson, he had been offered the ministership to Siam, but he turned this down in favor of the Peking job, which he had always wanted. His time in Peking further reinforced the view of Asia and diplomacy that he had already been forming.

Peking in the 1910s was a fascinating city that boasted a constellation of talented younger diplomats, many of whom MacMurray first got to know during this period. At the Dutch Legation he met William Oudendijk, or Oudendyk (1874–1953)—"Uncle Ou"—longtime dean of the diplomatic corps, who had first gone to China as a young man in 1894 and returned for a year on the eve of World War I.[25] At the Italian Legation, MacMurray came to know Daniele Varè (1880–1956), linguist and novelist as well as diplomat, who had been posted to an eight-year stint as first secretary in 1912.[26] At the French Legation, MacMurray became acquainted with the consul, Damien, Comte de Martel (1872–1942), and at the British, with Miles Lampson (1880–1964, first Baron Killearn), an impressive figure—more than six-and-a-half feet tall, an old Etonian first posted to Asia in 1908 and from 1916 to 1919 first secretary of the British legation— who proved an able and enlightened diplomat.[27] Without doubt the best

[24]MacMurray Diary, January 21, 1910, MacMurray Papers; Cohen, *America's Response,* pp. 77–84.

[25]William Oudendyk, *Ways and By-Ways in Diplomacy* (London: Peter Davies, 1939).

[26]Daniele Varè, *Laughing Diplomat* (New York: Doubleday, Doran, 1938), pp. 298ff. Among Varè's novels is *The Maker of Heavenly Trousers* (New York: Doubleday, Doran, 1936), a romantic evocation of the Peking he knew.

[27]Obituary, *The Times,* September 19, 1964; E. T. Williams and C. S. Nicholls, eds., *Dictionary of National Biography, 1961–1970* (Oxford: Oxford University Press, 1981), pp. 627–28; for Lampson's service as minister, see Harold Edwin Kane, "Sir Miles Lampson at the Peking Legation, 1926–1933" (Ph.D. dissertation, University of London, 1975).

informed of the group was Kenkichi Yoshizawa (1874–1965), a graduate of the Imperial University of Tokyo whose career had already taken him to Hankow and London, among other posts, before he arrived in Peking.[28]

Historians succumb all too easily to the temptation to see Peking of the 1910s and early 1920s through distorting lenses, and to accept it as inscrutable and romantic.[29] Certainly continuity with Manchu China was strong: The emperor, after all, still reigned in the Forbidden City, though only within those narrow precincts. The memory of the Boxer Uprising, just a decade or so before, was strong, too. Finally, World War I had missed Peking, allowing the ritual and *politesse* of prewar Europe to continue to rule diplomatic etiquette there until the mid-1920s.

These impressions, taken alone, are misleading. China in the early twentieth century was in the throes of rapid change. Railroads, industry, and the development of modern armies were transforming economy, society, and politics. In the north, landless Chinese immigrants poured into Manchuria, which was little more than a raw frontier territory dominated by official and unofficial violence, speculation, and money making, and dotted with boomtowns. These developments posed threats to China's stability, unity, and sovereignty—threats of which the Chinese government was acutely aware.

Power in Peking during the first part of this period was in the hands of Yüan Shih-k'ai (1859–1916), whose government was committed above all to military modernization, and to frustrating Japan and other countries in their designs on China.[30] The gradual loss of territory to Russia and Japan had contributed to the military mutiny that forced the abdication of the Manchu dynasty in 1912, and the belief that a republican form of government was inherently stronger than monarchy and thus better able to enforce territorial claims had been one of the factors impelling Chinese to support such a system. Yüan Shih-k'ai, the most powerful military figure at the Ch'ing court, quickly became president of the new Chinese Republic. He had cut his teeth on the Japanese in the war of 1894–95, and thereafter

---

[28]Gaimushō gaikō shiryōkan, comp., *Nihon gaikōshi jiten* (Tokyo: Okurashō, 1979), p. 963; Ikuhiko Hata, ed., *Senzenki Nihon Kanryōsei no seido, soshiki, jinji* (Tokyo: Tokyo University Press, 1981), p. 257; see also the memoir, Kenkichi Yoshizawa, *Gaikō rokujū nen* (Tokyo: Jiyū Ajiasha, 1959).

[29]As did contemporaries. See the French minister's novel: D. de Martel and L. De Hoyer, trans. D. De Warzee, *Silhouettes of Peking* (Peking: China Booksellers, 1926).

[30]For Yüan, see Ernest P. Young, *The Presidency of Yüan Shih-k'ai: Liberalism and Dictatorship in Early Republican China* (Ann Arbor: University of Michigan Press, 1977).

devoted his formidable political and strategic gifts to pulling the Ch'ing Empire back together again.

With Russia out of the picture after 1914, Yüan understood that Japan was China's most dangerous adversary, and he sought to offset Tokyo by cultivating cordial relations with Britain and other foreign powers. Yüan's close friend, Admiral Ts'ai T'ing-kan (1861–1935)—a former Yung Wing scholar[31] and a naval hero of the Sino-Japanese War—was a friend of MacMurray and of many other foreigners. *Times* correspondent G. E. Morrison (1862–1920) advised Yüan, and the British minister, Sir John Jordan (1852–1925), was a sincere admirer.[32] It was not hard to respect the skill with which Yüan made the best of bad situations. When World War I broke out, Yüan himself told Paul S. Reinsch (1869–1923), the American minister and MacMurray's superior, that "the Japanese intend to use this war to take control of China."[33] Understanding this, Yüan had impressively mobilized foreign pressure to frustrate the most offensive of Japan's Twenty-one Demands by purely diplomatic means in 1915.[34] His success provided a model for subsequent governments in Peking.

As for MacMurray, his time in the Chinese capital was both personally happy and intellectually formative. Among the foreign advisers that Yüan brought in, ostensibly to help him reform his government, was Mac-Murray's old teacher, Frank J. Goodnow, president of Johns Hopkins University and an expert on constitutional law, whose daughter Lois would marry MacMurray in 1916.[35] In his understanding of Sino-Western diplomacy, MacMurray took naturally to what was current in Peking, an

---

[31]That is, one of the students supported in the United States between 1872 and 1881 by the official Ch'ing Chinese Educational Mission, administered by Jung Hung (or Yung Wing in Cantonese; 1828–1912), of the Yale class of 1854, the first Chinese to graduate from an American university.

[32]For Jordan, see Kit-Ching Lau, "Sir John Jordan and the Affairs of China, 1906–1916, with Special Reference to the 1911 Revolution and Yüan Shih-k'ai" (Ph.D. dissertation, University of London, 1968).

[33]Paul S. Reinsch, *An American Diplomat in China* (New York: Doubleday, 1922), p. 129.

[34]See Madeleine Chi, *China Diplomacy, 1914–1918*. Harvard East Asian Monographs, no. 31 (Cambridge, Mass.: East Asian Research Center, Harvard University, 1970).

[35]Goodnow, constitutional consultant to Yüan Shih-k'ai from 1913 to 1914, was the author of *China: An Analysis* (Baltimore: Johns Hopkins University Press, 1926). On his activities in China, see Noel H. Pugach, "Embarrassed Monarchist: Frank J. Goodnow and Constitutional Development in China, 1913–1915," *Pacific Historical Review* 42 (1973), pp. 499–517.

approach that may be called the "northern perspective." At the time of the open door notes and the Boxer Rebellion, diplomats in Peking had determined that it was essential for them to work together to manage relations with a weakened empire that posed problems in the East similar to those posed by the Ottoman Empire in the West. At the same time, however, most of these diplomats were profoundly pro-Chinese in their sympathies, and they applauded the efforts of Yüan and his successors to frustrate the Japanese. MacMurray viewed Chinese politics from precisely this perspective.

Yüan Shih-k'ai, however, had two important enemies. The first was the Japanese. Although such Japanese statesmen of the older generation as Masataka Terauchi (1852–1919) and Aritomo Yamagata (1838–1922) tended to worry very much about Russia and therefore to foster a strong China as a counterweight, the younger generation, impressed by their own military success, were aware only of the degree to which a strong China obstructed their more ambitious continental goals. The problem became acute when Yüan managed to force the authors of the Twenty-one Demands to withdraw the portions of their ultimatum that really threatened China. This diplomatic humiliation led the Japanese, some of whom had previously supported Yüan, to resolve to get rid of him.[36] Yüan made the task easier by unwisely seeking to become emperor of China.

One of the weapons that the Japanese employed in their all-out attack on Yüan Shih-k'ai in 1916 was support for his second enemy, Dr. Sun Yat-sen (1866–1925) and his followers, in what would become the Chinese Nationalist party. Because the Nationalist party came, during the 1920s, to control China, most histories of the period concentrate on it and pay far less attention to its adversaries. As a result the Nationalist victory is thought of almost as a foregone conclusion, and historians forget just how little influence Sun's party had in its early stages, and how likely it seemed to contemporaries that China's future belonged to the Northern Government, and not Sun's followers in Canton. Yüan was an old court insider who had fought the Japanese both militarily and diplomatically, and around him were men who seemed a logical choice to rule China after the Ch'ing—the generals and officers of his modern army. Sun, by contrast, was a classically marginal person. A Cantonese, he had spent much of his life abroad and lacked a firm base inside China. He lacked as well a sense of the need to

---

[36]*Nihon Gaikō Nempyō Narabini Shuyō Bunsho* (Tokyo, 1955), 1: 418–19; Kitaoka, "China Experts in the Army," in *The Japanese Informal Empire in China, 1895–1937,* ed. Peter Duus, Ramon H. Myers, and Mark R. Peattie (Princeton: Princeton University Press, 1989), pp. 352–60.

foster a diplomatic balance that would hold off the nation's enemies. A sincere patriot with a variety of visionary schemes for the regeneration of China but an outsider in the Chinese political system, he had little hope of success unless someone put him in power. In search of such patronage, he turned from the Japanese to the Germans and to the Russians, all powers that opposed the Peking Government because it threatened their interests.[37]

After Yüan's death, the internal struggle that was already stirring during his rule became more acute and gradually began to interfere with China's consistent pursuit of foreign-policy goals. Yüan's successors, the so-called warlords, were increasingly weak, and their governments tended not to last long. A power vacuum developed in China, which invited foreign intervention. All such foreign intervention, however, was either genuinely private (e.g., the Englishman "General" Frank "One-Arm" Sutton [1884–1944] who, to London's distress, taught the Manchurian militarist Chang Tso-lin [1872–1928] how to make trench mortars) or at least ostensibly so (the Japanese had many "unofficial" military advisers and intelligence officers in China). For the last thing the Powers wanted was an actual disintegration and partition of China. Rivalries between the Powers there had already indirectly brought Russia and Japan to blows; the possibility of a new "scramble for concessions" was a nightmarish prospect. So even as internal forces were tearing China apart, the Powers sought to keep it intact and unified.

A number of ad hoc measures served these goals: the arms embargo proclaimed in 1919, the consortiums that regulated foreign lending, and the regular consultation by which the Powers sought to adjust and arbitrate their own potentially competitive interests.[38] What promised to be a master framework for defusing competition and thus fostering Chinese unity, however, was outlined shortly after MacMurray returned to the United States. After service as counselor in Tokyo in 1917 and as chargé in Peking in 1918, he became chief of the Far Eastern Division of the State Department. A Wilsonian, MacMurray believed that cooperation among the Powers and gradual revision of China's international status offered the key

---

[37]On Sun, see in particular C. Martin Wilbur, *Sun Yat-sen: Frustrated Patriot* (New York: Columbia University Press, 1976), and Marius B. Jansen, *The Japanese and Sun Yat-sen* (Cambridge, Mass.: Harvard University Press, 1954).

[38]On the arms embargo, see Ch'en Ts'un-kung, *Lieh-ch'iang tui chün-huo chin-yün* (Taipei: Chung-yang yen-chiu-yüan, 1983); for the consortiums, Frederick V. Field, *American Participation in the China Consortiums* (Chicago: University of Chicago Press, 1931); also Roberta Allbert Dayer, *Bankers and Diplomats in China, 1917–1925: The Anglo-American Relationship* (London: Frank Cass, 1981).

to enduring order in Asia. He wrote at the time of his hope that "all claims of all nations to special interests [should] be abandoned" and that "leased territories should be rendered."[39] He believed that international law provided a framework for doing just that, and he would soon have an opportunity to prepare for that outcome.

The Washington Conference is best known for its naval agreements, but at least equally important was the path it attempted to clear for a normalization of China's legal and diplomatic status. This was a topic on which MacMurray had made himself an expert. While in Peking he had devoted himself to a compilation of treaties. Ever since the military defeats of the nineteenth century, China's sovereignty had been restricted by international agreements, which prescribed everything from foreign territorial and personal privileges in China to the levels at which tariffs could be levied. By the twentieth century hundreds of treaties had been concluded, and while they formed the legal framework for China's international relations, they had never been systematically gathered or analyzed. In 1904 Rockhill had published a volume containing all the treaties concluded up to that year, but the work of bringing it down to the present was incomplete when the former ambassador died in 1914.[40] MacMurray's decision to revise and complete his mentor's work probably owed as much to an outlook that valued international law as it did to MacMurray's personal admiration for the older man. Published by the Carnegie Endowment in 1921, the two volumes of MacMurray's *Treaties* were an impressive piece of scholarship, and they did much to enhance his reputation as a China expert.[41]

This background fitted MacMurray unusually well for the role in the conference to which his office entitled him, as chief of the American technical staff dealing with Pacific and Far Eastern questions, and adviser to Charles Evans Hughes, whom he admired intensely. Opening with some splendor in the Pan American Union building on Saturday November 12, 1921, the Washington Conference was an American-sponsored attempt to create a new, multilateral, international framework for foreign relations in East Asia, one that would assure China's territorial integrity and the gradual elimination of foreign privilege there. Although it was intended to supersede the Anglo-Japanese alliance, the conference would nevertheless secure those vital interests that were Japan's price for participation.

---

[39]MacMurray to Roland Morris, February 5, 1919, MacMurray Papers.

[40]William Woodville Rockhill, *Treaties and Conventions with or concerning China and Korea, 1894–1904, Together with Various State Papers and Documents Affecting Foreign Interests* (Washington, D.C.: U.S. Department of State, 1904).

[41]J.V.A. MacMurray, *Treaties and Agreements with and Concerning China* (New York: Carnegie Endowment, 1921).

Many diplomats concerned with Chinese questions were represented. One of four Japanese delegates was the future foreign minister, Kijūrō Shidehara (1872–1951), who would champion a policy of noninterference in the internal politics of China and seek instead to use internationalist and economic means to maintain Japanese interests.[42] Others in the Japanese delegation with whom MacMurray would deal repeatedly were Sadao Saburi (1879–1929), who would later serve as Shidehara's particular contact man in the Washington embassy, and Katsuji Debuchi (1878–1947), a specialist in Asian affairs who would eventually become ambassador in Washington. MacMurray's later contacts with Japan, and his view of Japan's needs and possibilities, would be largely formed by his work at the Washington Conference. The other key presence at the conference was Britain, and among its delegates was MacMurray's old friend from Peking, Miles Lampson.

As for the Chinese, they sent their best team, headed by the ambassadors to Washington and London, Sao-ke Alfred Sze (Shih Chao-chi, 1877–1958), and V. K. Wellington Koo (Ku Wei-chün, 1887–1986), the latter a brilliant Columbia-educated international lawyer who may be considered the originator of twentieth-century professional Chinese diplomacy. The Chinese delegation, as even the most superficial reading of the conference proceedings makes clear, was bent on eliminating as many as possible of the then-existing foreign privileges and the treaties guaranteeing them. China had already enjoyed some success in this regard: World War I had eliminated extraterritorial jurisdiction and residential concessions for Germans and Austrians and, following the revolution, for the Russians as well. Koo had larger plans, however; he was a master of the loopholes in the international legal system and clearly intended to use the methods and doctrines of that system to undermine the treaty system that controlled China. Specifically he would champion the previously little-known doctrine of *rebus sic stantibus,* which declared that treaties and laws might be considered valid only so long as the circumstances surrounding their original conclusion had not changed.[43]

This Chinese approach posed a particular threat to the Japanese. Tokyo's special position in China, which was still being expanded as World

[42]Unfortunately, no full study of Shidehara exists in a Western language. See Toru Takemoto, *Failure of Liberalism in Japan: Shidehara Kijuro's Encounter with Anti-Liberals* (Washington, D.C.: University Press of America, 1978), and Sidney DeVere Brown, "Shidehara Kijūrō: The Diplomacy of the Yen," in *Diplomats in Crisis,* ed. Burns and Bennett, pp. 201–26.

[43]T. Young Huang, *The Doctrine of Rebus Sic Stantibus in International Law.* Foreword by V. K. Wellington Koo. (Shanghai: Comacrib Press, 1935).

War I drew to a close, rested on the foundation of just this treaty system that Koo and his colleagues were attacking. Furthermore, since 1896 some form of alliance between London and Tokyo had been the basis of Japan's international position, accepted "variously as the marrow, the sheet-anchor, the corner-stone, the crux, of the country's diplomacy." In the spirit of this alliance, Japan had assisted Britain with its navy in the dark days of World War I when unlimited U-boat warfare threatened to sink all Allied shipping. Japan, however, had exacted a price for its support: succession to the German position in the strategically important Shantung peninsula. At Washington, Japan was asked to return Shantung to China and to end the alliance with Britain. This it did, putting a good face on things, though the end of the alliance with Britain left the Japanese feeling "isolated and lonely *(sabishii)*."[44] The belief was that Japan's other privileges, embodied in treaties, were safe—or at least if they were to be modified, it would only be in concert with actions of other Powers. At Washington, then, Japan in effect traded certain tangible guarantees of its position in Asia—Shantung, the alliance with London—for intangible promises of cooperation.

It was understood at Washington that Japan's interests in Manchuria could not be threatened. Since before the turn of the century, the Japanese had consistently endeavored to obtain international recognition for what they called their "special interests" there. The Root-Takahira agreement of 1908 and the Lansing-Ishii agreement of 1917 had ostensibly provided such recognition. MacMurray had little use for these documents, however; years later he would describe the second as "the miserable little agreement . . . foist[ed] on Mr. Lansing (or perhaps it was on President Wilson)."[45] He also recognized, nonetheless, that without some guarantee to Japan regarding Manchuria, the new Washington system could never get started: The Japanese simply would not join a system that put Manchuria in jeopardy, and they had the power and the resources to stand alone, if necessary. Eventually they were convinced, by extensive consultations in Washington, that the guarantee they sought was implicitly contained in the so-called security clause of the Nine-Power Treaty, which pledged the Powers

> to refrain from taking advantage of conditions in China in order to seek
> special rights or privileges which would abridge the rights of subjects or

---

[44]See Ian H. Nish, *Alliance in Decline: A Study in Anglo-Japanese Relations, 1908–1923* (London: University of London Press, 1972), pp. 383, 391.

[45]MacMurray to Hornbeck, September 24, 1936. Papers of Stanley K. Hornbeck, Hoover Institution.

citizens of friendly states, and *from countenancing action inimical to the security of such states* [emphasis added].[46]

The problem, of course, was that despite verbal understandings at Washington, this clause was not an explicit guarantee of Japan's position. In addition, taken as a whole, the treaty texts—with their emphasis on China's rights—could be read against all special foreign positions, including those of Japan. Much of the diplomacy of the next decade thus depended on how the treaties were understood.

Despite these ambiguities, the Washington Conference ended in an atmosphere of optimism. The lesson of World War I, at least so it seemed to many professional diplomats, was that national self-assertion could lead only to disaster; firm multinational systems, by contrast, could secure the peace. In the 1920s many attempts were made to reach such agreements (Washington, Genoa, Geneva, Locarno, Kellogg-Briand), just as in the 1930s these same agreements were repudiated. The reasons for the change are far too complex to be summarized here, but they did reflect a single pattern: an increasing turn toward unilateralism, both by the victors and by the defeated or aggrieved powers, in which internal politics was often the motivating force.

As chief of the Division of Far Eastern Affairs, MacMurray could champion this internationalist approach with the full backing of his secretary of state, Charles Evans Hughes, who considered him "the great American expert on Far Eastern affairs."[47] But when, in 1925, Coolidge appointed MacMurray as minister to Peking, and Frank Kellogg (1856–1937) as secretary of state, this began to change. One reason was Kellogg's acute sensitivity to U.S. public opinion, and his lack of East Asian expertise. An even more important reason was change in China itself.

How one evaluates MacMurray depends very much on how one evaluates China and the changes it was undergoing during his service there. For MacMurray, China was at best "a mere congeries of human beings," while Japan and Thailand, the other two independent countries in Asia, were much more like functioning nation-states. This condition began to change during MacMurray's ministership. The China that many had thought

---

[46]*Conference on the Limitation of Armament, Washington, November 12, 1921–February 6, 1922* (Washington, D.C.: Government Printing Office, 1922), p. 1625; Asada Sadao, "Japan and the United States, 1921–1925" (Ph.D. dissertation, Yale University, 1963), p. 287 and *passim;* also "Japan's 'Special Interests' and the Washington Conference, 1921–1922," *American Historical Review* 56 (1961), pp. 62–70.

[47]L. Ethan Ellis, *Frank B. Kellogg and American Foreign Relations, 1925–1929* (New Brunswick: Rutgers University Press, 1961), p. 106, cited in Collester, p. 36.

somnolent and ineffective seemed suddenly galvanized by a new nationalistic consciousness; in the course of what some termed a "revolution," the country appeared to be radically reshaping itself in a way that promised ultimately to strengthen the Asian international order, but which in the short run crashed like a powerful tide against the vast structure of treaties, privileges, and even new policies, including those hammered out at Washington. Critics at the time, and later scholars as well, felt that MacMurray erred in not understanding this elemental force. Certainly MacMurray's own view of what was going on was quite different (see memorandum, p. 62).

The changes in China had a variety of sources. One was a dispute with France over the "gold franc," which had delayed the ratification of the Washington Treaties and therefore the concessions to China for which they provided. Another was the way that the previously marginal Kuomintang in South China had been greatly strengthened by infusions of Soviet aid and advice, provided through Mikhail Gruzenberg (1884–1951), a Comintern agent who used the *nom de guerre* Borodin. Perhaps most important, however, was the way the Peking government, which had been the most powerful force in China by far, had wasted its military power and destroyed its always tenuous organizational cohesion in a series of increasingly bloody civil struggles, culminating with the fiasco of the second Chihli-Fengt'ien war of autumn 1924. A series of violent antiforeign incidents followed in the next spring. The result was a China far less organized and far more angry than the one MacMurray had left six years earlier. In place of one reasonably secure government that could negotiate and compromise, there were competitive political factions that engaged not so much in serious international relations as in domestically directed bidding wars over nationalistic issues.[48]

Arriving once again in China, MacMurray recognized that he confronted a new situation. As he would write to Assistant Secretary Nelson T. Johnson (1887–1954), he had "deceived himself [while in Washington], going on thinking under the illusion that China was the same last May as it was in 1918," and confessed that he had spent his first seven months as minister "unlearning whatever ideas I had formed as counselor in days gone by."[49] Although his superiors in Washington were increasingly convinced that the new situation required fundamentally new responses, MacMurray continued to believe international cooperation—particularly now that Japan

[48]For this concept, see R. S. Milne, *Politics in Ethnically Bipolar States: Guyana, Malaysia, Fiji* (Vancouver: University of British Columbia Press, 1981), esp. p. 184ff.
[49]Quoted in Thomas Buckley, "John Van Antwerp MacMurray: The Diplomacy of an American Mandarin," in *Diplomats in Crisis,* ed. Burns and Bennett, p. 36.

was so much more directly threatened than before—to be the *sine qua non* of Asian policy.

MacMurray's disagreements with Washington on these points began even before he had arrived in Peking, while he was still at sea aboard the *President Pierce* in May 1925. What later became famous as the May 30th Movement had begun with demonstrations on that date in Shanghai, which led to the killing of nearly a dozen Chinese by police in the International Settlement, and unleashed a wave of antiforeign agitation that soon engulfed much of South and Central China. Among the demonstrators' demands was the immediate abolition of the foreign privileges, which the treaties had guaranteed.

MacMurray was upset to learn that while he was at sea Secretary of State Kellogg had responded positively to a Chinese demand for treaty revision outside the framework of the Washington Treaties. The two men were soon involved in the first of a series of increasingly bitter and personal disagreements that plagued American diplomacy of the period. While Washington increasingly favored unilateral concessions to China, Mac-Murray recommended that existing treaties be enforced until they could be revised, even if troops or gunboats were required to do so.

MacMurray's policy was nearly followed in 1926 when the forces of Feng Yü-hsiang's Kuominchün mined navigation channels at Taku, near Tientsin, and fired on foreign shipping in an attempt to provoke foreign intervention in their struggle with Chang Tso-lin's government at Peking. This was in violation of the Boxer Protocol of 1901, which guaranteed foreigners free access to Peking from the sea, and MacMurray, in collaboration with the representatives of the other Powers, urged a strong naval demonstration. The secretary of state was not in Washington at the time, and in his absence Under Secretary Grew endorsed MacMurray's recommendations. When Kellogg returned, however, he was outraged, thinking that Grew had "declared war on China." Both Chinese sides eventually backed down, however, and access to the river was restored.[50] Influential China missionaries and others criticized MacMurray's approach, and he went from being "our top China expert" to "America's gunboat minister," as the *Nation* called him.[51]

As the situation in China changed, the cooperative Washington Powers began to go their own ways. Britain's shift toward unilateralism, exemplified by the so-called Christmas memorandum of 1926, and the retrocession

[50]Grew to MacMurray, March 23, 1926, MacMurray Papers; Buckley, "Mac-Murray," p. 37.
[51]Ibid.

of the Han-k'ou and Chiu-chiang Concessions in 1927, made the situation worse. MacMurray saw his task as working with the other Powers within the Washington framework, but Kellogg was increasingly concerned lest unilateral concessions such as those made by the British lead to a perception that America was not responsive enough to China. MacMurray saw "orderly negotiation . . . with insistence upon full respect for existing obligations" as the wisest policy.[52] Kellogg by contrast wished to move as rapidly as possible to meet Chinese demands. The question came down to priorities for Asia. Was the maintenance of the Washington system paramount? Or did a changed situation give precedence to China's new demands?

Troubled by this conflict of policies, MacMurray had written to Kellogg in December 1926. He was concerned by the "lack of mutual understanding as to the purpose which it is my duty to serve under your direction. I do not feel that I have made clear to you the facts of the situation that day to day confronts us here, and I infer from your instructions that you find my various recommendations and suggestions unresponsive to your desires."[53] Plans were made for an early 1927 visit to Washington, for what to MacMurray was the most pressing need, "personal consultation with you who are my Chiefs—the President, the Secretary and [Under Secretary of State Joseph Grew]."[54] MacMurray was deeply disappointed when these plans were abruptly canceled, ostensibly because the situation in China would not allow his absence. He suspected the real reason to be "the desire of certain influences not to have me at home and accessible to the White House and the Hill while Congress is in session."[55]

The rise of the Nationalists in China was making U.S. policy there far more controversial at home. Stephen G. Porter (1869–1930), chairman of the House Foreign Affairs Committee, had introduced a resolution on January 4, 1927, supporting unilateral U.S. moves to give up extraterritoriality and other privileges, a development in which some have detected the hands of Chinese ambassador Alfred Sze and the secretary of the International Missionary Council, A. L. Warnshuis (1877–1958). Passed by the House, the bill expired, much to MacMurray's relief, in the Senate.[56]

[52]*Foreign Relations of the United States,* 1926, 1:919–21; MacMurray to Silas Strawn, December 23, 1926, MacMurray Papers; Buckley, "MacMurray," p. 38.

[53]MacMurray to Kellogg, December 30, 1926, MacMurray Papers; Buckley, "MacMurray," p. 38.

[54]MacMurray to Grew, February 12, 1927, MacMurray Papers.

[55]MacMurray to Willys Peck, February 12, 1927, MacMurray Papers.

[56]Iriye, *After Imperialism,* pp. 107–8; Dorothy Borg, *American Policy and the Chinese Revolution, 1925–1928* (New York: American Institute of Pacific Relations, 1947; reprint ed., with new introduction by the author, New York: Octagon Books, 1968), pp. 238–39; Buckley, "MacMurray," pp. 38–39.

Within the Department, however, two officials in particular were far more sympathetic to the unilateral approach than was MacMurray. As chief of the Far Eastern Division, Nelson T. Johnson counseled Kellogg in favor of greater flexibility. A full fight broke out in 1927 when Johnson was promoted to assistant secretary of state and Stanley Hornbeck was nominated to succeed him at the Far Eastern Division. Neither man shared MacMurray's interpretations of international law as applied to China, and both took less seriously than he the threat posed by Japan. MacMurray was profoundly opposed to Hornbeck's appointment in particular, and exerted all the influence he could behind the scenes to block it. He was unsuccessful, however, and U.S. China policy under Kellogg increasingly moved away from MacMurray's conceptions.

The policy shift was evident in Kellogg's response to the action of the Congress. Without any prior discussion with MacMurray, Kellogg announced on January 26, 1927, that "the United States is now and has been, ever since the negotiation of the Washington Treaty, prepared to enter into negotiations with any Government of China or delegates who can represent or speak for China not only for the putting into force of the surtaxes of the Washington Treaty but for entirely releasing tariff control and restoring complete tariff autonomy to China," and that it was "prepared to put into force the recommendations of the Extraterritoriality Commission" subject only to Chinese guarantees.[57]

MacMurray promptly communicated this offer to the Nationalists, although they did not respond.[58] Kellogg's action had completely undercut MacMurray's position in both Washington and Peking, and in a letter to his friend Grew written in February 1927 he candidly expressed his frustrations. MacMurray listed seven instances since his arrival in which he felt that policy coordination between Washington and Peking had been poor and that as a result his position had been undermined. It seemed to him that "with the increasing confusion and bewilderment of the chaotic situation in China, the Department has traced over the line of China policy with a hesitating and unsteady hand that has criss-crossed back and forth across the line it has been following." He realized, "of course, that the dragging of Chinese affairs into home politics has had much to do with this." But would it not be possible, he asked, "for the Department to take a stand more definitely upon the realities of the situation in this country and the

---

[57]*Foreign Relations of the United States,* 1927, 1:350–53; the original press release is in the MacMurray Papers.

[58]See Hallett Abend, *My Life in China, 1926–1941* (New York: Harcourt, Brace, 1943), pp. 94–95.

necessary protection and defense of American interests here, against the importunities of those sentimentalists who conceive that the responsibilities of our Government in China are toward the Chinese rather than toward our own people?"[59]

While on one level MacMurray clearly wished to maintain U.S. interests, the ultimate justification for his position was found in his concern for international law and proper diplomatic procedures. The politicization of Chinese foreign policy, particularly after 1925, posed the risk that the Chinese, forgetting how their enhanced international position had been achieved, would tear down the structure that had made it possible, thus creating a situation that would threaten both their own interests and the peace of Asia. He feared above all "a policy of renunciation, of pacifism, and of defeatism—a policy that would frustrate the hope of cooperation among China and the interested foreign nations, and substitute for it what they call 'an independent American policy,' which in effect would mean that we disinterest ourselves in China as an *international problem,* and invite the others to resume a new battle for concessions and spheres of influence; whereas in the Battle of Concessions of thirty years ago, the basis was the professed desire of each foreign Power to protect China against encroachments upon its territorial integrity on the part of other Powers, the basis today would be that of protection of the abstract idea of Chinese national sovereignty against 'inequalities' and 'servitudes'—with just the same results as before."[60]

Disagreement with Washington worsened in March 1927, when Nationalist troops advancing north killed a number of foreigners in Nanking and forced others to be evacuated by foreign gunboats. The British now called for joint sanctions, but Kellogg considered that public opinion would never tolerate such an action. Rumors circulated of MacMurray's resignation, but he stayed on. Once the Nationalist Government was securely established, he reached a settlement with it over the Nanking incident, and signed as well a tariff treaty on July 25.[61]

It is tempting, when considering MacMurray's conflict with Kellogg, to adopt the popular language of nationalism and talk about the impossibility of constraining China's developing aspirations in a "narrow legalistic framework." It is important to bear in mind, however, that an Asia without such a framework—that is, without the Washington Treaties—would probably have not been a very attractive place, particularly for China. Whether

---

[59]MacMurray to Grew, February 12, 1927, MacMurray Papers.
[60]MacMurray to Grew, February 12, 1927, MacMurray Papers (emphasis added).
[61]Buckley, "MacMurray," p. 41.

allied with Britain or not, Japan would almost certainly have carried out extensive naval building and quickly beome the preeminent power in the region. Japan's power would have been transformed into effective hegemony over China; no European power would have been able to block her. The United States would probably have been unwilling, and the Soviet Union was absorbed with its own problems. Strong Japanese influence at Canton might well have meant no Russian aid for Sun Yat-sen, and hence no Northern Expedition; the lack of a strong British presence would have left the Peking Government with no possible counterweight to Japan. China's independence would have disappeared in short order. China, therefore, could attack the Washington Treaties only so long as someone was leashing Japan. In the 1920s Japan was constraining itself, as it attempted to join an international system governed by international law. Remove that incentive, however, and all bets about Japanese behavior were off. MacMurray understood all this. It may be doubted whether Kellogg, Hornbeck, and Johnson understood as well.

MacMurray held out some hope that the Hoover Administration would prove more supportive, but if anything his conflicts with Washington grew more acute after 1928, when Henry Stimson replaced Kellogg as secretary of state. The Kuomintang had by then conquered the North, and fresh from this triumph moved simply to sweep away extraterritoriality and the treaties. In April 1929, Wang Cheng-t'ing (1882–1961) addressed identical notes to six Powers, including the United States, calling for steps to be taken "to enable China, now unified and with a strong central government to rightfully assume jurisdiction over all nationals within her domain."[62] In response the United States offered negotiations "which would have as their object the devising of a method for the gradual relinquishment of extraterritorial rights," but ruled out immediate abolition as premature.[63] The Nationalists would not accept this, and on December 26, 1929, the National Government issued a mandate terminating all extraterritorial rights for foreigners as of the first of the following year.[64] These escalating Chinese demands led to tension between Stimson and MacMurray. The secretary of state was inclined to accept Chinese proposals, but in 1929 when he inquired of MacMurray whether some new policy might be appropriate in light of the seemingly new situation in China, the minister was negative. The Nationalist victory, MacMurray argued, simply reflected a shift in the

---

[62]*China Yearbook*, 1929–1930, quoted in Liu Da Jen, *A History of Sino-American Diplomatic Relations*, p. 173.
[63]*China Yearbook*, 1929–1930, pp. 905–7, quoted in Liu Da Jen, *History*, p. 174.
[64]Liu, *History*, pp. 174–75.

internal balance of Chinese politics and should be treated cautiously. Certainly any changes in the intricate system of treaties and agreements that regulated relations among the Powers, and their relations with China, should not be rashly undertaken. Stimson thought otherwise. Like Mac-Murray's other critics, he believed, as he put it early in 1929, that the Nationalists represented "the beginning of a permanent change in the Chinese Government and character."[65] When, as just described, the Nationalists moved toward unilateral repudiation of the treaties later in the same year, 1929, and MacMurray urged the secretary to make clear that the United States would not "tolerate any further disregard of our rights," Stimson was therefore astonished. The comment, he remarked, raised "the question of whether the hour may already have passed when anything can be accomplished by the Powers through such means as suggested by you."[66]

The chronic conflict damaged MacMurray's career. His advice to the secretaries of state fell on deaf ears, and men like Nelson T. Johnson and Stanley Hornbeck, who had ranked far below him at the time of the Washington Conference, were now drawing even within the foreign service. Johnson would succeed him in the Peking Legation, while Hornbeck had already taken over his old job as director of Far Eastern Affairs. The Chinese learned of the disagreements and began to short-circuit Mac-Murray's Legation and take their requests directly to Washington. In October 1929, deeply frustrated, MacMurray not only resigned as minister to China but also left the foreign service. His ostensible reason was to take up the directorship of the Walter Hines Page School of International Relations at Johns Hopkins University, which he did, but he seems really to have been concerned, as he put it in a personal letter, to "get my handcar off the track before the train comes by."[67] One senses unfinished business, however. From Greenfields, his forty-acre country place near Baltimore, MacMurray deflected an approach to become president of Princeton.[68] The ambassador wanted to get back to diplomacy.

Origins of the Memorandum

Events in Asia unfolded much as MacMurray had feared. The willingness of the Washington Powers to ignore the provisions of those treaties, which

---

[65]Quoted in Iriye, *After Imperialism,* p. 258.

[66]Stimson to MacMurray, July 9, 1929, *Foreign Relations of the United States,* 1929, 2:582.

[67]MacMurray to Ferdinand Mayer, October 21, 1929, MacMurray Papers.

[68]Starkey, "MacMurray," p. 43.

became evident during his ministership, may have assuaged public opinion in China and the United States, but had quite the opposite effect in Japan. There China policy became ever more controversial, beginning after the Katō Government lost its parliamentary majority in 1925 and had to rule by coalition. Developments on the continent convinced an increasing number of Japanese that the internationalism promised by the Washington system was not going to guarantee their interests. Splits developed between government agencies in China, Manchuria, and Japan, and to some extent between the military and civilians as well. The result was first the more interventionist policy of Giichi Tanaka (1863–1929), who served as prime minister from 1927 to 1929, and then, after a final internationalist interlude, the independent moves of the Kwantung army to take control of Manchuria starting on September 18, 1931.

This Far Eastern Crisis was exactly the sort of development MacMurray had long warned against, and he could feel a certain vindication. Pierrepont Moffat (1896–1943), Joseph Grew's son-in-law, was at a tea in Washington on November 13, 1931 where he had

> a chat with Jack MacMurray. The latter asked about [Grew's] work in Turkey, and as I described it said that it was very much like his work in Peking—fighting to protect our institutions against the rising tide of nationalism. He said that China was reaping where she had sown in Manchuria, and that the events of the past six weeks in that neighborhood were no surprise to him.[69]

MacMurray's stock rose as events bore out his analysis. Two years later Franklin Roosevelt brought him back into the foreign service, appointing him in 1933 to serve as minister to the Baltic States, a vitally important task at a time when Riga was America's listening post on the as-yet-unrecognized Soviet Union.[70] Even as he immersed himself in Soviet affairs, however, preparing for what he hoped would be an eventual appointment as first U.S. ambassador to Moscow, MacMurray kept up his interest in East Asia.

Japan's actions in Manchuria meant that U.S. policies toward East Asia were ripe for reevaluation. Manchuria itself was an area of unclear cultural affiliation. The homeland of the Manchu nation, which had conquered China in 1644, it had become in the late nineteenth century a territory

---

[69]Moffat Diary, November 13, 1931. Papers of Jay Pierrepont Moffat, Houghton Library, Harvard University.

[70]On the importance of the Riga mission, see Natalie Grant, "The Russian Section, a Window on the Soviet Union," *Diplomatic History* 2 (1978), pp. 107–15.

contested by Russia, Japan, and China. After their victory over Russia in 1905, the Japanese expanded their economic position there considerably, sending immigrants to open up farms and, drawing on the area's abundant natural resources, to create heavy industrial complexes, which were felt to be essential to Japan's national security, and whose protection was one justification for a Japanese policy toward continental Asia that disregarded the views of the other Powers.[71] By the 1920s, certain Japanese, and particularly the long-serving foreign minister, Kijūrō Shidehara, had come to believe that the most basic of these interests could best be assured within an internationalist framework such as that worked out at Washington, and had therefore steered Japan to a cooperative course. Such calculations were challenged, however, by developments in China during the 1920s and the lack of coordinated international response to them. These led to Shidehara's political eclipse, and an increasing trend toward unilateralism in Tokyo. The result was the triumph of those in Japan who believed that interests could be secured only through direct military action. The Kwantung army moved without governmental approval in 1931, but once Manchuria was occupied Tokyo willingly established the client state of Manchukuo in 1932 under the sovereignty of the old Manchu ruling house of the Ch'ing dynasty.

As mentioned at the outset, these developments confronted the United States with difficult choices. One was, in effect, to accept Japan's actions. If that course was rejected, there remained two alternatives, neither particularly palatable. One was to go to war with Japan, a power not to be trifled with; the other was to pound the table about Japan's perfidy, year in and year out, while doing nothing about it, a course that gradually became ridiculous. Since the use of force was never contemplated, the choice had to be the last, so-called non-recognition, originated by Secretary of State Henry Stimson.

Even this passive policy had risks, however. The rights and wrongs of the Manchurian situation were in fact more complex than might at first be evident, and they had to be dealt with flexibly. In formulating America's response, Stimson, like many distinguished jurists before him, "[used]

---

[71]For a summary of the importance of Manchuria, see Justus D. Doenecke, comp., *The Diplomacy of Frustration: The Manchurian Crisis of 1931–1933 as Revealed in the Papers of Stanley K. Hornbeck* (Stanford: Hoover Institution Press, 1981), pp. 3–10; also Donald G. Gillin and Ramon H. Myers, eds., *Last Chance in Manchuria: The Diary of Chang Kia-ngau* (Stanford: Hoover Institution Press, 1989), pp. 1–18; for issues of its legal status, see C. Walter Young, *Japan's Special Position in Manchuria* (Baltimore: Johns Hopkins University Press, 1931).

precedent to create what amounted to new law.''[72] He drew up an impressive bill of indictment that traced precedents from the open door through the Washington Treaties up to Japan's violation of them, greatly reducing the possibility for any compromise with Japan. This legal argument was so tight as to deny his client any room to maneuver; it made an out-of-court settlement almost impossible, yet the only court that could hear the case, the League of Nations, could not make its judgments stick. Stimson had created a "wrong without a remedy"[73] and a difficult problem for the incoming Roosevelt Administration.

War in Asia in 1935 was not in the interest of most of the Powers. Britain and the other European Powers were extremely worried about Germany and would be stretched thinly enough just defending their homelands. The United States was pacifistic by inclination, and it faced severe economic problems at home; furthermore, the navy was not yet sufficiently powerful to ensure success in a Pacific war. China was sure to lose a war fought with Japan in 1935—better for her to bide her time while preparing for war, and hope that changes in the international situation might improve her position. China's best hope was to deflect the Japanese thrust against the country that most military men in Japan saw as the major enemy, the Soviet Union. The latter, however, was the one country that would benefit from war in Asia, provided it was between Japan and China, so the possibility that the Japanese could be redirected in this way seemed small.

Understandably, then, from its first days in office, the Roosevelt Administration appeared to want to wriggle out of the legal straitjacket that Stimson had devised. Japan had to be pressured, and also accommodated, if peace were to be secured. Roosevelt moved in both directions. Naval building was stepped up, which strengthened the hand of those in Tokyo who argued that war with the United States would be a disaster and that Japan should compromise. Diplomatic relations were established between the United States and Japan's number one potential adversary, the Soviet Union, in 1933. This put pressure on Tokyo as well. The United States also sought to reassure Japan. Hull maintained Stimson's theoretical position, but with a shift in emphasis: "The United States would avoid debating, provoking, or challenging Japan. It would acquiesce in, but not assent to, Japanese expansion already undertaken at the expense of China. It would not invoke, but not discard, the Nine-Power Treaty."[74]

---

[72]Waldo Heinrichs, *American Ambassador: Joseph C. Grew and the Development of the United States Diplomatic Tradition* (Boston: Little, Brown, 1966), p. 175.
[73]Ibid.
[74]Ibid., p. 220.

It was against such a background that in 1934 MacMurray first floated the idea that would lead to the memorandum. Stanley Hornbeck was then director of Far Eastern Affairs, and in January MacMurray wrote him from Riga in connection with a projected conference to revise the Washington Treaties the following year. Speaking of the original conference, Mac-Murray recalled the difficulties the Americans had "in extemporizing and presenting in usable form for our delegation the relevant information that we had available [at Washington]." He continued:

> So, on the chance that it may not yet have occurred to you, I am making bold to offer the suggestion that it may not be too early to plan for the coordinating and presentation of the Far Eastern material that our people may find necessary for their use at the next Conference.[75]

Early in the summer of 1935 MacMurray returned to Washington on leave from his post, and began actively to reestablish his connections among policymakers. On June 14, William Phillips (1878–1968), under secretary of state, invited

> Jack MacMurray, now on leave from his post at Riga and at home in Baltimore, to come and see me this afternoon to discuss Far Eastern matters. I wanted to get his reaction to our policy of "hands off." There is probably no one better informed than Jack on the historical aspect of the Far East. He entirely agreed with our conclusions, and recommended the utmost caution in any approaches to Japan.[76]

A few days later Phillips talked to the Chinese ambassador, Alfred Sze, and "Jack MacMurray dropped in for a few minutes."[77]

MacMurray's intention, as he explained to Hornbeck on August 22, had been to prepare the way for his own employment as consultant on East Asian questions. He had

> put it to those in authority, who were available at that time, that for compelling personal reasons I [was] anxious to stay in this country until it

---

[75]MacMurray to Hornbeck, January 18, 1934, Hornbeck Papers.

[76]Phillips Diary, June 14, 1935. Papers of William Phillips, Houghton Library, Harvard University. Warren Cohen, *America's Response,* p. 137, quotes this passage and appears to suggest a connection between the meeting with Phillips and the preparation of the memorandum, a connection that does not seem to be borne out by either the diary or other documents.

[77]Phillips Diary, June 18, 1935.

is time to attend the October session of the Wheat Advisory Committee, in London, on my way back to Riga. . . . Several sympathetic souls— among them Max Hamilton[78]—suggested that it might be possible to arrange for an assignment to the Department for consultation.

He wondered whether Hornbeck would "have any actual or constructive use for me as a consultant 'elder statesman' in the present juncture of Far Eastern affairs."[79]

The idea had also occurred to Hornbeck, who two days later wrote to Cordell Hull, reminding him that he had

on two or three occasions, when preparing for you memoranda with regard to our Far Eastern relations in broad outline, suggested that it might be of advantage for us to have Mr. MacMurray come to the Department to do some intensive work, in cooperation with FE, on that subject.

MacMurray's availability would now make that possible, and Hornbeck recommended that the project, which he called a "rather comprehensive study of the problem of our Far Eastern relations," be started.[80] Hull approved the idea two days later; Hornbeck wrote MacMurray with the news, and a telegram was sent ordering him back to the Department and authorizing payment for travel as well as a "per diem of $5.00 while on consultation." Initially thirty days, the consultancy was subsequently extended to two months for a job that Hornbeck thought should easily have taken six.[81]

The memorandum was submitted on November 1, 1935. Initially it seems to have had little influence on the way Asian policy was formulated. That task, though contested by others, was securely in the hands of Stanley Hornbeck, who, as has been mentioned, tended to underestimate the risk of war with Japan. An incident on November 11, 1935, the day MacMurray "dropped in [on Phillips] to say goodbye on his way back to his post," is revealing.[82] Rear Admiral John D. Wainwright (1878–1965) had called on

---

[78]Maxwell M. Hamilton (1896–1957), assistant chief of the Far Eastern division, 1931–37.

[79]MacMurray to Hornbeck, August 22, 1935, Hornbeck Papers.

[80]Hornbeck to Secretary of State (Cordell Hull), August 24, 1935, Hornbeck Papers.

[81]Hornbeck to Secretary of State (Cordell Hull), August 24, 1935, Hornbeck Papers; Hornbeck to MacMurray, August 26, 1935, MacMurray Papers; Hull to MacMurray, August 26, 1935, Hornbeck Papers and MacMurray Papers.

[82]Phillips Diary, November 11, 1935, Phillips Papers.

Phillips the same day and rather grimly predicted that within a year or at most eighteen months, "the Yangtze would be under the exclusive control of the Japanese and all of China north of the Yangtze under their domination." The admiral was not quite right in his timing (Wuhan did not fall until 1938), but he had a much better understanding of the situation than did Phillips's next informant, Hornbeck, who told him "not to take the Admiral too seriously."[83] Certainly Hornbeck did not expect war.

Nor did the pessimistic appraisal in MacMurray's report seem to Hornbeck any sounder than the admiral's views, and it seems not to have left his office. From the start, he had viewed its commissioning more as a favor granted at a difficult time in the author's personal life than as a real opportunity to obtain an outside appraisal of the situation.[84] The outbreak of full-scale hostilities between China and Japan in the wake of the Marco Polo Bridge incident on July 7, 1937, however, had an effect on the Roosevelt Administration similar to that of the Manchurian incident on the Hoover Administration. In both cases the Administration determined that war was to be avoided at all costs. At the same time the aggressor had to be penalized somehow, even if only verbally. Even such small steps, however, increased the threat of war. Gradually the Powers switched onto collision courses, and the threat of general war became ever more palpable.

Under these inauspicious circumstances, as mentioned previously, the memorandum first came to the favorable attention of an important decision-maker, Ambassador Grew in Tokyo. The autumn after war broke out in China found MacMurray on a brief mission to Japan. He arrived at Yokohama on November 20, and immediately plunged into diplomatic business. Accompanied by Grew, he called on Kōki Hirota (1878–1948) at the Foreign Ministry, where the minister alluded to the possibility of "some kind of agreement" regarding the security of the Philippines. At lunch MacMurray met many leading Japanese, and later Katsuji Debuchi raised a question about the Nine-Power Treaty.[85] Grew recalls that he and the visiting minister spent much of the afternoon talking, reminiscing in particular about the Taku incident in 1926, which had led Kellogg to decide to remove Grew as under secretary of state and had damaged MacMurray as well.[86] It was in the course of this conversation that MacMurray spoke of his memorandum, of which Grew had never heard, and followed up by giving the ambassador the copy alluded to at the beginning of this essay. It all made sense, for

---

[83]Ibid.

[84]Dorothy Borg to author.

[85]Grew Diary, 1937, p. 3570, Grew Papers.

[86]Ibid., pp. 3573–74.

MacMurray's interpretations of Asian policy unfortunately looked far more persuasive illuminated by the flames of the Asian war than they ever had in peacetime.

Contents of the Memorandum

Developments in Asia and in MacMurray's career form the immediate background for understanding the memorandum. The document itself is no simple complaint or apologia; rather, it is a carefully structured argument, not so much about MacMurray's own diplomatic service, or even about China, as about the United States, international law, and the balance of power, three of the most basic issues of interwar diplomacy. It is MacMurray's treatment of these topics that makes reading the document intellectually rewarding even today. Such reading can be a challenge, however. Although written with the crystal clarity on which MacMurray always prided himself, the memorandum describes many events that are now largely forgotten. Furthermore, the analysis is often at odds with what modern writers say about the same period. The reader who acquires the information to overcome these obstacles—and it is provided here in notes—can still feel the memorandum's power.

Subheadings divide the memorandum into four parts: "The Aftermath of the Washington Conference," "The Period of Chinese Agitation (1922–1926)," "The Period of Chinese Nationalist Violence," and "The Present Situation." The document has one single purpose, made clear in the first pages: to consider what U.S. Asian policy should be in "a situation so essentially altered" from that which formed the Washington Conference approach that neither "ultimate objectives" nor "strategic and tactical methods" for securing them could be taken for granted (memorandum, p. 61).

Its subject, in other words, is not China (which is first mentioned at the end of the third paragraph) but rather Asia. MacMurray begins by sketching the changes that had transformed that part of the world in the ten years since he returned to China as minister, and that forced reconsideration of policy. These include the new assertiveness of Japan, the reconsolidation of Russian power under the Soviet Government, and the development in China of what MacMurray calls "a type of nationalism." These developments, each marking the greater assertiveness of one or another power, have been matched by an opposite tendency on the part of the United States: withdrawal, not only from Asia (MacMurray mentions the decision to grant Philippine independence, p. 60) but also from Europe (although this is not stated explicitly).

MacMurray believes that the best remedy for the disequilibrium these factors created was the system devised at the Washington Conference, which was animated by much the same impulse that led MacMurray's mentor, Woodrow Wilson, to sponsor the League of Nations. Meeting from November 12, 1921, until February 6, 1922, the Conference had produced agreements guaranteeing the Pacific possessions of the Powers (the Four-Power Treaty); setting ratios to limit naval competition (the Five-Power Treaty); and providing for China's independence and Japan's eventual return of Chiao-hsien (Kiaochow) in Shantung (the Nine-Power Treaty); as well as for the convening, within three months of ratification, of special conferences to consider the Chinese customs tariffs, which were set by treaty with foreigners rather than by the Chinese themselves, and extraterritoriality, the system that removed foreigners from the jurisdiction of Chinese law.

Some commentators understood these treaties as, in effect, guaranteeing China's security and promising reform. At the outset, MacMurray takes pains to explain the precise significance of the legal language of the treaties. He points out that, while "giving [to the principles of the open door and of Chinese integrity] a definiteness of interpretation such as had never before been internationally accepted," the treaties still "did not create or imply an obligation of a positive character on the part of the signatories . . . to maintain China's independence or integrity." Nor did the treaties require any treaty revision. Under the terms of the treaties, the United States or any other Power could "[hold] aloof from any controversy involving Chinese rights or interests." Nevertheless, it was expected that the Powers would work together to deal with the universally recognized defects of the old system. As MacMurray put it, "the international cooperation envisaged was to have been not a merely legalistic or formal procedure but a wholehearted effort." Note, however, MacMurray's belief that "this intended structure of cooperation" had been "allowed during 1925–29 to fall into desuetude," thus rendering its provisions inapplicable in the present crisis. This view was quite different from that of Stimson and successive U.S. Administrations, which took the Washington Treaties as one of the legal bases for condemnation of Japan (memorandum, pp. 63, 64–65).

Much of the memorandum is devoted to explaining just how the Washington Conference order broke down. Historians agree that cooperation in Asia initially appealed to different Powers for different reasons. All were concerned to avoid ruinously expensive military competition—the British above all, for after World War I their forces were already stretched to the breaking point, and their government was bankrupt. The United States was less determined, not so much because it could not afford a military buildup as because it lacked the inclination to join the race. The Japanese were least concerned of all—theirs had been a good war, their economy had made gains, their military needs were clear, and a powerful section of public and governmental opinion favored an improvement in the nation's military capacity. Therefore, while the other Powers might be important actors, Japan was critical, and the folly, as MacMurray saw it, of policy during the decade of the 1920s was that it did not deal with the requirements of the Power that was both strongest in the area and most reluctant to join the international system.

MacMurray uses a series of diplomatic incidents to tell how the Washington system broke down. The first important test was the Special Tariff Conference, convened in Peking in the autumn of 1925, and which, if successful, would have made much-needed revenue available to the Chinese Government. It foundered because of the increasingly bitter political division between North and South in Chinese politics. The summer before the meeting had been difficult. The death of Sun Yat-sen had cast doubt upon the future of the southern Nationalist forces, but at the same time the new success of xenophobic appeals in stirring up large numbers of Chinese, demonstrated at the time of the May 30th incident, was leading both the northern and the southern groups to compete to run ahead of the mob. The Tariff Conference had been planned at Washington when the political situation in China was more stable and the atmosphere calmer. Its agenda was limited, too, although if it were successfully completed, it would be but the first step toward further modifications of the treaty system.

MacMurray's guiding principle in approaching the conference was that existing law should be maintained, and changes made only through recognized legal processes. Thus he was equally unhappy with the British, whom he saw as obstructive of the granting of changes already agreed upon, and with the Chinese, whom he saw adopting rhetorical postures rather than serious negotiating positions. He recognized that, "to them the conference was merely an opportunity to further their personal political fortunes by dramatizing their contempt for the foreigners and their rights" and, old-school diplomat that he was, scorned their grandstanding. He was irritated when, at a private evening conference, the U.S. delegation "received [C. T. Wang, the Chinese negotiator's] fulsome thanks for the fairness and generosity of the American proposals—and, at the next morning's meeting, found itself snubbed and upbraided by the same Chinese chairman for having made such 'manifestly objectionable proposals.' " He also recognized the seriousness, indeed almost the menace, of the concern expressed by Mr. Saburi, the Japanese representative known to be Shidehara's "pet,"[87]

---

[87]Barbara J. Brooks, "China Experts in the Gaimushō, 1895–1937," in Duus, Myers, and Peattie, eds., *Japanese Informal Empire,* p. 378.

lest U.S. policy regarding China "might develop an unrealistic altruism which we Americans could afford to indulge in view of the relative unimportance of our material involvements in China, but which would create an intolerable situation for Japan, to whose economic and political existence China is an absolutely necessary complement" (pp. 73, 78, 80–81).

MacMurray manifested the same overriding concern for the maintenance of the integrity of the international legal framework in his analysis of another test of the Washington system: namely, the unilateral decision by the Nationalist Government at Canton to begin enforcing the 2½ percent customs surtax, which had been among the topics of negotiation at the Tariff Conference before it was adjourned in the chaos of the summer of 1926. The Washington Conference had not envisioned any unilateralism, nor any such regionalism. The Japanese were so· profoundly concerned by its appearance that they "considered a conference of the Washington Conference Powers advisable." The U.S. State Department, swayed (as Mac-Murray saw it) by pressure from the missionary community endorsing such unilateral repudiation of treaties, and also by the resolution of Congressman Stephen Porter, which had placed the Administration on the domestic political defensive, turned down Japan's request, not perceiving "the urgency of initiating discussions with Great Britain and Japan" (p. 87). This was a serious blow to the trust between Tokyo and Washington.

That had been October 1926. An even more serious challenge to the Washington system developed in the following spring. The systematic looting and killing as Nationalist troops took control of Nanking in March 1927 had created "throughout the countryside an ominous tension. . . . Missionaries reluctantly abandoned their work in the interior, merchants gave up the attempt to carry on business in the outports, and foreigners either gave up and went home or concentrated in Tientsin or Shanghai to wait until the storm had blown over." Yet again the United States failed to cooperate with the other Powers. In spite of having participated in drawing up the joint protest letter, it was unwilling to join in sanctions against the Nationalists, and thus "paralyzed [the action of the other Washington Powers] and left them in a false position" (pp. 95, 96).

According to MacMurray, the U.S. response in the matter of the Belgian treaty, which China sought to repudiate in the autumn of 1926, was yet another betrayal of the principles of international law and cooperation. Although Belgium was hardly an important force in China, its treaty was nevertheless "one of the typical treaties establishing the basis of the relations of the Powers with China." If it could be abrogated unilaterally, in violation of its provisions, then all other treaties were vulnerable was well. From a legal point of view this was a profoundly serious matter. Kellogg, who looked at the matter from a domestic perspective, dismissed

MacMurray's concerns, and instead told the press that he "did not know of any reason why this Government should support the Belgian Government in any protest against the denunciation by China of its treaty with Belgium" (p. 100).

The most fateful of the steps undermining the Washington system, however, was the Chinese abrogation of the Japanese treaties of 1896 and 1903. MacMurray believed that the U.S. Government should perhaps have been impressed in September 1928 when Count Yasuya Uchida (1865–1936) made a special call at the State Department to express the concern of the new Tanaka Government (which had come to power partly because of dissatisfaction at the failures of Shidehara's policy in China) at the lack of cooperation among the Powers, and the seeming impunity with which the Chinese could break their treaty commitments. These were matters of utmost seriousness for Japan. The U.S. response was evasive and dilatory (it came in February of the following year). To Japan's concern about China's disrespect for treaties, it responded with classic policy double-talk, saying the Administration,

> believing that the National Government [of China] desires to conform its practices to the best standards of international practices, hopes that the National Government's acts will demonstrate that such is its intention.

Given such a "rebuff" by the United States, and the conclusion without consultation of a new treaty between the United States and the Nationalist Government beginning in July 1928, it was not surprising that Japan should have turned to her own military power to guarantee her interests, where hitherto she had relied on multilateral diplomacy. These examples, and others like them, led to MacMurray's conclusion: China and the United States had unwittingly done much to create the aggressive Japan that now menaced them both (pp. 117, 118).

What should be done? We have already seen that, when the memorandum was prepared, U.S. policymakers were deeply divided about approaches to Japan. Some favored coming to terms with the seemingly irreversible reality Japan had created on the mainland of Asia; others wanted resistance. MacMurray proposed a slow and deliberate disengagement, one that would not compromise U.S. principles, but would make their application moot, given that the means of enforcement would no longer exist. Above all, MacMurray hoped to avoid the war that he believed was likely, and was persuaded could bring no advantage to the United States. For as he pointed out, the problem in Asia was not Japan, but rather the whole system of relationships among the Powers. Even if Japan, the putative aggressor, were defeated, the result would almost certainly not be peace, but rather her replacement by the USSR as the dominant power in the region, a development that would be detrimental to U.S. interests. Mac-Murray feared, however, that the U.S. tendency to make policy emotionally, and to shift capriciously, might nevertheless bring about a conflict. MacMurray's final counsel for dealing with the new situation in Asia was similar to his original recommendation for dealing with Chinese nationalism: The United States should not adopt rhetorical positions that it was unwilling to back up, with force if necessary.

Evaluation of the Memorandum

When he composed the memorandum, MacMurray had achieved new diplomatic success and reestablished his reputation as an Asian specialist. In 1936 he was promoted from Riga to Ankara, and in 1937 Roosevelt demonstrated his confidence by again offering him the ambassadorship to China. MacMurray declined the post, however, and stayed on in Turkey.[88]

No full study of MacMurray's service in China has yet been made, so evaluations are scattered and incomplete. As with the memorandum itself, these are easiest to understand against the background of the times in which they were written, and their authors' concerns. They fall into two general categories: those written by specialists on Japan or Asia in general, which are by and large sympathetic, and those written by specialists on China or on U.S.-Chinese relations, which tend to be more negative.

This division reflects in turn two distinct sets of preoccupations. The Pacific war was a great catastrophe, and the first group of scholars generally took Pearl Harbor as their starting point, retrospectively scanning the horizon to find something that could have helped avoid it. The memorandum suggests one such policy: greater attention to international law in the 1920s, which might have changed the course of Japan's history, and therefore the world's. Akira Iriye's treatment of the period 1921 to 1931 is the best example of this approach, which stresses the possibilities initially offered by the Washington System, or what he calls "The Lost Opportunity."[89]

Pearl Harbor, however, is not the only site of disaster from which historians have looked back for alternatives. For those chiefly interested in

---

[88]See Franklin D. Roosevelt to Secretary of State, April 5, 1937, Official File (OF) 20; FDR to Secretary of State, December 18, 1940, OF 1274; also cross-references March 31, 1937; April 12, 1937; and December 18, 1940; OF 909. Papers of Franklin D. Roosevelt, Franklin D. Roosevelt Library, Hyde Park, N.Y.

[89]Chapter 1 in Iriye, *After Imperialism*.

China, "The Great Aberration," as Warren Cohen labels it, of estrangement between Peking and Washington following the Communist victory in 1949, and the many events deemed its consequences—for example, the Korean War and the Vietnam War—is as serious as Pearl Harbor.[90] Here the retrospective prescription—namely, U.S. identification with Chinese national aspirations—is rather different.

United States' diplomacy could not possibly have achieved both sets of goals. Keeping Japan part of the international system in the 1930s would have meant maintaining a certain distance from China. Such distance, however, would have cooled even more the lukewarm backing for Chinese aspirations in the interwar years, one of the factors that China specialists regularly mention as having contributed to later problems with that country. If Japan specialists often see the estrangement of the 1930s as a more severe form of a problem that had been evident in the 1920s and even before, China specialists have a similar tendency to view the U.S. response to China after 1949 as an intensified version of the fundamental flaw of U.S. China policy over the preceding decades—namely, the failure to get the United States firmly on the side of "Chinese nationalism." It seems that ultimately one must be forced to take sides in a zero-sum game, for or against one of the "two ascendant nationalisms, Japanese and Chinese," in which many scholars see the conflict as being rooted.[91]

Few analysts have attempted to resolve this dilemma.[92] Students of China and Japan have gone their separate ways; the result, as Waldo Heinrichs has pointed out, is that while specialized studies abound, very little work deals comprehensively with the large questions of U.S. Pacific policy (the very kind of issues the memorandum addresses).[93] Almost by default, therefore, MacMurray has been judged not against the appropriate

---

[90]Cohen, *America's Response,* p. 217. Cohen's use of the term is ironical; the earlier, A. Whitney Griswold generation of writers on U.S.-East Asian relations considered American engagement there to be the "aberration."

[91]Doenecke, *Diplomacy of Frustration,* p. 3.

[92]The theme is repeatedly treated by Akira Iriye; see also, among other works, Alvin D. Coox and Hilary Conroy, eds., *China and Japan: Search for Balance since World War I* (Santa Barbara: ABC-Clio, 1978), and Shinkichi Etō, "China's International Relations, 1911–1931," in *The Cambridge History of China,* vol. 13, *Republican China, 1912–1949, Part II,* ed. John K. Fairbank (Cambridge: Cambridge University Press, 1986), pp. 74–116.

[93]Waldo Heinrichs, "The Middle Years, 1900–1945, and the Question of a Large U.S. Policy for East Asia," in *New Frontiers in American–East Asian Relations: Essays Presented to Dorothy Borg,* ed. Warren I. Cohen (New York: Columbia University Press, 1983), pp. 77–106.

international background, but rather within the single context of Chinese politics of the 1920s, and this has led to misunderstandings.

Most scholars, Chinese and Western alike, see the 1920s as dominated by a sudden rise in Chinese nationalism. Following this analysis, students of foreign policy identify the chief issue facing the Powers as "response to nationalism": Are the new Chinese demands to be embraced or resisted?[94] Most of these scholars then fault MacMurray and his colleagues for making what they interpret as the second choice. Michael Hunt, for example, writes:

> The 1920s found the United States and China locked in an antagonistic phase, as Chinese nationalists more sharply than ever attacked the unequal treaties. . . . A group of increasingly influential career American diplomats schooled in the principles of pre-1914 China policy reacted with predictable dismay, even hostility, to this rising tide of Chinese nationalism and the disorder that accompanied its challenge to foreign interests. John V. A. MacMurray, the most outspoken of that group, regarded the intensifying Chinese protest as a kind of "folly," a venting of spleen by humiliated Chinese whipped into a frenzy of "hysterical self-assertion" under the influence of "Bolshevik and juvenile nationalistic influences." Even appearing to make concessions on the major issue of treaty revision was dangerous. . . . Nelson T. Johnson and Stanley K. Hornbeck . . . followed the general drift of MacMurray's analysis though they expressed their views in less strident terms.[95]

As for the memorandum specifically, Dorothy Borg's evaluation is scathing:

> While Minister in China, MacMurray had become bitterly, almost passionately, critical of the activities of the Chinese and especially of the nationalist antiforeign movement which he felt, under the direction of the Kuomintang, had taken the form of an unrestrained and outrageous defiance of the treaty powers. The memorandum showed that MacMurray's views had in no way altered and, among other matters, had led him to look upon Japanese aggression in the 1930s with a measure of tolerance.[96]

---

[94]The "response to nationalism" formulation seems ubiquitous in the scholarly literature, e.g., in the title of Warren I. Cohen's article, "America and the May Fourth Movement: The Response to Chinese Nationalism, 1917–1921," *Pacific Historical Review* 35 (1966), pp. 83–100.

[95]Michael H. Hunt, *The Making of a Special Relationship: The United States and China to 1914* (New York: Columbia University Press, 1983), pp. 304–5.

[96]Dorothy Borg, *The United States and the Far Eastern Crisis of 1933–1938* (Cambridge, Mass.: Harvard University Press, 1964), pp. 171–72.

The limited Chinese scholarship on the topic is even more condemnatory. It portrays MacMurray and his colleagues as little more than agents of the U.S. imperialism they believe was seeking at the time to establish total domination over China.[97]

All such criticisms are premised on an understanding of the political events of the 1920s that is arguably incomplete and oversimplified. Nationalism in particular is by no means a straightforward political entity, nor did the struggle, first within the Northern camp, and then between the Northern forces and the Kuomintang, pose anything like the simple choices for or against it that the "response to nationalism" paradigm assumes. Applied to MacMurray, the oversimplified "nationalism pro or con?" view of the 1920s distorts and misrepresents both his concerns and his purposes. The U.S. minister was in fact no enemy of Chinese aspirations; far less was he a sympathizer of Japan. As a diplomat whose concerns embraced both countries, however, he had perforce to consider seriously, as most subsequent scholars have not, the effects on each of developments in the other.[98] Earlier experience had impressed on him the gravity of the threat Japan posed to China, and during his ministership he was particularly concerned lest measures to modify China's international position should unleash that menace again. He believed, perhaps wrongly, that such a catastrophe could be avoided if treaty revision were carried out by the Powers cooperatively and within a strict framework of international law. The analysis that follows will deal with these issues in succession, examining first MacMurray's attitudes toward international law, and second the nature of Chinese nationalism during the period in question.

---

[97]For mainland Chinese scholarship, see Rongqu Luo and Xiangze Jiang, "Research in Sino–American Relations in the People's Republic of China," in *New Frontiers in American–East Asian Relations,* pp. 1–16; also Arnold Xiangze Jiang, *The United States and China* (Chicago: University of Chicago Press, 1988), esp. pp. 66–88. MacMurray is distinguished from other Americans only by his argument "that America should act together with the other imperialist powers," i.e., not unilaterally, in pursuit of domination. See Chung-kuo k'o-hsüeh-yüan, chin-tai-shih yen-chiu-so, comp. *Chin-tai lai-hua wai-kuo jen-min tz'u-tien* (Pei-ching: Chung-kuo k'o-hsüeh-yüan, 1981), p. 306. For a Nationalist Chinese account, see Ta Jen Liu, *A History of Sino-American Diplomatic Relations, 1840–1974* (Taipei: China Academy, 1978), pp. 152–77.

[98]Neither of the authors mentioned addresses the issue squarely. Hunt observes, without further explanation, that "the revived Japanese menace in the late 1920s began to alter the dynamics of the Sino-American relationship," *Special Relationship,* p. 305; Japanese aggression is similarly a given in Borg's *The United States and the Far Eastern Crisis.*

We have already pointed out that the underlying theme of the memorandum is a concern for international law and multilateral diplomacy in East Asia, and a sense that, had these been pursued, the outcome would have been better. Thus, after recounting the developments that have given Manchuria to Japan and brought that country to the brink of war in China proper, MacMurray remarks:

> Some easing of the tensions created by these developments might have been expected if there had remained any practical or moral effectiveness of those Treaties and Resolutions of the Washington Conference of 1921–22 which aimed to establish a policy of cooperation among the signatory Powers, including China. Since, however, the intended system of cooperation was allowed during 1925–29 to fall into desuetude, the formulation of principles upon which it was to have been based has inevitably lost its authority. The Washington Treaties have therefore ceased in practical fact to be available as a means of accommodating such strains as may arise from the changes of equilibrium that lately have taken place in the Far East.[99]

This sense of the need to cooperate and work within the Washington system had clearly been shared by MacMurray's colleagues in Peking. In the 1920s many of his friends from the 1910s returned to head legations— Yoshizawa in 1923, de Martel in 1924, Lampson in 1926, Varè in 1927—and they formed what they called "The Old Firm,"[100] a congenial group who tried to coordinate policies in a way that would obviate the danger of competition among themselves over their positions in China.

Their approach made sense. These diplomats belonged to a generation that had just emerged from a horrific war that was arguably the product of diplomatic failure; they were all internationalists in one way or another, and not solely, or even primarily, in connection with China. All diplomacy of the time was carried out in the shadow of the European peace, and particularly of Versailles. Even the end of the Anglo-Japanese alliance was not so much an aspect of British Asian policy as it was of London's United States policy. Similarly, France's position on Chinese treaty revision reflected no special animus against Peking; rather, it was an aspect of its insistence that the Versailles settlement and German reparations not be diluted. Even Japan's China policy was sometimes subordinated to its desire to retain membership in the larger, Europe-centered club of nations.

This means that many of the issues MacMurray and his colleagues addressed were thus only coincidentally about China. The treaties they

---

[99]Memorandum, pp. 60–61.
[100]Yoshizawa, *Gaikō rokujū nen,* p. 82.

made and the precedents they set in China were important primarily because of the influence they would have in Europe, where international law was, in theory at least, the basis of the postwar order. The world of the 1920s saw a proliferation of international documents and international organizations, animated, sincerely or cynically, by a desire to keep peace through cooperation. Some of these could not be faulted on any ground (except perhaps practicality); the Kellogg-Briand pact outlawing war, signed in 1928, the same year MacMurray settled with the Nationalists, was a good example. Others were objectionable, at least to certain groups: The majority of Germans disliked the Versailles treaties because, like the treaties regulating China with which MacMurray was concerned, they had been imposed by force and their provisions were "unequal," a fact played on by agitators of both left and right. The problem was that, in the eyes of the diplomatic system, all duly concluded treaties were equally valid. To repudiate one would jeopardize all. As Hornbeck stated with regard to international law, "disturb the fabric at any point and you produce disturbances throughout its entirety."[101]

Such "unequal treaties," however, produced grievances within the countries upon which they had been imposed, which in turn fed internal instability. If their provisions were not adjusted in a timely manner, the treaties might be repudiated, and the nations involved take their own courses. This in turn would upset the international balance of power. Chinese treaties were part of this web. Were repudiation to be countenanced there, far more powerful states—Germany, for example—might follow suit. International diplomats were therefore faced with the delicate task of tailoring and reweaving the fabric of international law without rending it at any point.

In China the outstanding issues were tariff revision and extraterritoriality. The former was important because customs were a chief source of revenue for the Chinese Government, and shortage of that revenue, because of low tariffs, was one of the factors slowly choking that government. The latter was important for symbolic reasons. The privileges and immunities enjoyed by foreigners under the treaties were deeply offensive to the pride of Chinese, and rather than modestly enjoying them, many foreigners reveled in them in a way that compounded the insult. The Washington Treaties provided mechanisms to revise the tariff and reexamine extraterritoriality. The authors of these provisions probably expected that negotiations would produce the sort of gradual abolition of unequal treaties that they had already witnessed (and in some cases participated in) in Thailand and Japan.

---

[101]Doenecke, *Diplomacy of Frustration,* p. 35.

The arcana of international law, however, were the province of a relatively small group of professional diplomats, and the practical men who guided much foreign policy in the interwar period proved less particular about punctilious observation of every legal point. Like the paper money of the time, diplomatic agreements were gradually devalued: The more treaties that were signed, the less, it seemed, each was worth. For a treaty to mean anything, it had to include real sanctions for enforcement, even, as a last resort, military action, which threatened war. Was one to take such provisions seriously? With increasing frequency the answer was "no." To many people treaties became no more than words, "black and big on paper," as Ramsay MacDonald said of his promises to aid France; they were, in A.J.P. Taylor's words, no more than "a harmless drug to soothe nerves."[102]

Concern about this point is at the core of MacMurray's memorandum. He felt that politicians at home were undermining international law for their own short-term purposes, with little concern for the larger future. He was not alone in this opinion. George Kennan had similar reactions less than a decade later, when he found himself posted to Moscow to help with the negotiation of new U.S.-Soviet treaties. Like Peking in MacMurray's day, Moscow in 1933 was the seat of a government that sought to repudiate or remake much of international law. Like MacMurray working for Kellogg, Kennan found himself serving under an ambassador, William Bullitt (1891–1967), and an administration that for reasons of their own were eager that all should go well.

Earlier, in Riga, Kennan had been interested in the degree to which commercial treaties of the new Soviet Government "had or had not afforded real protection to the interests of other governments."[103] In Moscow, Kennan decoded the impressive-looking but essentially meaningless guarantees in proposed treaties with the United States. Despite this, the higher levels in the State Department went along with the drafts proposed by Soviet foreign minister Maksim Litvinov (1876–1951), and signed treaties embodying, as Kennan recalled, "weak verbiage that had failed to be effective in protecting the interests of other countries."[104] Kennan pondered the political implications of such sloppiness, saying that he never learned whether or not Roosevelt "knew this and did not care, considering merely that to an uncritical public, and particularly to a congressional public, the passage would look good."[105] It was, he said, his first lesson on

---

[102]A.J.P. Taylor, *English History, 1914–1945* (Reading: Pelican Books, 1970), p. 277.
[103]George F. Kennan, *Memoirs, 1925–1950* (Boston: Little, Brown, 1972), p. 50.
[104]Ibid., p. 53.
[105]Ibid.

one of the most consistent and incurable traits of American statesman-
ship—namely, its neurotic self-consciousness and introversion, the tendency to make statements and take actions with regard not to their effect
on the international scene . . . but rather to their effect on . . . American
opinion.[106]

MacMurray would certainly have agreed.

What about nationalism? The kind of American opinion to which
Kennan referred would fault MacMurray for being hidebound and unresponsive to broad Chinese national aspirations. Scholars have generally
portrayed him as having an outdated understanding of China. Thomas
Buckley, for example, explains that "it was the China of the nineteenth
century, dying in the twentieth, that impressed itself upon MacMurray's
mind." As a result he was unable, in the 1920s, fully to appreciate the "new
forces building in Peking."[107] Although theoretically favoring reform, he
could not grasp the revolutionary changes it would require, which overtook
that society during the period of his ministership. As Warren Cohen puts
it:

> Not merely recognizing China's need to modernize, but encouraging the
> process, the United States nonetheless demanded order, seemingly un-
> aware that the ancient scales of Chinese society could hardly be scraped
> away without the sword. A combination of sterile legalism and a rigid
> insistence on order shaped American policy.[108]

Cohen's comment about "the sword" points up the belief, shared by many
of MacMurray's critics, in revolutionary transformation, a belief that keeps
apparent parallels between the 1920s and later periods never far from the
surface. Dorothy Borg, for example, evidently considers that MacMurray's
inability to cope with the revolution of his day prefigures the problems of
U.S. China policy during the late 1940s; as Warren Cohen observes, her
"praise for Kellogg was not without implicit advice for the Truman
administration: let the Chinese fight their own civil wars and revolu-
tions."[109] To explain MacMurray's alleged failure, at least one author has
turned to psychology, maintaining that childhood left him with weaknesses
and insecurities that made Chinese national assertion deeply threatening.[110]

---

[106]Ibid.

[107]Buckley, "MacMurray," pp. 29, 28.

[108]Cohen, *America's Response,* p. 113.

[109]Cohen, *New Frontiers,* pp. xviii–xix.

[110]Janet Sue Collester, "J.V.A. MacMurray, American Minister to China, 1925–1929:
The Failure of a Mission" (Ph.D. dissertation, Indiana University, 1977).

Such a critique is based on a superficial understanding of MacMurray and of nationalism. MacMurray was not a die-hard opponent of treaty revision and Chinese rights. Quite the opposite: He was well aware of the precedents for peaceful and orderly abolition of unequal treaties in other Asian states, and he favored the same process for China. Some longtime foreign residents of China seem even to have viewed him as a hopeless naïf. His earlier experience in China was ignored, as witness the following exchange, in a novel evoking the time, between a prissy American lady and her British friends in Amoy:

> "Now our new Minister in Peking, Mr. MacMurray, takes a very sympa-
> thetic view of Chinese aspirations, he . . ." "How long has he been in
> China?" Mrs. Theobold suddenly turned round. "Why, it must be eight
> weeks now." But you could not catch Esther Mary Smith that way. "It's
> the fresh eye we need, of course. . . ."[111]

Nor did MacMurray particularly oppose the Nationalist party. He simply held the same very low opinion of its members that he held of most Chinese politicians. His staff was regularly in contact with them, and in September 1926 he became the first minister of any foreign government to visit the Nationalist Government at Canton. From Eugene Ch'en and T. V. Soong he "gathered an extremely strong impression that the Kuomintang has a real desire to adopt toward the powers a policy of conciliation." He was hopeful about working with them, because both men made a "partic-ular effort . . . to impress on me that treaty obligations had not been repudiated by them and that they were ready to accept those obligations as the point for beginning negotiations."[112] After the Nationalist Government moved to Wuhan, MacMurray continued to maintain contact. In early summer 1928, when the Nationalists were established in Nanking, Mac-Murray rapidly negotiated a new tariff treaty, which was signed on July 25.[113]

Thus the nature of MacMurray's diplomacy was far more complex than the "response to nationalism" paradigm grasps. What MacMurray opposed was not Chinese aspirations or treaty revision, but rather the adoption of a competitive or unilateral approach to China policy that, while ostensibly serving those ends, would in fact undermine them. This was the lesson of the Conference on the Chinese Customs Tariff, mentioned earlier. When it finally opened after long delay on October 26, 1925, promising important

---

[111] Averil Mackenzie-Grieve, *A Race of Green Ginger* (London: Putnam, 1959), p. 116.
[112] *Foreign Relations of the United States,* 1926, 1:868.
[113] Text in *Foreign Relations of the United States,* 1928, 2:475–77.

steps toward modification of the treaties, MacMurray expended a great deal of effort to support the undertaking. As he feared, however, it was upset by both political competition among Chinese factions and insufficient cooperation among the Powers. And China was left no better off than before.

Furthermore, MacMurray understood that nationalism was not, as some believed, a new arrival on the Chinese scene. Nationalistic policies had been followed consistently by the post-1912 Government, as the examples of Yüan Shih-k'ai and Wellington Koo demonstrate; in fact, both were far more subtle and effective diplomats than their initial Kuomintang counterparts. What changed in the mid-1920s was not the goals or the substance of Chinese diplomacy, but rather its role in Chinese society and politics. The institutional framework that had hitherto enabled China to make her nationalistic demands with one voice broke down, and several groups began competing for control of nationalist issues. What Elie Kedourie calls "The Politics of Nationalism" took command, a game of capture-the-flag between the Peking Government in the North and the Kuomintang in the South.[114] Each side sought to outdo the other in its nationalist zeal, with the result that however satisfactory or extreme the position one side took, the other had to go one better, which meant that no settlement of issues could be reached. Of course, the point of the game, for the Chinese players at least, was not to reach a settlement; rather, it was to use such competition to win political power. The positions of foreign powers on the actual issues of nationalism were thus rendered irrelevant by the dynamic of Chinese internal politics.

How this worked was very clear in the bidding war that ensued between North and South as the military balance of power began to shift after the fall of the Tuan Ch'i-jui Government in the face of student protest in March 1926. The Tariff Conference was an important arena. If it worked out as planned, the Northerners stood to receive a significant income, between 90 and 100 million Chinese dollars, which would permit the Northern Government to ameliorate its finances and strengthen its domestic position. Therefore it was in the Northerners' interests to negotiate seriously and moderately, and they did. Extreme demands would only hurt them; what they wanted was the granting of reasonable demands. The Southerners, not being the recognized government of China, had no such incentive. They would be excluded from any share of the new customs revenue, so they followed a strategy of disrupting the conference in such a way as to deny the money to their northern rivals, while at the same time appearing to be the truer champions of China's dignity.

---

[114]Elie Kedourie, *Nationalism,* 2d ed. (London: Hutchinson University Library, 1985), pp. 92–140.

Another example of such a bidding war took place in the second half of 1926, this time to the disadvantage of the Southerners. MacMurray had visited the South that autumn, and been impressed by the moderation shown by the Kuomintang leaders. For the United States to begin to deal with the Southerners, however, would have been a disaster for the North. Wellington Koo's abrogation of the Sino–Belgian treaty on November 6, 1926 (though part of a larger diplomatic strategy as well), had the political effect of forcing the Kuomintang's hand. If the North was to be repudiationist, the South could be no less. Two weeks later, in Nanchang, Chiang K'ai-shek told a foreign correspondent that he endorsed Koo's action, rejected the idea of treaty revision, and called for the immediate abrogation of all existing treaties.[115] The Chinese sides were now stalemated. Neither could expect what each very much wanted—namely, a working relationship with the Powers that could be translated into political ascendancy within China.

Faced with this situation, which MacMurray immediately understood, the minister's concern was not to support or to reject specific Chinese demands, but rather to neutralize the political competition by cobbling together a joint Chinese delegation that could negotiate about the treaties with a single voice. This expedient had been adopted at Versailles and at Washington, and without it in both cases foreign policy might have been crippled by internal contention. The solution had been effective: The May 4th Movement, instead of growing more extreme, had largely subsided after the restoration of Shantung, and nearly all Chinese had accepted the Washington Treaties. Experience taught that if Chinese factionalism could be checked and the Powers kept together, genuine concessions could be made, and these in turn would do much to assuage legitimate and authentic nationalist demands.[116]

For such a strategy to work, however, foreigners as well as Chinese had to speak with a single voice. MacMurray unbendingly opposed any action that would undercut this requirement. Sometimes this undercutting took place in Peking, as when British minister Macleay failed to consult with his colleagues or insisted that, in the face of civil war in China, the Tariff Conference should be adjourned rather than simply suspended, as his colleagues urged, which would have kept open the possibility of its resumption. More often the undercutting came from home governments, which

---

[115]Chiang's interview with Associated Press correspondent Bruno Schwartz appeared in *Hankow Herald,* November 23, 1926, enclosed in Lockhart to Kellogg, December 4, 1926, State Department Files, 893.00/7993. I am indebted to Zhitian Luo for this reference.

[116]*Foreign Relations of the United States,* 1926, 1:857, 868–69.

(perhaps understandably) never quite grasped the political dynamics so important to China's diplomats. London did not consult Miles Lampson about the new China policy launched in December 1926, nor did Washington alert MacMurray to the American response a few months later.

Nevertheless, even during a period of domestic Chinese chaos, the representatives of the Powers in Peking sought to work within the legal and diplomatic structures that could peacefully accommodate the interests of all concerned. They were building on precedents for treaty revision elsewhere in Asia, and on the basis of discussions that had been carried out with the Chinese at least since the Washington Conference. Their own claims to the contrary notwithstanding, the Nationalists were not the first Chinese to call for treaty revision, or to pursue it as a political goal.[117] Nor were the Powers unalterably opposed to such a goal. The issue was not so much whether to make concessions (though just how far to go was highly contentious), as how to make them without jeopardizing the international legal order, a question that had implications not only for China but for post-Versailles Europe as well.

Unfortunately, the Nationalists proved extremely effective in gaining support even for treaty revision of a sort that would implicitly undermine international law and procedure. Their organization moved into the vacuum created by the breakdown of the Northern Government after the civil wars of 1924–25, and their spokesmen took the sort of uncompromising positions that proved very popular domestically. The Nationalists were also able to mobilize opinion abroad. In the United States, where it was brought to bear particularly through missionary organizations, such pressure led to the adoption of policies tilted in favor of the Nationalists.[118]

Such influences converged to make the period after 1925 generally one of unilateral initiatives, not only from Washington, but from London and Brussels as well. Japan, however, appears to have been the exception, still trying to work within an internationalist framework. For longer than those of the other Powers, Shidehara's foreign policy "laid stress on the mainte-

---

[117]For example, Thomas Millard, *The End of Extraterritoriality in China* (Shanghai: A.B.C. Press, 1931). For a balanced treatment see Wesley R. Fishel, *The End of Extraterritoriality in China* (Berkeley: University of California Press, 1952); also Thomas H. Etzold, "In Search of Sovereignty: The Unequal Treaties in Sino-American Relations, 1925–1930," in *China in the 1920s: Nationalism and Revolution,* ed. F. Gilbert Chan and Thomas H. Etzold (New York: New Viewpoints, 1976), pp. 176–96.

[118]Paul A. Varg, *Missionaries, Chinese, and Diplomats: The American Protestant Missionary Movement in China, 1890–1952* (Princeton: Princeton University Press, 1958), pp. 180–211.

nance of the Washington system of cooperation,"[119] even when that seemed to jeopardize immediate Japanese interests. When Japanese policy finally changed, it did so in a way that proved catastrophic for everyone else.

The process was clear in the policies of the coalition government formed in 1924 by Takaaki Katō (1860–1926). Largely responsible for the imposition of the Twenty-one Demands on China in 1915, Katō was clearly no liberal on China policy. In this as in other areas (electoral reform, for instance), his government pursued policies that had the effect of strengthening Japan's credentials as a full member of the liberal postwar international community.[120] In his speech to the Diet on July 1, 1924, Foreign Minister Shidehara took great care to associate Japan with the other Powers, stressing that future actions in China would be carried out within the framework of the Washington Treaties.[121] During the Chihli-Fengt'ien war two months later, when Wu P'ei-fu seemed to challenge Japan's position in Manchuria, he threatened to resign rather than approve military intervention on behalf of Chang Tso-lin.[122] Scholars have confirmed MacMurray's account of the continuing influence of internationalists within the Japanese government until the 1930s, and their deep dismay at the lack of foreign seriousness about their concerns.[123] From these facts flowed MacMurray's central contention: that if the Powers had been more scrupulous in their observance of the Washington Treaties, the hand of the internationalists in Tokyo would have been strengthened, the nascent diplomacy of the Taishō period (1912–1926) saved, and the hostilities of the 1930s perhaps avoided.

Could the Washington system have avoided war? Was it, in fact, "wounded in the house of its friends," as MacMurray contended, or had it perhaps been crippled even at birth? These questions raise large and contentious issues about the origins of the Pacific war that lie beyond the scope of a simple introduction to an archival document. Nevertheless, a few specific points about MacMurray's analysis (p. 126) are in order.

The events that led to war began in Manchuria. One of the most uneasy

---

[119]Hosoya Chihiro, "Britain and the United States in Japan's View of the International System, 1919–1937," in *Anglo-Japanese Alienation, 1919–1952,* ed. Ian Nish (Cambridge: Cambridge University Press, 1982), p. 12.

[120]Sheldon Garon, "Katō Takaaki," in *Encyclopedia of Asian History,* 2:283.

[121]Masaru Ikei, "Dainiji Hōchoku sensō to Nihon," in *Tai-Manmō seisakushi no ichimen: Nichi-Ro sengo yori Taishōki ni itaru,* ed. Ken Kurihara (Tokyo: Hara Shobō, 1966), pp. 193–94.

[122]Masaru Ikei, "Dainiji Hōchoku sensō to Nihon," p. 210.

[123]See, for example, Akira Iriye, "The Failure of Economic Expansionism: 1918–1931," in *Japan in Crisis: Essays on Taishō Democracy,* ed. Bernard S. Silberman and H. D. Harootunian (Princeton: Princeton University Press, 1974), pp. 237–69.

linkages in MacMurray's argument is the one between the breakdown of cooperation among the Powers in China proper and the development of the Manchurian crisis. Recall that even at the Washington Conference itself, when China was relatively feeble militarily and Japan overwhelmingly strong, the issue of Manchuria had to be fudged, because even if there was a consensus among the Powers that Japan's position there should not be challenged, public opinion would not permit this to be stated explicitly.

From the start, therefore, Japanese diplomacy rested uneasily on two foundations. One was a commitment, shared even by such internationalists as Shidehara, to the maintenance of the status quo in Manchuria. The other was the desire to work cooperatively with the other Powers. It was believed that if only the framework of international law could be guaranteed, these interests would be maintained. During the crisis in the Chihli-Fengt'ien war, Shidehara noted that existing treaties governing Manchurian railways would provide a sufficient basis for Japanese military action against the Chinese if they tried to move in Manchuria.[124]

In this approach Shidehara was not unlike many other internationalist thinkers of the time. The British foreign secretary, Lord Curzon (1859–1925), told the Japanese ambassador, Viscount Sutemi Chinda (1856–1929), that the future of China did not lie in subdivision among the Powers, nor "did it lie in the assumption by Japan of the overlordship of the Far East," because the day of empires had passed.[125] Curzon was probably not visualizing actual independence for the entities of the British empire, or any similar real diminution in Japan's holdings. Rather, he believed that a middle way could be found between domination and independence, one based on agreements that would be legally binding and enforced judicially, and thus obviate the need for police, military occupation, colonial governors, and so forth, and yet that would guarantee something like the existing state of affairs. Unfortunately, this appealing middle way may simply not have existed.

Certainly this way did not exist in the form in which the Powers tried to find it. MacMurray perhaps shares their unrealism when he describes their close cooperation. In fact, all were involved in unilateralism very early. The United States saw an open door policy as the best guarantee of its rights; the British had fixed interests in Shanghai and the South and were willing to trade off to favor those, even if that meant undermining cooper-

[124]Masaru Ikei, "Dainiji Hōchoku sensō to Nihon," p. 212.

[125]Quoted in William Roger Louis, *British Strategy in the Far East, 1919–1939* (Oxford: Clarendon Press, 1971), p. 21.

ation. The Japanese did much the same. At the Tariff Conference, Shidehara agreed to autonomy in principle, subject only to special local regulations for Manchuria. Furthermore, after the summer of 1925 when the Katō cabinet lost its parliamentary majority, China policy became one of the foci of internal political competition in Japan. Even as originally conceived, then, the Washington system did not so much adjust differences as paper over them.

Nevertheless, international cooperation might have worked if China had been stronger and more united. MacMurray is certainly correct when he explains that the "frenzied impulse of defiance and self-assertion" that had swept China in the year 1925 was to some extent simply the result of the delay in implementing the Washington agreements. He is also correct that Comintern policies stirred up and directed this sentiment. He is peculiarly unaware, however, of the extent to which institutional developments in China made all this possible. The civil wars that reached a climax in 1924 transformed a government that had some hope of cohesion, and therefore the credibility and stability necessary to negotiate realistically, into simply another faction competing in the nationalist game (p. 60).

If the Chinese "asked for it," it was not as a result of a conscious (or even unconscious) choice, but rather for institutional reasons that led to a polarization of politics. Furthermore, it was the wars that this polarization brought about, far more than the abstract breakdown of international law, that ultimately galvanized the Japanese. MacMurray implicitly accepts the argument that the Manchurian incident and the war that followed were caused by the rise of militarists in Japan, and that their rise had been caused by the breakdown of the Washington system and the consequent undermining of the internationalists. This is the familiar *nijūgaikō* (dual-diplomacy) argument, which contrasts military with civilian policies in Japan. As diplomats at the time realized, and Shin'ichi Kitaoka has convincingly shown since, what happened in Japanese policy did not reflect a difference between the military and the foreign office so much as the development in China of an unforeseen and unwelcome situation.[126] Its source was thus less the failure of the Powers to coordinate their policies than it was the emergence of new threats to Japanese interests in China (p. 64).

It is hard to see how the Powers could have averted this, although if the Washington Treaties had been ratified sooner, a stronger Northern Govern-

---

[126]Kitaoka, "China Experts in the Army." Much the same analysis was made by foreign diplomats at the time. See, for example, Sir Charles Eliot (British Ambassador, Tokyo) to Ramsay MacDonald, October 3, 1924, F 3554/15/10, and F.S.G. Piggott (Military Attaché, Tokyo) to Eliot, September 30, 1924, F 3583/19/10 in FO 405/254, Public Records Office, London.

ment would have emerged. But would it have accepted a permanent "special position" for Japan in Manchuria? Probably not. If a strong Northern Government looked set to destroy that special position through diplomacy (as Wellington Koo was), then Japan might have repudiated the Washington system and moved unilaterally. If, on the other hand, a strong Northern Government had been unsuccessful diplomatically, would it not have eventually felt compelled to challenge Japan militarily? And if it had, would the Powers have been willing to commit the forces necessary to restore the system? That seems unlikely, but even if they had, could they have been any more successful against China than the Japanese were?

Even though the usual criticism of MacMurray for being unresponsive to nationalism is incorrect, one can nevertheless ask whether the central contention of his memorandum is sustainable. Could the kind of position the Japanese wanted in Manchuria have been assured simply by international cooperation? MacMurray perhaps overestimates the compatibility of Japanese and Chinese interests in Manchuria, however adjusted, and he never mentions the increasing strength of Chinese armies, which caused much anxiety among the Japanese. Arguably, developments in China would have led sooner or later to conflict with Japan over Manchuria no matter what the other Powers did.[127] If so, even a United States that had scrupulously followed MacMurray's internationalist prescriptions would have faced dilemmas similar to those the memorandum blames in part on U.S. unilateralism.

Nevertheless, continued dominance by liberal and internationalist politicians in Japan, coupled with a stable situation in China, might have made it possible for Japan to redefine her goals in Manchuria in such a way as to permit acceptance of real Chinese sovereignty. It is only a possibility, but postwar experience suggests that Japan need not be aggressive. Given the tight balance of policies within Japan in particular, closer cooperation along the lines that MacMurray envisioned could only have been positive.

Conclusion

MacMurray retired from the foreign service in 1944 as special assistant to the secretary of state.[128] Three years later Dorothy Borg published her study, *America and the Chinese Revolution*, which still remains the most

---

[127]Shin'ichi Kitaoka, "China Experts in the Army," in *The Japanese Informal Empire in China 1895–1937*, pp. 330–68.

[128]Obituary, *New York Times*, September 26, 1960.

comprehensive account of U.S.-Chinese relations during the period MacMurray was in Peking, and which also did much to establish the image of MacMurray that this essay has sought to qualify—as a diplomat who responded in inexplicable and counterproductive ways to the Chinese aspirations for modernity and dignity. MacMurray knew the book and was sufficiently troubled by it to consider, as he wrote George Kennan, "publishing the memorandum in light of the misunderstanding by Dr. Borg by way of apologia."[129]

MacMurray never shared his thoughts with a wider public as Kennan did, and as a result the misunderstanding of his mission and his larger approach to diplomacy has persisted. What was that larger approach? As has been seen, it was in many ways similar to that which Kennan himself followed in his early career. Indeed, Thomas Buckley's summary of it, with a few modifications, could apply to the author of the "X" article:

> Strongly "realistic" in his approach to policy, he believed that the basic interests of the United States in China were immutable. Thus MacMurray deplored the unilateral, vacillating, idealistic tendencies he detected in many American proposals and preferred cooperative policies with other nations, the use of force when necessary, and deliberate, cautious negotiation.[130]

In many ways it is the standard profile of a certain, often admirable, type of American diplomat.

Despite his accomplishments, which are substantial when judged by conventional diplomatic standards, MacMurray has rarely been admired by specialists on U.S.-Chinese relations, who see him as having failed at a crucial moment. The judgment is based on a blending of a particular view of modern Chinese history with balance-of-power analysis. The view of history is what may be called the revolutionary paradigm: This sees the rise of nationalism and social radicalism, under the auspices first of the Nationalists and then of the Communists, as indispensable ingredients in a process of historical development whose eventual product would be a strong and stable China. Balance-of-power theorists, in turn, often see such a strong and stable China as essential to the peace of Asia. Both views continue to condition our understanding of China's political history and diplomacy, and even help to frame our foreign policy. The second leads to a desire to get on the right side of China, which is considered, as MacMurray put it, the "sun" to which in Asia even Japan was "planetary" (p. 62), and the first

---

[129]MacMurray to Kennan, March 25, 1951, Kennan Papers.
[130]Buckley, "MacMurray," p. 27.

suggests the degree of flexibility that may be necessary to do so. The approach has continued to have great persuasive power; arguably it provided the rationale for the Nixon visit in 1972.

In the years since Mao Tse-tung's (1893–1976) death, the revolutionary paradigm just mentioned, which has conditioned our understanding of China since the 1920s, has begun to lose its power to persuade. Scholars have increasingly marked down their evaluations of revolutionary change in China. Businesspeople no longer expect vast profits there. Geopoliticians no longer think of Japan as planetary. As the situation in Asia becomes more like what it was in MacMurray's day—with a strong Japan and a weak and internally divided China—his analyses become more relevant. Even his fears have some transferability. Japan no longer has the fatal stake on the Chinese mainland that it held in the 1930s, but a repetition of the pattern he describes, in which disorder in China gradually spreads by ripple effects into the rest of Asia, is still conceivable. The answer to it seems likely to be the same as advocated by MacMurray: international cooperation to sustain a legal order, rather than tilts designed to win favor with one country or another.

At root, the problems scholars encounter in evaluating MacMurray have less to do with his diplomacy than with their own personal expectations about China. MacMurray was a highly competent, and by no means unconventional, diplomat. His memorandum is a classic example of the diplomat's art. Had he chosen Europe as the stage for his career, he probably would have gotten better reviews. He chose China, however, and that made the difference. Perhaps George Kennan, the fellow Princetonian whose career echoes MacMurray's in so many striking ways, should be allowed the last word. Kennan has remarked on the American belief in Chinese exceptionalism, whose origins he finds "in our own emotional complexes."[131] This must be borne in mind when we consider evaluations of MacMurray, for against the exceptional standards and unusual expectations that, in the U.S. mind, go with China, an approach to diplomacy that would in other circumstances have been easily understood has seemed puzzling.

---

[131]Kennan, *American Diplomacy*, p. 52.

Memorandum

Note on the Text of the Memorandum

A carbon copy of the memorandum as submitted to the State Department is found in the papers of Stanley K. Hornbeck in the Hoover Collection (67008-9.25), Box 284. A photostatic copy is found in the State Department Files, National Archives, 711.93/383, and a typescript with corrections, in the Papers of John Van Antwerp MacMurray, Seeley Mudd Library, Princeton University. This text follows the Hoover version. Two variants found in the Princeton version are given in the notes.

Strictly Confidential

Developments Affecting American Policy in the Far East

THE BASES AND OBJECTIVES OF AMERICAN POLICY IN THE FAR EAST REQUIRE reappraisal in the light of fundamental developments during the past ten years.

Chief among these developments is the assertion by Japan, since 1931, of a forthright "positive" policy in eastern Asia, as exemplified by her aggressions in Manchuria and (to a lesser degree) in China proper, her withdrawal from the League of Nations, and her denunciation of the Washington and London Naval Treaties. These facts give evidence of Japan's determination to make herself dominant in the Far East, of a jealous attitude toward the claims of Western Powers to a participation on equal terms in the development of China, and of a hypersensitive intolerance of anything that she deems to be an interference with her course of action.

During the past decade the Soviet Union has reconsolidated the Russian East: and while constrained by immediate internal necessities to adopt a yielding attitude whenever its interests in Asia conflict with those of Japan, gives nevertheless the impression of a spring bent tighter and tighter and ready to recoil the more violently when released. Moreover, the Soviet Government (in its other manifestation as the Third International) has, in furtherance of the world revolution, propagated in China with a considerable measure of success certain of the political principles of Bolshevism, and very largely influenced the form and the purposes of the present Nationalist Government of China.

In China there has grown up a type of nationalism, in which the immemorial Chinese dislike of foreigners and the consciousness of grievance were directed by Communist advisers into a frenzied impulse of defiance and self-assertion: and although the force of that emotional outburst has largely spent itself, it has left the Chinese disillusioned and cynical, and less than ever to be counted on for cooperation even with those whose assistance they may bespeak.

Concurrently with these diverse forms of self-assertion on the part of Japan, Soviet Russia, and China, our own country has moved in the opposite direction, seeking to disembarrass itself of responsibilities for its only holdings in the Far Eastern area by granting independence (effective after ten years) to the Philippine Islands.[1]

Some easing of the tensions created by these developments might have been expected if there had remained any practical or moral effectiveness of those Treaties and Resolutions of the Washington Conference of 1921–22 which aimed to establish a policy of cooperation as among the signatory Powers, including China.[2] Since, however, the intended system of coopera-

---

[1]*Philippine independence:* The United States received the Philippines from Spain in 1898 following the Spanish-American War; American control, however, was not fully imposed until Philippine armed resistance ended in 1902. The Jones Act of 1916 conceded the rights of self-rule and eventual independence, while the Tydings-McDuffie Act of 1934 provided for independence after ten years, with a commonwealth form of government in the interim. In 1937 MacMurray was appointed chairman of the Joint Preparatory Committee on Philippine Affairs, a body established by Roosevelt and Philippine president Quezon to examine the problems, chiefly economic, that would arise with independence, and to evaluate how such factors might affect the possibility of moving independence forward to 1938 or 1939. Plans were disrupted, however, by the Japanese invasion, which began in December 1941; independence came on July 4, 1946. *References:* United States, Department of State, Conference Series: Joint Preparatory Committee on Philippine Affairs. *Report of May 20, 1938* (Washington, D.C.: U.S. Government Printing Office, 1938); David A. Rosenberg, "Philippines," in *The Encyclopedia of Asian History,* ed. Ainslie T. Embree (New York: Charles Scribner's Sons, 1988) 3:246–51.

[2]*The Washington Conference:* Organized by U.S. secretary of state Charles Evans Hughes, the conference met from November 12, 1921, until February 6, 1922. Its purpose was to reduce tension in the Pacific area, most importantly by limiting naval armaments, establishing a common approach to fostering the integrity of China, and creating a multilateral substitute for the Anglo-Japanese Alliance. The chief treaties guaranteed the Pacific possessions of the Powers (the Four-Power Treaty); provided for China's independence and Japan's eventual return of Shantung (the Nine-Power Treaty); and set ratios to limit naval competition (the Five-Power Treaty). Other important provisions called for the convening, within three months

tion was allowed during 1925–29 to fall into desuetude, the formulation of principles upon which it was to have been based has inevitably lost its authority. The Washington Treaties have therefore ceased in practical fact to be available as a means of accommodating such strains as may arise from the changes of equilibrium that lately have taken place in the Far East.

These developments confront us with a situation so essentially altered from that in which the traditional American policy grew to its eventual formulation at the Washington Conference, that we must, in order to be on safe ground, recognize the changes and inquire to what extent they should modify either our ultimate objectives or the strategic and tactical methods by which we may best pursue them.

I. The Aftermath of the Washington Conference

The essence of our traditional Far Eastern policy was that China, with its vast potentialities for economic development, was the crux of the whole

---

of ratification, of a conference to revise the Chinese customs tariff, and the establishment of a commission to examine the questions of extraterritoriality. In addition to leading figures from the countries involved, many diplomats who would later play key roles in China participated in the conference at junior levels. Thus, MacMurray, Stanley Hornbeck, and Nelson Johnson were all in the American delegation; Miles Lampson, with the British; Katsuji Debuchi and Sadao Saburi, along with Kijūrō Shidehara, in the Japanese. Alfred Sze, Wellington Koo, and Ch'ung-hui Wang (all senior) were the major figures in the Chinese delegation. The personal acquaintance and shared enterprise of these diplomats, as much as the treaties they concluded, served as the basis for the "Washington system" in practice. This fact became particularly evident in the 1920s, when ambiguities in the wording of the treaties (particularly in regard to the Japanese position in Manchuria), political turmoil in China, and increasing unilateralism by their home governments reduced the ability of the Washington diplomats to coordinate China policy. *References: Conference on the Limitation of Armament, Washington, November 12, 1921–February 6, 1922* (Washington, D.C.: Government Printing Office, 1922); Sadao Asada, "Japan's 'Special Interests' and the Washington Conference, 1921–1922," *American Historical Review* 56 (1961), pp. 62–70; Stanley J. Granat, "Chinese Participation at the Washington Conference, 1921–1922," (Ph.D. dissertation, Indiana University, 1969); Thomas H. Buckley, *The United States and the Washington Conference, 1921–1922* (Knoxville: University of Tennessee Press, 1970); Akira Iriye, *After Imperialism: The Search for a New Order in the Far East, 1921–1931* (New York: Atheneum, 1969); Wunsz King, *China at the Washington Conference, 1921–1922* (New York: St. John's University Press, 1963); William Roger Louis, *British Strategy in the Far East, 1919–1939* (Oxford: Clarendon Press, 1971); John Chalmers Vinson, *The Parchment Peace: The United States Senate and the Washington Conference, 1921–1922* (Athens: University of Georgia Press, 1955).

problem. Our actual trade with Japan has long been far greater than with China; and our political relations with Japan have had such additional importance as is consequent upon the fact that she might prove to be a contestant with us, economically or even militarily. China, by contrast, was a mere congeries of human beings, primitive in its political and economic organization, difficult and often troublesome to deal with in either aspect, and by its weakness constantly inviting aggressions that threatened such interests as we might have or hope for. Yet the possibilities which China prospectively afforded, as a supplier of raw materials and as a market for our exports, were so great that the maintenance of a right of fair participation in the trade of China was an objective justifying a degree of effort and solicitude out of all proportion to the present commercial value of the trade. We wanted nothing but an equal chance: but our claim to it was one of vital principle, justifying abnormal efforts and sacrifices.

The very difficulties of maintaining our right of opportunity, more-over, against the encroachments of particularistic action on the part of certain other Powers, led to such enunciations as that of Hay's correlated policies of the open door and the territorial and administrative integrity of China;[3] and the particular case of China thereby became a touchstone of our general claim to a right of fair and unimpeded trade in all quarters of the world. And the emphasis which reasoned policy thus placed upon the question of the open door in China was the more readily supported by the popular opinion of the country because of the widespread and genuine (though perhaps somewhat nebulous) feeling of sentimental interest in the Chinese people which resulted from several generations of American mis-sionary and cultural activities there. So it was natural and right that our governmental policy as well as popular opinion put China at the center of its thinking on Far Eastern affairs—made it the sun to which Japan and even our own Philippine possessions were merely planetary. It was equally a matter of course that the dominant purpose of American diplomatic activity in the Far East was to retain unimpaired the right of Americans to share in the commercial benefits of China's anticipated economic development,

---

[3]John M. Hay (1838–1905), secretary of state (1898–1905), authored a note (September 6, 1898) that sought to head off the threat, acute after the defeat in the Sino-Japanese War of 1894–95, that China would be partitioned into spheres of influence. Hay proposed that Britain, Germany, and Russia agree to respect treaty ports and refrain from discriminatory economic practices. Langer observes that "the note had little immediate importance, but set up an ideal policy often referred to later." William L. Langer, ed. *An Encyclopedia of World History* (Boston: Houghton Mifflin Co., 1968) p. 791; see also Kenton J. Clymer, *John Hay: The Gentleman as Diplomat* (Ann Arbor: University of Michigan Press, 1975).

while "holding the ring" so as to enable the Chinese to proceed with that development so far as possible unembarrassed.

That manner of thought found its culmination at the Washington Conference of 1921–22 at which, in a happy set of circumstances, it proved possible to obtain the concurrence of the interested Powers in a group of agreements concerning Far Eastern affairs, as the basis and implied condition of the agreement on the limitation of naval arrangements. Virtually all those Far Eastern agreements—all those, in fact, which in the eyes of their makers had any substantive importance—related to China: even the Four-Power Treaty concerning Insular Possessions was consciously formulated for the primary purpose of making a decent end to the Anglo-Japanese Alliance because of its adverse effect upon the situation with regard to China. Those agreements not only were predicated upon the theses of the open door and Chinese integrity with which our Government had particularly identified itself, but gave to those related principles a definiteness of interpretation such as had never been before internationally accepted. So much the Washington Conference accomplished—or, at least, so much opportunity it gave for constructive achievement in building up a system of security and peace in the area of the Pacific Ocean.

But, important as it is to realize the significance and potentialities of the Washington Treaties, it is no less necessary to avoid misunderstanding of their scope and purport. The most important of them, and the one whose meaning is most frequently misconstrued, is the Nine-Power Treaty concerning Principles and Policies in China, which provides that:

> The Contracting Powers, other than China, agree:
> (1) To respect the sovereignty, the independence and the territorial and administrative integrity of China; . . .

The obligation undertaken by the signatory Powers (other than China) was indeed a very important one, but one of purely negative character—of self-abnegation only. It did not create or imply an obligation of a positive character, on the part of the signatories, collectively or individually, to maintain China's independence or integrity. It neither made China a protectorate, nor constituted a treaty of guaranty or a defensive alliance. Any such construction would certainly have been repugnant alike to China and to the United States, as unquestionably it would have been to the other signatories.

An equally erroneous notion which yet has some currency in this country is that, by taking leadership in the formulation of principles beneficial to China, and giving the Chinese support at the Conference for certain of their contentions, the American Government so far committed itself to special trusteeship for Chinese interests that it cannot now honorably withhold further championship of the cause of China against other Powers—that we in effect estopped ourselves from holding aloof from any controversy involving Chinese rights or interests. Not only is that idea without factual basis; it is true, on the contrary, that throughout the Conference a tendency on the part of the Chinese delegation, in their informal discussions with us, to take for granted such a commitment on our part was repeatedly met by explicit statements that such support as we gave them was prompted not by any sense of obligation to China or special commitment of our Government to her interests, but by what we considered an enlightened self-interest, and that only disillusionment could come out of an assumption of more altruistic motives.

There has also rather widely prevailed among our people (particularly during 1925 and the ensuing period when there was considerable sympathy with the professed aims of the Chinese Nationalist party) a belief that in acknowledging and undertaking, at the Washington Conference, to remedy certain inequitable conditions which had been imposed upon China in the past, the signatories had conceded the injustice of the whole special *régime* built up during generations of contact with the West and had forgone all claim to insist upon the validity of what the Chinese term the "unequal treaties." No such claim was even made by the Chinese at the Conference: on the other hand, they concurred in express provisions establishing the terms on which changes might be made in respect to the two most vital matters (the tariff, and extraterritoriality) arising out of the "unequal treaties"; and in regard to most of the incidental points of the treaty *régime* that came under discussion, they volunteered assurances that the Chinese Government had no intention of making any change. And the other Powers, on their part, made it quite clear that they were prepared to relinquish their rights, under the established treaty system, only as, and to the extent that, the Chinese might bring about normal conditions which would do away with the *raison d'être* of the traditional system. There was nothing, either in the conclusions of the Conference or in the deliberations leading up to them, by way of a general renunciation of all special rights and privileges such as differentiated the international status of China from that of other states politically more normal.

The whole purpose and effect of the Treaties and Resolutions was to lay down principles on the basis of which the signatories would find it to their interest to cooperate in practicing a policy of live-and-let-live, each respecting the rights and interests of others (and refraining in particular from infringement upon China's political entity), claiming no special privileges, and agreeing to frank consultation when any situation should arise that might bring into question the obligations so assumed. The international cooperation envisaged was to have been not a merely legalistic or formal procedure but a whole-hearted effort, on the part of all the governments concerned, to work out, with mutual good will and helpfulness, practical solutions to such complex questions as had in the past bedeviled the inter-relations of all those that had or asserted interest in the Far East. It was predicated in the first place upon an assumption of China's readiness to collaborate with the other Powers in validating the fundamental principle of the open door, instead of playing off one foreign interest against another, regardless of any principle involved. To reassure itself on that point, our Government had, on the eve of the Conference, taken the occasion (in connection with a dispute involving the contract rights of an American company as against a Japanese claim to a monopoly of wireless telegraphy in China)[4] to obtain through the Chinese Legation concurrence in a state-ment of the open door policy which was subsequently adopted by the

---

[4]*A monopoly of wireless telegraphy:* In 1921, the Federal Telegraph Company negoti-ated a contract with China. This was immediately challenged by the Danish, British, and Japanese, all of whom claimed their right to do so by virtue of prior contracts. For the State Department, the issue raised was that of equal opportunity for American business in China. But a second and more serious problem was money: Federal Telegraph could fulfill its contract only if the Chinese government floated a four-million-dollar foreign loan. At the time all loans to the Chinese Government were supposed to be made through the International Banking Consor-tium (England, France, Japan, and the United States). The purpose of this arrange-ment, proposed by the United States in 1918 and approved by Japan in 1920, was to rehabilitate China's credit by limiting loans to those that were sound, and thus ending the practice of making loans on no security for political purposes, as the Japanese had done frequently. Although from an international standpoint the consortium was thus a means of containing Japan, it had the incidental effect of making it hard for Peking to obtain funds, and thus it weakened the Government there, while limiting the amount of business that could be carried out by that Government with American or other companies. Thomas Lamont, acting for the American group of banks, declined to underwrite the Federal Telegraph loan: this action aroused bitter argument in the United States, and the State Department sought vainly to persuade him to help a fellow American company, while inciden-tally strengthening the U.S. position in China. But Lamont held firm and was accused of putting British interests first as a result. In fact, the Federal Telegraph loan would almost certainly never have been paid back. The same people who argued for making it, in company with the American bankers who collectively were owed more than 50 million dollars in China by 1922, and the many American firms who had never been paid for goods supplied, would have returned to demand that Washington somehow force China to make good. *References:* Warren I. Cohen, *The Chinese Connection* (New York: Columbia University Press, 1978), pp. 105–7; Iriye, *After Imperialism,* p. 31; Harry W. Kirwin, "The Federal Telegraph Company: A Testing of the Open Door," *Pacific Historical Review* 22 (1953), pp. 275–86.

Conference as the basis of the formulation of that doctrine in the Nine-Power Treaty. The type of cooperation in view was not a matter of a coincidence of particular interests among certain signatories of the treaties, but one of all-round effort to give effect to principles accepted by all the signatories alike. And as these principles had especial bearing upon the situation of China, that country was involved, if anything, more deeply than the others, in the obligation to such cooperation. China herself accepted as an actuality the fact that the special *régime* of the "unequal treaties," however distasteful to her, did indeed exist as the basis of a *status quo* to be modified only through prescribed courses of action in collaboration with the Powers. Her cooperation was implicit in the conclusions of the Conference (as indeed it had been explicit in the arguments of her spokesmen) in pledging the Chinese Government to participation in the endeavor of the interested nations to work out satisfactory solutions to the unsatisfactory situation. In greater degree than, say, Belgium or Japan, therefore, though in like manner, China acknowledged herself to be a necessary factor; and her defection from the covenanted principles of cooperative action would warrant and require common counsel and effort to bring the dissident nation back into the agreed system of working together to a common end.

Secretary Hughes was well justified in stating in the course of his address to the American Historical Association, at New Haven, on December 29, 1922:

> The Washington Conference, if its work continues to enjoy the same support in public sentiment which was so emphatically expressed at the time, will not only afford a better assurance of peace and the continuance of friendly relations, but will serve to illustrate the method of effective international cooperation which fully accords with the genius of American institutions.

The hope thus expressed seemed for some time likely to be realized. Despite the delay in bringing them into force, because of the action of the French Government in withholding for more than three years its ratification of the Conference Treaties concerning China, as a makeweight for bargaining in a financial dispute with the Chinese Government,[5] the principles and

---

[5] *A financial dispute with the Chinese Government:* This is the so-called gold franc controversy, which delayed France's ratification of the Nine-Power Treaty until 1925, thus postponing for three years the beginning of work by the Tariff Conference and the Commission on Extraterritoriality. MacMurray largely blames this delay, "which gave occasion for the suspicion that the Treaty Powers had been

policies formulated by the Conference were in fact observed meanwhile with a faithfulness creditable to all the signatory Powers. It may be said that, on the whole, the three countries with lesser interests (Belgium, Portugal, and the Netherlands) have, throughout, been exact in the observance of their obligations. France and Italy, though in a few instances capitalizing their position to drive hard financial bargains with the Chinese in a way that might be thought scarcely to accord with the spirit of the agreements, have nevertheless kept actually within the letter of them. The Japanese Government for almost ten years (up to the beginning of the invasion of Manchuria, in September 1931) was, in the belief of the

---

insincere in their undertakings, and had in fact sought only to lull into quietude the movement for 'rights recovery' " (memorandum, pp. 68–69), for the fundamental change in Chinese attitudes toward the Powers so evident by 1925. In question were payments under the Boxer indemnity, made in gold since 1905. The Allies suspended all Boxer indemnity payments for five years from December 1, 1917, when China entered the war, and some remitted them thereafter, but France required resumption of payment, calculated on the basis of prewar gold francs rather than in the depreciated currency then being used in France itself. Why France was unwilling to yield is difficult to say. Ostensibly, Paris wished to use the funds to rehabilitate the Banque Industrielle de Chine, whose failure in 1921 had weakened her position in the East, but the *China Weekly Review* was probably closer to the truth when it remarked that "the interest of France in world affairs is centered almost entirely in a solution of the Reparations Problem and a strict enforcement of the Treaty of Versailles," and that her China policy was designed to pressurize Britain and the United States into backing her in Europe. In any case, Italy and Belgium strongly supported France, while the other Powers went along for the sake of speeding the ratification of the Nine-Power Treaty. But the issue was delicate in China, and Wellington Koo in particular was adamant against accepting France's terms. Settlement seemed near at several moments in 1922 but slipped away each time: in August when the hard-line T'ang Shao-yi (1860–1938) cabinet replaced that of Liang Shih-yi (1869–1933), in November when the Wang Chung-hui cabinet fell, in part over the issue, and in December when Parliament blocked the Wang Cheng-t'ing cabinet's decision to accept the French position. Productive negotiations, with China making the concessions, began only when the second Chihli-Fengt'ien war brought Tuan Ch'i-jui to power in November 1924. The issue was finally settled, essentially on French terms, on April 12, 1925. *References:* H.G.W. Woodhead, ed., *The China Year Book 1925* (Peking and Tientsin: The Tientsin Press, 1925), pp. 1296–1300; Ku Wei-chün, *Ku Wei-chün hui-yi-lu* (Pei-ching: Chung-hua shu-chü, 1983), 1:320–22; Hosea Ballou Morse and Harley Farnsworth MacNair, *Far Eastern International Relations* (Cambridge: Houghton Mifflin, 1931), pp. 709–10; Wesley R. Fishel, *The End of Extraterritoriality in China* (Berkeley: University of California Press, 1952), pp. 83–85; "What's the Matter with China?" *China Weekly Review* 29.1 (June 7, 1924), pp. 3–4.

diplomatic representatives of all countries in China at the time, scrupulously loyal in its adherence to the letter and the spirit of the Washington Conference. It is true that that statement must be qualified by a recognition of the effects of that curious dualism in the Japanese system, which made it possible for officers in active Army service to participate, like the patriotically inspired irresponsible individuals known as *rōnins*,[6] in intrigues and adventures designed to further their conception of Japan's imperial destiny in Asia; and that their interventions in Chinese affairs had some effect in frustrating the efforts of the Chinese to attain unity and ordered political conditions. But those in closest touch with Chinese affairs at the time were disposed to concede unreservedly that the Japanese Government, as such, was endeavoring in unimpeachable good faith to live up to its undertakings.

The issue of success or failure for the policies evolved at the Washington Conference was actually in the hands of China herself, of Great Britain, and of the United States—the three that had the most obvious interests, and that had in fact cooperated closely at the Conference. The eventual failure to maintain that cooperation disappointed the hopes that the Conference had created. The story of that failure is not one of consciously adverse intentions, but of confused purposes, of drift, and of futility.

II. The Period of Chinese Agitation (1922–1926)

The attitude of the Chinese, who had come to the Washington Conference as suppliants and had been genuinely thankful for the measure of satisfaction which its conclusions gave to their national aspirations, changed fundamentally during the three-year period of delay in bringing the treaties into effect, and convening the Tariff Conference and the Extraterritoriality Commission. The change of attitude was to a large extent the result of the mere delay, which gave occasion for the suspicion that the Treaty Powers had been insincere in their undertakings, and had in fact sought only to lull into quietude the movement for "rights recovery" which had already been

---

[6]In Japanese, a *rōnin* is a masterless samurai, or by extension an adventurer, an unsuccessful examination candidate, or a jobless person. Chou Tso-jen (1885–1967) describes the type in China: "They think of China as a territory of Japan, and imagine themselves as coming to a colony of which they are the masters to practice on the inhabitants the *bushidō* [warrior] tradition they have inherited. They proceed to give full vent to the wild impulses they cannot let loose in their own society. In Peking, there are many such disruptive and violent types among the Japanese merchants, and the situation in other places can well be imagined." Chou Tso-jen, "Jih-pen yü Chung-Kuo," in *Tán hu chi* (Pei-ching: Pei-hsin shu-chü, 1928), vol. 2, p. 500. Cited in Nancy E. Chapman, "Zhou Zuoren and Japan" (Ph.D. dissertation, Princeton University, 1990), p. 171.

espoused by the student element and begun to have an influence even with the normally conservative mercantile and scholarly classes of the country. And that distrust had been zealously and ably fostered by Borodin and other Bolshevik agents[7] in pursuance of the Third International's declared policy of furthering the world revolution by rousing China and other "semi-colonial" countries against the capitalistic and imperialistic Powers. Their influence had prevailed on Sun Yat-sen, the leader of the Kuomintang or Nationalist party, to abandon his efforts to purchase by new concessions the support of the United States or of Japan, and to make "anti-imperialism" and the abolition of the "unequal treaties" the cardinal doctrine of his system for the rejuvenation of China. It had proved a doctrine so congenial to typical Chinese political thinking that in the spring of 1925 Sun had been welcomed and acclaimed in Peking by his bitterest political opponents; and dying there with something of the semblance of a patriotic martyr, and having had attributed to him by his followers a political testament[8] pro-

---

[7]*Borodin:* Mikhail Markovich Gruzenberg (1884–1951) was born in Belorussia, attended Valparaiso University (Indiana) from 1908 to 1909, lived in Chicago, returned to Russia in 1918, and went to work for the Comintern. He became adviser to Sun Yat-sen in 1923 and was intimately involved with Kuomintang plans, at the center, until the split with the Communists. He was one of the ruling group in the Hankow Government. Upon returning to the Soviet Union he worked initially in the state paper and lumber industry, then was involved in various publishing ventures for the expatriate American community, such as Anna Louise Strong's *Moscow News.* He was arrested, with Strong, in 1949. She was allowed to return to the United States, but Borodin died in a prison camp near Yakutsk, Siberia. *References:* Lydia Holubnychy, *Michael Borodin and the Chinese Revolution, 1923–1925* (New York: University Microfilms for East Asian Institute, Columbia University, 1979); Dan N. Jacobs, *Borodin: Stalin's Man in China* (Cambridge, Mass.: Harvard University Press, 1981).

[8]*A political testament:* On February 24, 1925, the dying Sun Yat-sen approved a 145-word testament that mentioned his political programs and the need to abolish unequal treaties but made no reference to the USSR. On March 11, he signed the testament as well as a private will, bequeathing his books, papers, house, and so forth to his wife Soong Ch'ing-ling. MacMurray, however, refers to yet another document, which "appeared at Dr. Sun's bedside" the same day. A text in English, prepared by Eugene Ch'en in consultation with Borodin, it was first made public by *Pravda* on March 14 and is addressed to the Central Executive Committee of the Union of Soviet Socialist Republics. It states in part that through the heritage of the immortal Lenin the victims of imperialism are destined to secure their freedom. A report by Borodin to Moscow relates that the dying Sun kept repeating, "Only if the Russians continue to help." But as Professor Wilbur notes, "Given the circumstances, many leading members of the Kuomintang declined to treat it with the

claiming that in the Soviet Union alone could China find a savior from her servitude to the imperialistic Powers, he had given tremendous emotional impetus to the Chinese feeling of resentment against their whole relationship with foreign nations.

A few months later, with the bloodshed at Shanghai and Shameen (Canton),[9] the smouldering revolt was fanned into flame; the articulate

---

respect they accorded [to the other documents]." *Reference:* C. Martin Wilbur, *Sun Yat-sen: Frustrated Patriot* (New York: Columbia University Press, 1976), pp. 277–80.

[9] *The bloodshed at Shanghai and Shameen (Canton):* MacMurray is referring to two incidents in 1925, one at Shanghai on May 30, the other at Canton on July 23. The events at Shanghai were an explosion of feeling that had been brewing for months, made possible by the breakdown of national and local administration following the Chihli-Fengt'ien war of the previous autumn. A wave of labor troubles had begun in Shanghai in December 1924, and in February 1925 strikes began against Japanese cotton mills. When, in mid-May, a Chinese worker was killed in an encounter with Japanese plant security personnel, both Communist and Nationalist groups in Shanghai organized protests, which reached a climax on Saturday, May 30. Crowds in central Shanghai demonstrated against the Japanese. When some were arrested and taken into custody, the crowds besieged the Louza police station, just off the Nanking road. At 3:37 P.M., after issuing a warning in English and Chinese and waiting ten seconds, the Settlement police fired 44 shots, killing four Chinese and wounding nine, of whom seven later died. This incident, which unleashed protests throughout the Yangtze valley and beyond, is generally considered to mark the beginning of mass nationalist protests in China. Attempts to settle the incident proved extremely difficult, for they brought many latent conflicts into the open. Negotiations between the Powers and the Chinese Government initially produced a package of strong measures: Police Superintendent McEuen was to be dismissed; Chinese officials on whose territory the demonstration had been organized were to be punished; and, if necessary, the foreign-run Shanghai Municipal Council was to be dissolved. These recommendations, however, were too strong for many foreigners and too weak for most Chinese. While Chinese increasingly called for the abolition of the entire treaty system, foreign residents of Shanghai felt that even the measures proposed posed unacceptable threats to their autonomy. The residents thus brought pressure to bear on consulates, legations, and home governments. Ultimately, British foreign secretary Austen Chamberlain (1863–1937) vetoed the original recommendations and called for a new inquiry, which proved unsatisfactory in its turn. The inept handling of the incident by the Powers fed already potent antiforeign feeling, strengthening radicals within China while badly shaking the unity of the diplomatic community and undercutting those Chinese moderates who had attempted to deal with them. The events at Canton took place near Shameen, or Shamien, a sandy island in the Pearl River adjacent to the city, which in 1859 was set aside as a foreign settlement. On July 23, 1925, a parade of Chinese demonstrators, numbering about 60,000, attempted to march across the bridge that connected

elements among the Chinese burst into a furious antiforeign feeling, and indulged in a frenzy of racial self-assertion against what they claimed to be the stigma of inferiority imposed on them by the existing treaty system. The incidents at first aroused the especial animosity of the Chinese against the British and the Japanese alike, but (apparently on the recommendation of the Bolshevik advisers of the Kuomintang) the agitation was almost abruptly concentrated upon the British, who were made the bullseye at which the antiforeign movement was aimed—the Japanese being the first ring, the Americans the second, and the other Powers the outer rings of the target. For more than a year there was in force against British trade and shipping a boycott that was particularly effective in the South, and a strike directed against the British Crown Colony of Hong Kong. The Peking Administration, which enjoyed the *de facto* recognition of the Powers, asked in reasonably moderate terms for an outright revision of the treaty system with particular reference to extraterritoriality and the tariff. But behind that moderate official request for revision was manifest, on the part of the officials, an attitude of defiant indifference to treaty obligations, which reflected the ill will of the less responsible elements throughout the country. The Powers, realizing that the situation would compel them to go further along the line of concessions than the Washington Conference had provided, but still hoping to attain the cooperation with China which it had contemplated, replied in identic notes on September 4, 1925, to the Chinese request for treaty revision that:

> (The United States) is now prepared to consider the Chinese Government's proposal for the modification of existing treaties in measure as the Chinese authorities demonstrate their willingness and ability to fulfill their obliga-

---

it to the mainland, and into the settlement. The march had been carefully organized, and within its ranks were armed cadets from the Kuomintang's Whampoa Military Academy. The British had made preparations to defend the settlement, trying as much as possible to avoid any provocation; thus their units were deployed so as not to be visible from the Canton side of the Shaki (Sha-chi) River, which separated the settlement from the city. According to foreign eyewitnesses, the firing that broke out was initiated by the Whampoa cadets. It lasted about ten minutes, until the British gave the order to cease; casualties are not known, but estimates range from one to well over 100. *References:* Nicholas R. Clifford, *Shanghai, 1925: Urban Nationalism and the Defense of Foreign Privilege,* Michigan Papers in Chinese Studies, no. 36 (Ann Arbor: University of Michigan, 1979); Richard W. Rigby, *The May 30 Movement: Events and Themes* (Canberra: Australian National University Press, 1980); Donald A. Jordan, *The Northern Expedition: China's Revolution of 1926–1928* (Honolulu: University Press of Hawaii, 1976), pp. 8–9.

tions and to assume the protection of foreign rights and interests now
safeguarded by the exceptional provisions of those treaties. It is because of
a most earnest desire to meet the aspirations of the Chinese Government
that the Government of (the United States) desires to impress upon the
Chinese Government the necessity of giving concrete evidence of its ability
and willingness to enforce respect for the safety of foreign lives and
property and to suppress disorders and antiforeign agitation which embit-
ter feeling and tend to create conditions unfavorable for the carrying on of
negotiations in regard to the desires which the Chinese Government has
presented for the consideration of the treaty Powers. . . .

The questions of the conventional tariff and the extraterritorial rights
under which nationals of treaty Powers reside in China . . . received
consideration at the Washington Conference and it is the belief of the
Government of (the United States) that the most feasible method for
dealing with them is by a constant and scrupulous observance of the
obligations undertaken at that Conference.

By the time that this Special Tariff Conference was convened in Peking
(in the autumn of 1925) to implement the provisions of the Washington
Customs Treaty, the temper of the Chinese had become so antagonistic to
the spirit of the Washington Conference that the feeling prevalent among
virtually all political factions was not unfairly represented by the shrillest of
the radical spokesmen, Eugene Chen,[10] who declared that for the Powers to
talk of the principles of the open door and of the integrity of China was to
insult a people which (to quote a later utterance of his) had once known
greatness and was again conscious of renewed strength.

---

[10]*Eugene Chen:* Eugene Ch'en (Ch'en Yu-jen [1870–1944]) came to China when he
was in his thirties from Trinidad, the land of his birth and early schooling, where
he was a successful lawyer. In 1911 he traveled to London, where he served as a
barrister and came to know Sun Yat-sen. Returning to China with Sun, he served as
his foreign affairs adviser until 1913, and then as editor of the English-language
Peking Gazette. When Sun returned to Canton in 1923, Ch'en rejoined him as foreign
affairs adviser; in 1926 he joined the Central Executive Committee of the Kuomintang; and in May 1926 he was named foreign minister of the Canton *régime.*
MacMurray met him in Wuhan in September 1926 and was well acquainted with
the negotiations he carried on with the British chargé, Sir Owen O'Malley (1887–
1974), leading to the retrocession of the British Concessions in Hankow and
Kiukiang early in 1927. When the Wuhan Government split, Ch'en was among
those who fled to Moscow and, except for brief service as foreign minister in 1932,
he never again played a central role in Chinese politics. He died in Shanghai in 1944.
Reference: Howard L. Boorman, ed., *Biographical Dictionary of Republican China* (New
York: Columbia University Press, 1967), 1:180–83.

The Tariff Conference[11] began its deliberations under the guidance of Chinese political leaders who (with certain honorable but impotent exceptions) had all of the extreme radicals' defiant and truculent attitude toward the international obligations of the country, although lacking the fanatical idealism which might have restrained their venality. To them the Conference was merely an opportunity to further their personal political fortunes by dramatizing their contempt for the foreigners and their rights. The very agenda of the Conference, which their chairmanship gave them the opportunity to control, ignored the treaty basis on which the Conference had been convened. They refused to admit to the agenda the question of the establishment of a Board of Reference, which the Washington Conference

---

[11] *The Tariff Conference:* At Washington the nine Powers had signed a treaty regarding the Chinese customs tariff, which provided for the raising of the rate of duties on goods going to China to 5 percent, for the holding, within three months of its ratification, of a Conference to consider the abolition of *likin* [see note 12], and the granting of a further customs surtax of 2.5 percent. After a long delay caused by the French position in the gold franc case, the Conference opened in Peking on October 25, 1925, with a large and impressive array of delegates, including Mac-Murray and Silas Strawn (1866–1946) for the United States, Macleay for Britain, de Martel for France, Oudendyk for the Netherlands, Yoshizawa for Japan, and Shen Jui-lin, W. W. Yen, C. T. Wang, and Alfred Sze, among others, for China. But by the time the Conference got under way, the rise of antiforeign disorders had created an environment in which the basic Washington consensus had weakened. Without such a basis for agreement, it was difficult to decide how the money at stake, between 90 and 100 million Chinese dollars, should be apportioned, particularly between the needs of the Peking Government and the foreign demands for debt service. Nevertheless, before the end of 1925 the Conference agreed both to the immediate granting of the Washington surtaxes and to the principle of tariff autonomy for China. The political chaos of the following year, in particular the fall of the Tuan Ch'i-jui government in April and the launching of the Northern Expedition in July, made impossible the holding of a plenary session that would have ratified these agreements; they went unimplemented, and the Conference adjourned on July 3, 1926. The foreign delegates made clear, however, their willingness to continue once China's internal circumstances permitted. The work of the Conference prepared the way for the subsequent tariff reform, but its history illustrates both the willingness of the foreign powers to concede to Chinese nationalist demands and the ways in which China's internal situation could frustrate it. *References: Conference on the Limitation of Armament, Washington, November 12, 1921–February 6, 1922,* pp. 1630–39; *The Special Conference on the Chinese Customs Tariff* (Peking: n.p., 1928); Stanley F. Wright, *China's Struggle for Tariff Autonomy* (Shanghai: Kelly & Walsh, 1938), pp. 461–600; Morse and MacNair, *Far Eastern International Relations,* p. 711; Katsumi Usui, *Nihon to Chūgoku: Taishō jidai* (Tokyo: Hara, 1972), pp. 235–54.

had referred to the Peking Conference for decision; and while insisting upon "tariff autonomy" (by which it was intended that the Powers should completely relinquish all interest in the tariff rates and in the administration of the customs), they would not even consider accepting the 2½% surtax for which the treaty provided, or fulfill the obligation to make the stipulated increases in tariff rates conditional upon their effective abolition of the pernicious system of *likin* taxes.[12]

It is scarcely an exaggeration to say that the Chinese nullified and proclaimed their disdain of each individual paragraph of the Washington Treaties and Resolutions that had been designed to afford them opportunity to build up a sound national life and to cooperate with the Powers in doing away with the restrictions of the special *régime* that had grown up in consequence of their traditional unreadiness to adapt their polity to the norms of international relationship. They claimed as a vested right every concession that the Washington Conference had even conditionally granted them, but at the same time denied the validity of the Washington Treaties and Resolutions as being unresponsive to the needs and aspirations of an awakened China.

It was the Chinese, therefore—and not merely the single rather unrepresentative faction at Peking which enjoyed the *de facto* recognition of the Powers, but the mass of articulate political opinion, of all factions, throughout the country—which frustrated the genuinely earnest and loyal efforts of the Powers to give concrete effect to the spirit of the Washington

---

[12]*Likin (li-chin):* From a word meaning one-thousandth, *likin* was a tax on native goods in transit from province to province, or even from town to town within a province, introduced by the Ch'ing dynasty in 1853 to raise money to combat the Taiping rebellion. Such a tax was necessary because tax rates on exports and foreign trade had been set by treaty and could not be altered. Nevertheless, *likin* eventually came to be levied as well on foreign goods being shipped inland after regular duties had been paid. Rates were arbitrary, and the tax stifled trade. Its abolition was regularly advocated by both Chinese and foreigners. At the Special Conference on the Chinese Customs Tariff held in 1925–26, agreement was reached in principle that *likin* should be abolished, and proceeds from the new customs surtaxes be used in part to make good the resulting revenue loss to the Chinese Government. Dr. C. T. Wang, however, refused to admit any linkage between the abolition of *likin* and the granting of the new taxes; in the end it was agreed that the two should be simultaneous but unrelated. The inconclusive adjournment of the Conference meant that there was no further progress until after the consolidation of the Nationalist Government. Abolition of *likin* took place on January 1, 1931. *References:* Edwin George Beal, *The Origin of Likin (1853–1864)* (Cambridge, Mass.: Chinese Economic and Political Studies, Harvard University, 1958); Wright, *China's Struggle for Tariff Autonomy,* pp. 52–54, 446–53.

Conference in collaborating with China toward an evolution from the status of the "unequal treaties."

It is fair to recognize that the hostility of the Chinese, during this period of hysterical antiforeign agitation, bore hardest upon the British—a fact which in considerable measure explains and condones the rather Bourbon temper with which the British Government approached the cooperative efforts of the Powers. There was a Conservative Government in power, which placed a possibly exaggerated importance upon the maintenance of prestige and the notion of British primacy in Far Eastern affairs. And, most unfortunately for that purpose, the British Government had for some years been rather badly served by its representative in China (Sir Ronald Macleay)[13]—a Tory of the type that neither imagined good could come out of any liberal ideas hatched at Washington under the auspices of the American rebels, nor perceived that within China itself had been developing ideas which had already challenged and movements which had undermined British primacy;[14] so that the Chinese reaction to the Shanghai and Canton incidents would seem to have taken the British Government completely by surprise and found them at a loss to appreciate the new situation. They had in fact been taking their position too much for granted, and assuming that cooperation meant merely an acquiescence of other nations in whatever the British thought was wisest and least inconvenient

---

[13]*Sir Ronald Macleay:* Sir Ronald Macleay (1870–1943) was British minister in Peking from 1922 to 1926. He later served as minister in Czechoslovakia (1927–1929) and Argentina (1930–1933). MacMurray's low opinion of him seems to have been based on long acquaintance: Macleay's service as counselor in Peking (from 1914 until the latter part of the war) had coincided with MacMurray's as first secretary, and his time as British minister overlapped with the first part of MacMurray's term as American. Educated at Charterhouse and at Balliol College, Oxford, Macleay entered the diplomatic service in 1895, serving in Washington, Constantinople, Mexico, and Brussels before being posted to Peking, where he served under Sir John Jordan and probably acquired many of the approaches to Chinese politics, in particular some understanding of the "northern perspective," that were characteristic of that minister. Although Macleay's reports from Peking show a clear and detailed grasp of Chinese politics, the British handling of the May 30th incident and their role at the Tariff Conference, to both of which Macleay contributed, were unpopular with his colleagues and the Chinese alike. His replacement by Miles Lampson, in 1926, was widely welcomed. *Reference:* Obituary, *The Times* (London), March 8, 1943.

[14]Here the draft in the MacMurray Papers strikes out the bracketed words and reads: ". . . representative in China [(Sir Ronald Macleay)—a Tory of the type that neither imagined good could come out of any liberal ideas hatched at Washington under the auspices of the American rebels, nor] who had not perceived. . . ."

for British interests. That interpretation had been illustrated in 1923, when Sun Yat-sen had threatened to take over the Maritime Customs, at Canton—a threat to the whole treaty system, affecting the interests of all the Powers, but more particularly and immediately menacing the British control of the Customs Administration. In consultation with the British, our Government had whole-heartedly agreed that we should make a joint naval demonstration to challenge the threatened seizure, and sent four or five ships to Canton for the purpose, but the British, to the surprise of the Chinese no less than of ourselves, had sent only one. Yet in 1925, when the boycott virtually excluded all British shipping from Canton, the British Minister attempted to make an issue of the fact that American ships did not refuse to call at Canton and handle the cargoes that British vessels might otherwise have carried.

With such a predisposition to assume that it was the part of others to contribute toward the maintenance of a special status of British interests in the face of developments which had taken them aback, it is comprehensible that British efforts toward cooperation with the other Powers at that period were inelastic, spasmodic and not wholly realistic, and rather *de haut en bas* in manner. They seemed not to realize, as did the other foreign nations concerned, that a situation had arisen in which some degree of concession to Chinese feeling was imperative, and that to yield even a little with a good grace would ease the tension more than would a far greater concession grudgingly made under pressure. It was only with considerable difficulty and delay that the British were brought to agree to the identic notes of September 4, 1925 (referred to above), in reply to the Chinese request for treaty revision, without insisting upon a further postponement of the already overdue Commission on Extraterritoriality, for which the Washington Conference had provided. And the crucial Shanghai incident, which had occurred in the International Settlement and affected the relationships with the Chinese of other Powers in only somewhat less degree than those of Great Britain, they seemed to regard as a private British affair because the Settlement policemen involved were of British nationality; and for months they fought, with obstinacy and exasperation, the adoption of measures of appeasement which the other interested governments had considered self-evidently necessary from the first.

In the Tariff Conference, too, they maintained an attitude of reserve and aloofness, in conspicuous contrast to the relations of frankness and understanding that were quickly established between the Japanese delegation, for instance, and the American. In a situation in which the antagonistic attitude of the Chinese had forced a series of issues that presented for the Treaty Powers the problem of delicate adjustments and compromises to meet the Chinese views as far as possible without sacrificing their vital interests, the British continually complicated the issues by raising and insisting upon incidental matters which neither the other foreigners nor the Chinese considered essential. And when (in the summer of 1926) the further progress of the Conference was interrupted by civil commotions which led to the flight of the Chinese delegates and the disappearance of any such governmental organization as might have replaced them, the British, against the judgment of all the other foreign delegations, insisted upon adjourning the Tariff Conference until a recognized Chinese Government had been established, instead of having the foreign delegations hold themselves in readiness to continue the discussions whenever the opportunity should present itself.

But although the British insisted, during this time, upon some views that seemed shortsighted and unrealistic, they were nevertheless within the fair limits of their discretion; and while they sometimes made collaboration difficult, they did not deny or ignore the duty of cooperation.

The American Government may reasonably claim to have maintained, during this period, the leadership which it had assumed at the Washington Conference; even with the Chinese, who openly flouted the idea of cooperation, their relations were closer than those of any other nationality. The American delegation to the Tariff Conference, having worked out a plan of implementing the Washington Treaty concerning the Chinese tariff, and then proceeding to a further liberalization of the conventional tariff system with a view to Chinese "tariff autonomy," laid the plan frankly before the Chinese Chairman (C. T. Wang) of the appropriate Conference Committee,[15] acceded to every amendment that he suggested, received his fulsome

---

[15] *The Chinese Chairman (C. T. Wang):* Born to a Christian family in Chekiang and graduated from Yale in 1910, Wang Cheng-t'ing (1882–1961) served China in a number of important diplomatic and political posts. Active in the Peking Parliament until its dissolution in 1917, he subsequently went to Canton and served as its representative in the Chinese delegation at the Paris Peace Conference. After work in business and education, he returned to diplomacy in 1921, when he joined the Chinese delegation to the Washington Conference. In November 1922 he succeeded Wellington Koo as foreign minister at Peking, a post he was to hold under many governments in the following years. From mid-December 1922 to mid-January 1923 Wang served as acting premier. From March 1923 he handled Soviet relations for the Peking Government, and in March 1924 he arrived at agreements with the Soviet special envoy Lev Karakhan (1889–1937). Because they did not provide for the cancellation of the treaties the Soviet Union had made with Outer Mongolia, or for the withdrawal of Soviet troops from that state, these agreements were denounced by Koo, Wang's natural rival, both politically and personally. Wang served again as foreign minister in the cabinet of Huang Fu in 1924, and in 1926 he was a

thanks for the fairness and generosity of the American proposals—and, at
the next morning's Committee meeting, found itself snubbed and upbraided by the same Chinese Chairman for having made such "manifestly
objectionable proposals." Yet, in spite of that and other less striking
instances of bad faith, the Chinese continually sought and received advice
and assistance from the Department of State, from our Legation, and from
our delegation.

With the other interested nationalities (save insofar as the British held
themselves aloof) our relations—certainly at the Peking end of the wire—
were frank and mutually helpful. Particularly with the Japanese there was
established (thanks principally to Mr. Saburi,[16] who, though ranked only

---

delegate to the Special Conference on the Customs Tariff. He served again as foreign
minister from December 1925 through March 1926. Having established contact
with Chiang Kai-shek through Feng Yü-hsiang, he succeeded Huang Fu as foreign
minister in the Nationalist Government in June 1928. He served until September
1931, a period he described as the turning point in China's efforts to establish equal
treaties with foreign powers. Some opinion turned against him after the Japanese
invasion of Manchuria in September 1931. Students invaded and wrecked his office,
and he was extricated with difficulty. Shortly thereafter he resigned. From 1937 to
1938, Wang served as ambassador in Washington. He spent the war in Chungking,
then returned to Shanghai, and subsequently went to Hong Kong, where he died.
References: Biographical Dictionary of Republican China, 3:326–64; Wang Cheng-t'ing,
"Looking Back and Looking Forward," unedited typescript memoir available in
microform at the Rare Books and Manuscripts Library, Columbia University.

[16]*Mr. Saburi:* MacMurray singles out Sadao Saburi (1879–1929) for mention because,
as he notes, he was the "contact man" for Foreign Minister Kijūrō Shidehara. Two
years MacMurray's senior, Saburi had a diplomatic career that had certain parallels
with MacMurray's. Both men were professional diplomats, both participated extensively in international negotiations, and both put much stock in international concert
and agreement while opposing unilateral actions by their own governments. Born
in Fukuyama, Hiroshima, Saburi graduated from Tokyo Imperial University in 1905
and entered the diplomatic service in the same year. After postings in China (1905–
1906), Russia (1906), France (1906–1908, 1912–1918), and as first secretary in
Washington, Saburi was named chief of the commercial division (1924–1926) and
the treaty division (1926–1927) of Shidehara's foreign ministry. He attended the
Washington Conference (1921–1922) and the Special Conference on the Chinese
Customs Tariff in Peking (1925–1926), where although Eki Hioki (1861–1926) and
Kenkichi Yoshizawa (1874–1965) served as Japan's official delegates, Saburi's role as
the link to Shidehara made him the logical person to explain to the other delegations,
and particularly to the American delegation, the domestic political difficulties that
China policy posed in Japan. Broadly speaking, there was scope for complete
cooperation: there were "no concrete matters in which the course of action by his

as a Counselor to the Japanese delegation was in fact the "contact man" for Baron Shidehara,[17] the Minister for Foreign Affairs) a relationship of genuine intimacy. He recognized and accepted the fact that we Americans were disposed to be more indulgent toward the Chinese than were other nationalities—more ready to overlook their shortcomings, put faith in their potentialities, and believe in their assurances; but throughout the Tariff

---

government differed seriously from ours." Yet, while "indulgence" toward China was a popular policy in the United States, the same was not true in Japan. Japan had certain irreducible and critically important interests, notably in Manchuria, and Shidehara could no more yield them than could any other politician. Therefore Saburi impressed on the representatives of the other Powers that any breakdown of their cooperation with Japan could only lead to the eclipse of the cooperative Japanese policy, and its replacement by one worse for China and for the Powers. Saburi was appointed minister to China in 1929, but his life ended suddenly in November 1929. Saburi's death was determined to be a suicide, but there was much evidence that did not fit such a scenario (for example, Saburi had no known reason to commit suicide; the pistol used was not his own; the bullet entered through his right temple, though he was left-handed). Many scholars suspect, therefore, that he died at the hand of an army officer or right-wing *rōnin*, unhappy, perhaps, with the kind of diplomacy he stood for. Saburi was married to the daughter of the diplomat and former foreign minister Jūtarō Komura (1855–1911), who had pioneered for Japan the same use of treaties and negotiation to strengthen national position that Chinese diplomats emulated in the 1910s and 1920s. *References:* Gaimushō gaikō shiryōkan, comp., *Nihon gaikōshi jiten* (Tokyo: Okurashō, 1979), p. 329 (hereafter cited as *NGJ*); Barbara J. Brooks, "China Experts in the Gaimushō, 1895–1937," in *The Japanese Informal Empire in China 1895–1937,* ed. Peter Duus, Ramon H. Myers, and Mark R. Peattie (Princeton: Princeton University Press, 1989), pp. 369–94; Janet E. Hunter, comp., *Concise Dictionary of Japanese History* (Berkeley: University of California Press, 1984), pp. 99–100.

[17]*Baron Shidehara:* Kijūrō Shidehara (1872–1951) was the author of "Shidehara diplomacy," which sought to substitute economic and legal means for military in Japan's foreign policy. He joined the foreign service in 1896, being posted first to Korea. In 1903 he married Masako Iwasaki, younger sister of Takaaki Katō's wife. He was vice foreign minister in 1915, and served for the first time as foreign minister under Katō from June 1924 to April 1927. The approach toward China that he adopted at that time is frequently contrasted with that of his successor, General Giichi Tanaka (1863–1929), foreign minister from April 1927 to July 1929. Shidehara's China policies were complex, envisioning neither retreat nor conquest, but rather a pacific stabilization of Japanese interests within an international structure, such as discussed at Washington. Although conciliation with China was popular in the West, it was not in Japan, and Shidehara's diplomacy proved domestically controversial from the start. It grew more so as Chinese demands, and their ability to enforce them, escalated. Shidehara's problems were further exacerbated by the

Conference he indicated that there were no concrete matters in which the course of action favored by his Government differed seriously from ours. Yet, speaking as a Japanese liberal, he again and again expressed his apprehension lest American policy regarding China, based upon idealistic motives, might develop an unrealistic altruism in which we Americans could afford to indulge in view of the relative unimportance of our material

---

growth of unilateralism among the Washington Powers, and the weakness of his own government in Japan. Shidehara had only limited domestic support for his China policy. Even securing the acceptance of the Nine-Power Treaty had not been easy in Japan. When Shidehara was ambassador in Washington (1919–1923), his policies had been supported by Prime Minister Kei Hara (1854–1921) (who died just before the Conference) and the majority of the Seiyukai, as well as by the elder statesmen, against strong opposition. Hara's assassination by an ultra-nationalist gave some indication of the forces that would oppose the diplomacy he favored. After Hara's death, unity of the Seiyukai could not be maintained; his successor, Korekiyo Takahashi (1854–1935; prime minister November 1921–June 1922), was followed by the three nonparty cabinets of Tomosaburō Katō (1859–1923; prime minister June 1922–August 1923), Gonnohyōe Yamamoto (1852–1923; prime minister September 1923–December 1923), and Keigo Kiyoura (1850–1942; prime minister January 1924–June 1924). In such a competitive political environment it can be risky for a politician to appear to compromise the security interests of his country, and to Japan, security meant above all mainland Asia, including China. In the Japan of the 1920s, party politics weakened supporters of the Washington Treaties while providing an environment in which the army's traditional desire for a China policy independent of the Western Powers could revive. These trends ultimately undid Shidehara's policies. Shidehara became foreign minister for the first time in the cabinet of Takaaki Katō (1859–1926; prime minister June 1924–January 1926). Initially a coalition of the Kenseikai and Seiyukai, Katō's government became a minority in 1925 when the Seiyukai defected. Nonetheless it pursued a variety of politically difficult courses, introducing manhood suffrage and liberal social legislation (as well as antisubversive measures); reforming the House of Peers; establishing diplomatic relations with the Soviet Union; and reducing the size of the Army while modernizing it. Katō himself, who had been foreign minister in the cabinet of Okuma Shigenobu (1838–1922; prime minister April 1914–October 1916), which had presented the Twenty-one Demands, nevertheless supported Shidehara, who continued in office after Katō's death under his immediate successor, Reijirō Wakatsuki (1866–1949; prime minister January 1926–April 1927). In 1927, however, attacks on Shidehara's "weak" China policy were among the factors that brought Tanaka to power. Scholarly evaluation of Shidehara is varied and still inconclusive. Some see him and Tanaka as agreeing about imperial goals, while differing in means. Others see Shidehara as representing a civilian approach later overwhelmed by militarism. Both views contain truth, but equally they neglect the decisive impact on Japanese policy of the unexpected developments within China in

involvements in China, but which would create an intolerable situation for Japan, to whose economic and political existence China is an absolutely necessary complement. It was not until somewhat later, however, that these apprehensions were realized.

In the meanwhile, up to the autumn of 1926, there continued among the signatories of the Washington Treaties, other than China, a really extraordinary degree of cooperation toward the fulfillment and the extension of the purpose in which they all (including China) had concurred; it may fairly be said that the foreign Powers acted in concert, not in opposition to the fair and reasonable demands of China, but (despite the defection and intolerance of a revolutionized China) as trustees pledged to afford an opportunity for the fruition of the plans and hopes that had been worked out with the concurrence of the Chinese at Washington.

III. The Period of Chinese Nationalist Violence

The events which broke off the Chinese participation in the Tariff Conference, and frustrated the intentions of the foreign Powers to use it as a means of improving their relationships with China, were incidental to a new development in the domestic politics of that country. Out of the confused and meaningless struggles among innumerable petty aspirants for power, there were beginning to crystallize two major groups which, even if not representing definite political programs, yet did reflect recognizably different modes of thought. In the more stolid North, there had come into power a crude reactionary military dictator—Chang Tso-lin,[18] an ex-bandit,

---

the late 1920s, which rendered obsolete elements of both Shidehara's and Tanaka's approaches. *References: NGJ,* pp. 351–52; Kimitada Miwa, "Shidehara Kijūrō," *Encyclopedia of Asian History,* 3:439; Toru Takemoto, *Failure of Liberalism in Japan: Shidehara Kijuro's Encounter with Anti-Liberals* (Washington, D.C.: University Press of America, 1978); Sidney DeVere Brown, "Shidehara Kijūrō: The Diplomacy of the Yen," in *Diplomats in Crisis,* ed. Bennett and Brown, pp. 201–26; Nobuya Bamba, *Japanese Diplomacy in a Dilemma: New Light on Japan's China Policy, 1924–1929* (Kyoto: Minerva Press, 1977); Shin'ichi Kitaoka, "China Experts in the Army," in *The Japanese Informal Empire in China, 1895–1937,* ed. Duus, Myers, and Peattie, pp. 330–68.

[18]*Chang Tso-lin:* Chang Tso-lin (1873–1928), known as "the Old Marshal," controlled Manchuria during the 1920s. Born in today's Liaoning province, of peasant origin and without education, he started his military career young and fought in the Sino-Japanese War. Japanese patronage in the 1910s and the 1920s enabled him to establish a secure position in Manchuria, which he repeatedly attempted, by joining coalitions with other militarists, to transform into ascendancy in China proper. But

unenlightened and unscrupulous, but a shrewd and forceful leader, who in spite of his faults was honestly a patriot according to his lights. In the emotionally unstable South, the discordant factions of Sun Yat-sen's revolutionary party had been dragooned by their Russian advisers into working harmoniously together, so that the Kuomintang had at last become a coherent political force, unified in purpose, and appealing to large elements throughout the country. For the first time since the establishment of the republic, there began to emerge something like an issue of more significance than personal aggrandizement. On neither side did the leaders have personal records such as would have seemed to justify confidence on the part of their own people or of foreigners. And, from the foreign viewpoint, while the Northerners were less unfriendly, they were so obviously unresponsive to Chinese ways of thinking that the Powers could not bring themselves to regard them as a permanent factor in the situation, and in their case withheld the recognition that had theretofore been granted (if only as a matter of convenience in a confused situation) to the factions that had successively mastered the old capital (Peking) and the centralized administrations of the Maritime Customs, the Salt Gabelle and the Posts;[19] whereas the Southerners, although running with the tide of general popular support, did so largely by reason of their frenzied appeal to hatred of the foreigners and their interests. There would certainly seem to have been little to choose between them.

---

because this ambition threatened some Japanese plans for an autonomous Manchuria, it led to tension with Tokyo. After the collapse of Wu P'ei-fu's Chihli group in 1924, Chang's Fengt'ien military forces increasingly played the paramount role in northern China, sponsoring cabinets in Peking and deploying their own forces as far as Shanghai. Chang's forces proved no match for Chiang K'ai-shek's, however, and when the Nationalists arrived in Peking in 1928, the Old Marshal agreed to withdraw, thus preparing the way, in the eyes of some Japanese, for a stable and autonomous Manchuria under his control, able to coexist with a reunited China proper under Chiang. But without the knowledge of the Tokyo Government, extremists in the Japanese Army placed explosives on a bridge just outside Shenyang (Mukden); these were detonated on June 4, 1928, as Chang's train passed under, killing him and, in consequence, irretrievably destabilizing Manchuria. *References: Biographical Dictionary of Republican China,* 1:115–22; Gavan McCormack, *Chang Tso-lin in Northeast China, 1911–1928* (Folkestone, Kent: Dawson, 1972).

[19]All three were reformed, with foreign assistance, during the first part of the twentieth century, and revenues from customs and the salt gabelle (i.e., tax) were extensively hypothecated for loan service. See Stanley F. Wright, *China's Struggle for Tariff Autonomy: 1843–1938* (Shanghai: Kelly & Walsh, 1938) and S.A.M. Adshead, *The Modernization of the Chinese Salt Administration, 1900–1920* (Cambridge, Mass.: Harvard University Press, 1970).

There had, however, developed in several of the interested countries, and particularly in the United States and Great Britain, a strong popular sentiment in regard to China and her aspirations, of which the Southern or Nationalist group was the most ardent and audacious proponent. In this country, there would seem to be no reason to think that that movement was appreciably influenced by the Communist propaganda that did, in England, have considerable effect among the more radical elements. With us, the movement was natural, even through it was based upon rather naive and romantic assumptions with regard to Chinese conditions, and even though its vigor and intensity seemed out of all proportion to the average citizen's concern with Chinese affairs. The impetus of the movement was made possible by the widespread and general popular feeling of friendliness for the Chinese, based in part upon a somewhat patronizing pride in the belief that our Government had borne the part of China against selfish nations, but still more upon the fact that our church organizations had through several generations cultivated a favorable interest in China in support of their missionary enterprises therein. And at that juncture, the leaders of the American missionary movement were strong in their conviction that their work in China would best be furthered by a policy of sympathy with the political aspiration that the Chinese were asserting: and they therefore favored our Government's adopting an independent initiative in renouncing all the special treaty rights—particularly as regards extraterritoriality, tariff restrictions, and the special privileges of missionary institutions.

The popular sentiment thus created in the United States had at first been regimented in support of the so-called "Christian General," Feng Yü-hsiang;[20] but when, in 1926, Feng not only had been forced out of power but had also disillusioned his foreign partisans by openly seeking the

---

[20]*Feng Yü-hsiang:* Born in Hopei and known as "the Christian general," Feng Yü-hsiang (1882–1948) played perhaps his most critical role in the autumn of 1924, during the second Chihli-Fengt'ien war, when he abandoned the key northwestern front with which Wu P'ei-fu (1874–1939) had entrusted him and marched instead on Peking, causing the collapse of the Chihli military effort to unify China, and indirectly bringing about the ascendancy of Chang Tso-lin. The reasons for Feng's action are still debated but seem to include deterioration in Wu's position, sympathy with the Nationalists, and indirect suasion, through bribery, from the Japanese. Feng proved unable to capitalize on his coup, however; Chang Tso-lin drove him from Peking, and thereafter he played a marginal role in Chinese politics, dying in 1948 in a fire aboard a Russian ship in the Black Sea. *References: Biographical Dictionary of Republican China,* 2:37–43; James E. Sheridan, *Chinese Warlord: The Career of Feng Yü-hsiang* (Stanford, Calif.: Stanford University Press, 1966).

support of the Soviet Union, this vigorous pro-Chinese movement rather illogically transferred its adherence to the Nationalist faction in Canton. And Chiang Kai-shek; who soon rose to virtual control of the Kuomintang, later made sure of remaining the beneficiary of that element of foreign support, when it wavered somewhat in consequence of the outrage perpetrated by his armies upon American missionaries at Nanking, by himself professing conversion to Christianity. The vigorous partisanship of the religious organizations in this country was reflected in the press; it became popular to refer to the Chinese Nationalists as duplicating, under the leadership of Chiang Kai-shek as their George Washington, the patriotic spirit of 1776. The movement brought considerable pressure to bear both upon the Congress and upon the Administration. Representative Stephen Porter[21] succeeded in passing through the House a resolution requesting the President "forthwith to enter into negotiations with the duly accredited agents of the Government of China" for the purpose of treaty revision, and setting forth in its preamble these, among other, statements of opinion:

> . . . The Chinese people are entitled to such aid and encouragement as the United States may properly give them in their efforts to place upon a firm and efficient basis the republican form of government which they adopted in 1912 . . .;
> . . . It is highly unjust that a great and civilized people should be hindered by restraints imposed upon them in order to promote the interests of these powers . . .;
> . . . The United States has for many years taken the initiative in movements to secure just treatment for China, as was shown especially in establishing upon a firm and definite basis the principle of the open door in China . . .;

---

[21] *The Porter Resolution:* Introduced in the House of Representatives on January 4, 1927, by Stephen G. Porter (1869–1930), chairman of the House Foreign Affairs Committee, the Porter Resolution was designed to make it possible for negotiations over rights in China to be carried out even when there was no single Chinese government, by speaking of "the duly accredited representatives of the Chinese Government, authorized to speak for the entire people of China." The formulation was probably suggested by A. L. Warnshuis, secretary of the International Missionary Council, and the Chinese Legation in Washington is thought to have been involved as well. The Resolution increased pressure on the Department to "go it alone" and negotiate about China independently of what other Powers were doing, and without insisting on dealing with a single recognized Chinese government. *References:* Iriye, *After Imperialism,* pp. 107–8; Dorothy Borg, *American Policy and the Chinese Revolution, 1925–1928* (New York: American Institute of Pacific Relations, 1947; reprint ed., with new introduction by the author, New York: Octagon Books, 1968), pp. 238–39.

. . . The present situation in the Far East is one which renders it
especially expedient that the United States of America should now free
itself from entangling relations with other powers whose interests and
policies are not identical with those of the United States.

That Resolution (as evidenced by various references made to it by the
Secretary of State in conversations with the representatives of other countries, and in instructions to the Legation at Peking) carried considerable
weight with the Administration. The total effect of the pro-Chinese movement was in fact to place the Administration on the defensive for not having
done more for China by making unconditional relinquishment of our rights
under the "unequal treaties," regardless of the action or inaction of the
other Powers signatory to the Washington Treaties; the policy of cooperation was widely assailed as truckling to the selfish reactionary motives of
other less enlightened and altruistic nations; and instead of receiving credit
for the liberality and the patience with which it had tried to fulfill and even
to exceed its obligations to China, our Government was placed in the
position of having to justify itself for not going unconditionally to the
limits in acceding to Chinese demands. Those loyal American citizens and
staunch friends of China who furthered this movement could scarcely have
foreseen what an immense disservice their efforts would do to the interests
of both nations and to the ultimate situation in the Far East.

It was with such a background of popular sentiment—at its extremes
in the United States, but more or less prevalent among the people of other
interested countries—that the Powers found themselves under the necessity
of meeting a situation in which all semblance of a responsible national
administration in China had disappeared. With neither the Northern nor
the Southern group could the interested governments deal as with a
sovereign government. Neither possessed the authority to give more than
localized effect to its own decisions; neither felt itself strong enough to risk
the popular odium of undertaking any foreign obligations correlative with
the advantages demanded; and neither, in fact, had any policy with regard
to relationships with other countries beyond that of repudiating or whit-
tling down all foreign rights and interests. The several factions could not be
got to cooperate with each other, even for that purpose; but they competed
with each other in their defiance of the Powers.

It might have avoided some confusion and misunderstanding if (as was
in fact suggested by our Legation in November 1926, when the situation
had somewhat clarified) the Powers had frankly and publicly confronted the
fact that, in the absence of any government with which normal international
relations could be conducted, there was no further question of giving
countenance to one side or the other by dealing with it as a national

governmental entity, but that the necessary daily business of protection and the like would be handled locally by the consular representatives with whatever regional authorities might be in a position to act. Such an attitude, definitely announced, might conceivably have brought the Chinese to adopt their traditional compromise device of a delegation representing both factions for the purpose of negotiations; in any case, it might have minimized the jealousy with which each faction scrutinized and set itself to thwart all attempts of the Powers to come to any sort of understanding with the other. As it was, the attitude of the Powers remained confused and uncertain of the very nature of their relationship with the contending factions.

The mere suggestion of the Northerners that negotiations might be resumed for the purpose of putting into effect the promised 2½% surtax[22]

---

[22]*2½% surtax:* With the Northern Expedition getting under way in 1926, the Canton Government was in need of funds, and a local surtax on the customs revenue was an attractive way to raise them. Both both Chinese and foreigners had traditionally shied away from any measure that would dilute the power of the Inspectorate General of Customs, for by collecting and disbursing all tariff revenues, it denied a source of financial support to would-be local *régimes* and thus helped to foster China's unity. Nevertheless, attempts to appropriate customs revenue were not new. Early in 1918, legislators in Canton had claimed a right to a *pro rata* share of the customs surplus, and only when the Canton leadership split over who should get the money did the diplomatic body withdraw its approval and decide that the money should go to the internationally recognized government in Peking. In 1923, Dr. Sun Yat-sen had threatened to seize the Canton Customs House, to be deterred only by a naval demonstration by the Powers. Canton's move in 1926 thus posed a difficult challenge. In theory, the Powers subscribed to the idea of Chinese unity expressed by the nationwide authority of the Customs Inspectorate. But in the circumstances of 1926, their divergent interests made it difficult for them to support this, or any other, common policy. Once it was clear that no major power would support a joint naval demonstration against Canton, the question became how to give in with as little damage as possible to the structure of international law. MacMurray urged that the Powers should "by some means put in operation the Washington surtaxes as a fulfillment of the treaty obligations we have, rather than as a yielding to the Cantonese exactions." That, however, was exactly what the Nationalists did not want; their goal was not to divide the customs revenue, but rather to take it over intact from the Peking Government. The short-term interests of the Powers also argued against MacMurray's approach. Japan had hitherto been largely immune from the troubles of the British in South China, and for it to support MacMurray's position would invite retaliation in the form of anti-Japanese agitation, perhaps even in Manchuria. Britain, likewise, would be best served by a quick deal with Canton, which would relieve the pressure on Hong Kong. For the

brought from the Southerners a furious repudiation, in advance, of any agreement which might be effected. Shortly afterward, they themselves, in defiance of the existing treaties and with no attempt at negotiating conditions, put into force an equivalent surtax on imports into the territory under their control. That was manifestly a matter of joint concern to the signatories of the Washington Customs Treaty, and was in fact so considered and discussed by their Legations. Our own Legation reported (in a telegram of October 3, 1926), its judgment that

> . . . Against this indirect method of bringing about piecemeal repudiation of the treaties I feel that the powers principally interested should act resolutely even to the extent of affording naval protection to Canton Customs and taking whatever action might prove feasible to prevent levy of proposed taxes by Cantonese.
>
>   . . . I believe that no drastic action would in fact be necessary if Cantonese realized that the Powers were in earnest . . .
>
>   . . . In the circumstances I cannot too strongly recommend that the Department do everything possible to bring Great Britain, Japan and the United States into agreement to prevent the imposition of new taxes even to the point of a naval blockade or some similar feasible forceful measure. . . .

On the following day, the Legation reported that the Japanese Government had informed its Legation that "it opposes imposition of the new taxes and considers conference of 'Washington Conference Powers' advisable." A day later the Department instructed our Legation that

> . . . Department does not perceive the urgency of initiating discussions with Great Britain and Japan looking to naval demonstrations or other forceful means of preventing collection of taxes which have not yet been put into effect. . . .

In the circumstances of disunity thus manifested, the British undertook independent action in their own interest; they permitted their Consul General at Canton to reach with the so-called Nationalist Government there

---

United States alone to champion a legal and multilateral approach would draw Washington into China in ways that were becoming increasingly unpopular at home. Instead of cooperating, each Power adopted a unilateral policy of acquiescence, whose result, as Wellington Koo had foreseen, was the effective breakup of the Customs Service as a unifying factor in Chinese politics. *References:* Wright, *China's Struggle,* pp. 602–23; *Foreign Relations of the United States,* 1926 (Washington, D.C.: U.S. Government Printing Office), 1:203 (hereafter cited as *FRUS*).

an understanding by which Great Britain in fact acquiesced in the illegal
2½% surtax in exchange for the discontinuance of the anti-British boycott
and strike, although joining with other Powers in filing ineffectual *pro forma*
protests against the action of the Cantonese and against the similar action
which the Peking faction promptly took in emulation. This virtually
nullified the purpose of the Customs Treaty under which the Peking Tariff
Conference had been convened and was still technically in being, and was
the first overt and deliberate disregard of the policy of cooperation set up
by the Washington Conference.

The British had in fact been under fire for so long—their China trade
had suffered so greatly, and their Government had been so harassed between
the importunities of the "die-hard" element (who wanted more vigorous
protection) and the Labour party (who in opposition maintained that a
sympathetic attitude toward Chinese aspirations would purchase immunity
from anti-British feeling)—that the time had come to take the matter in
hand and make adjustments to the new conditions. For one thing, they
promoted to a European Embassy the Minister whose incomprehension
had been largely responsible for their troubles, and replaced him by Sir
Miles Lampson,[23] a younger but very keen and experienced official—one of
typical best of British civil servants, thoroughly competent and transparently honest and straightforward in all his dealings.[24] But without consult-

---

[23]*Sir Miles Lampson:* Sir Miles Lampson (1880–1964), later created Lord Killearn,
served as British minister in Peking from 1926 to 1933. Educated at Eton, he entered
the Foreign Office in 1903, serving as second secretary in Tokyo from 1908 to 1910
and first secretary in Peking from 1916 to 1919. After temporary service as acting
high commissioner in Siberia in 1919, he joined the British delegation to the
Washington Conference in 1921. In the period before his assignment to Peking he
served as head of the Central European department, then "probably the most
exacting task in the Foreign Office." His association with Sir Austen Chamberlain
in the difficult negotiations leading up to the Locarno Treaties of 1925 may have
contributed to his selection for Peking. He had knowledge of both the Chinese and
Japanese languages. In Peking, Lampson proved sympathetic and responsive to
Chinese aspirations. In 1930, however, his wife of eighteen years died. His second
wife, whom he married in 1934, may have influenced the increasingly hard-line
approach he took in later life, particularly in Egypt, where he was sent as high
commissioner in 1934. *References:* Obituary, *The Times,* September 19, 1964; E. T.
Williams and C. S. Nicholls, eds., *Dictionary of National Biography, 1961–1970*
(Oxford: Oxford University Press, 1981), pp. 627–28; Harold Edwin Kane, "Sir
Miles Lampson at the Peking Legation, 1926–1933," (Ph.D. dissertation, University
of London, 1975).

[24]The version in the MacMurray papers at Princeton strikes out the bracketed
material and reads: "they [promoted to a European Embassy the Minister whose

ing with him in advance, or awaiting his arrival at his post, his Government, in the middle of December 1926, communicated to the other signatories of the Washington Treaties a set of proposals as to a joint policy in China; and then, without allowing time for any adequate consideration or discussion, it published these in China as a formulation of British policy.[25] These proposals were in substance quite sound and practical—representing something not essentially different, in fact, from the way in which we and the other principally interested Powers had been feeling our way through the confused situation. But in manner the British document was exceedingly unfortunate. It took a self-righteous tone, scarcely justified by the facts, toward the other Powers; and toward the Chinese, whom its publication was intended to impress, it was ingratiating—almost wheedling—in its inflections. It contained passages such as this:

---

incomprehension had been largely responsible for their troubles, and] replaced [him] Sir Ronald Macleay by Sir Miles Lampson, [a younger but very keen and experienced official—one of the typical best of British civil servants, thoroughly competent and transparently honest and straightforward in all his dealings]."

[25] *A formulation of British policy:* This document, announcing a new and more yielding British approach to China, prepared in secret and made public with considerable fanfare on December 25, 1926, was intended to wrest for Britain the position of leadership in cooperation with China. It came as some shock to the other Powers. It originated in the aftermath of the May 30th incident, which saw popular unrest increasingly directed against a Britain whose position in China became economically and politically besieged, with little support from any of the other Powers. Under such circumstances, diplomats and politicians alike began to consider the advantages of some dramatic policy coup. Its outlines were sketched by Sir Victor Wellesley (1876–1954) in a series of memoranda in summer 1926, which stressed that since no military means were available to coerce China, Britain should welcome a speedy victory of the Kuomintang as the best hope of restoring order there. The Government therefore decided to show more public willingness to move unilaterally in such areas as tariff concessions, rather than being dragged along by a more liberal Japan and United States. Such unilateral angling for advantage went directly against the Washington spirit; it also proved embarrassing to Lampson, who was not informed of its contents in advance and thus was placed in a false position with his colleagues. In the end, Britain's move fell far short of what would have been necessary to assuage Chinese demands, but it did irritate her allies: Kellogg, in particular, was outraged that Britain should seek to appear a better friend of China than the United States. *References:* Text in *FRUS* 1926, 1:923–29; William Roger Louis, *British Strategy in the Far East, 1919–1939* (Oxford: Clarendon Press, 1971), pp. 142–44; William James Megginson III, "Britain's Response to Chinese Nationalism, 1925–1927: The Foreign Office Search for a New Policy" (Ph.D. dissertation, George Washington University, 1973).

. . . The Powers should recognize both the essential justice of China's claim for treaty revision and the difficulty under present conditions of negotiating new treaties in place of the old, and they should therefore modify their traditional attitude of a rigid insistence on the strict letter of treaty rights. . . .

. . . The basic facts of the present situation are that the Treaties are now admittedly in many respects out of date. . . . His Majesty's Government attach the greatest importance to the sanctity of treaties, but they believe that this principle may be best maintained by a sympathetic adjustment of treaty rights to the equitable claims of the Chinese. Protests should be reserved for cases where there is an attempt at wholesale repudiation of obligations, or an attack upon the legitimate and vital interests of foreigners in China. . . .

In the temper of the Chinese at the moment—particularly of the Nationalists who were sweeping victoriously into the Yangtsze valley in the guise of avengers of China's humiliation by the "mandarins" in corrupt league with the foreigners—such expressions as these had the effect of an invitation to contest the treaty rights of the foreigners. These ineptly made "proposals," so far from mollifying the Chinese by their professions of sympathy, were followed within a few days by the overrunning and seizure of the British Concessions at Hankow and Kiukiang by mobs incited by the Nationalist authorities.[26]

---

[26]*Seizure of the British Concessions at Hankow and Kiukiang:* Britain's Concessions at Kiukiang (Chiu-chiang), at the confluence of the Grand Canal and the Yangtze, and at Hankow (Han-k'ou), the major inland port of Central China, came under pressure as the Nationalists moved north in 1926. Kuomintang forces had arrived in Hankow in September 1926, and although they were initially welcomed by both the foreign and the Chinese communities, tension quickly developed as strikes and labor agitation began. It intensified after Borodin and the Canton Government moved to the city in November. Britain's response followed her approach to China as a whole; namely, to make large concessions in areas where British interests were relatively small in order to save the strong stand for Shanghai. Such was the approach London adopted when Hankow and Kiukiang were pressured, and it was further reinforced by the fact that large gunboats would not be able to sail upriver as far as Hankow until the following March or April. The crisis developed while Miles Lampson was on his way to assume the post of British minister, and he was instructed to stop in Hankow first. There, between December 8 and 17, he held talks with Eugene Ch'en, which led to an improvement in the situation. On January 4 and 5, however, Nationalist forces invaded the Concessions. Because this was done after an agreement had been reached whereby the British turned over responsibility for the safety of the Concession to the Chinese authorities, the move may perhaps be seen as an attempt by the left Kuomintang to undermine Chiang Kai-shek. But it hurt as well

But though ineffective for their purpose with the Chinese, the British "proposals" did have a prompt effect upon our own Government. Conscious of the strong popular pro-Chinese sentiment represented by the Porter Resolution, apparently afraid of having its hand forced by congressional action, and therefore the more reluctant that the British should assume leadership in the policy of indulgence toward Chinese aspirations, the Secretary of State, a month later (January 27, 1927), published a formal statement of our policy.[27] This statement, like the British "proposals," was sound in substance, but, like it, in its tone of ingratiating self-righteousness, it intimated a desire to appear in the light of being a better friend to China than were others. It contained these passages:

> . . . The Government of the United States has watched with sympathetic interest the nationalistic awakening of China and welcomes every advance made by the Chinese people toward reorganizing their system of government.
> . . . This Government wishes to deal with China in a most liberal spirit. It holds no Concessions in China and has never manifested any imperialistic attitude toward that country. . . ."

These words created strange impressions upon the British, on the one hand, whose Concessions had been seized by mob violence earlier in the month, and, on the other hand, upon the Chinese Nationalists who were in full cry against "British imperialism." During the period that followed, both the American and the British Governments, as their attitudes were reflected (for example) in the press, seemed to be vying with each other for

---

as helped the left: Hankow was to be their capital, and without some *modus vivendi* with the foreigners money would not be forthcoming. Talks were therefore undertaken by Owen O'Malley with Eugene Ch'en beginning on January 12, 1927. Agreement was reached on February 19, and on March 1 the Hankow Municipal Council transferred the Concession to Chinese control. A similar pattern was followed in Kiukiang. *Reference:* Megginson, "Britain's Response to Chinese Nationalism, 1925–1927," esp. pp. 500–515.

[27] *A formal statement of our policy:* Secretary Kellogg's statement sought to regain from Britain the position of foreign Power most sympathetic to Chinese aspirations. The 1926 volume of the *Survey of International Affairs* notes, "In the United States, the British memorandum caused an embarrassment almost indistinguishable in effect from disapproval, just because the British proposals advocated a fresh step forward on the very path in which the United States had long been accustomed to regard herself as the pioneer among foreign powers" (p. 330, quoted in Borg, *American Policy and the Chinese Revolution,* p. 231). *Reference:* Text in FRUS 1927, 1:350–53.

the favor of the Chinese, and encouraging, though unwittingly, their mood of irresponsibility and violence.

For it was a time of extreme and violent activity on the part of the Nationalists, made the more desperate by their internal dissensions which shortly afterward culminated in the discrediting and ejection of their Russian advisers and in General Chiang Kai-shek's making himself the virtual dictator of the movement. The tangled history of that time is of interest for the present purpose only insofar as it touched or threatened foreign lives and rights. Under the leadership of Chiang Kai-shek—who possesses all the traditional Chinese capacity for compromise and wangling and intrigue, but is unique among modern Chinese politicians in his ability to discern what he wants, make decisions and resolutely act upon them—the Nationalist armies had fought their way from Canton to the Yangtsze valley. The military campaign had been ably conducted with the assistance of the Soviet General Galen.[28] But the most remarkable phase of it (probably to the credit of Borodin rather than of Chiang) had been that the armies were preceded, at a considerable interval, by political or propaganda agents who persuaded the peasants, along the line of march, that the Cantonese armies were coming to redeem them from the bondage of the foreigners who were taking the bread out of the mouths of the Chinese. Sun Yat-sen's writings were quoted to them as proving that China's foreign trade—exports and imports alike—was a tribute to the imperialists, and that the age-long poverty and misery of the Chinese people were the results of a foreign commerce that had been forced upon the country against its will. There seemed to be no limit to the xenophobe credulity of the people; and through district after district that had previously resisted Cantonese attempts at control, Chiang's armies had passed unopposed and acclaimed as national redeemers. By the time that their administration had established itself on the Middle Yangtsze at Hankow, late in 1926, they were so elated with their successes that they not only dealt with the representatives of the

---

[28] *The Soviet General Galen:* Galen is one of the names of a man more commonly known as Vasilii Konstantinovich Bliukher (1889–1938; Blücher in German spelling; Galen is from Galina, his wife's name). An ordinary soldier in World War I, Bliukher made his career in the Far East. Fighting against Kolchak and Wrangel in the civil war, he became commander of forces in the Russian Far East (1921–1922) and fought the Japanese at Vladivostok (1922). He assisted Chiang K'ai-shek in the Northern Expedition but returned to the Soviet Union when Chiang discarded his Communist allies. He was dismissed and disappeared in 1938. *References:* A. I. Kartunova, *V. K. Bliukher v Kitae, 1924–1927 gg.: dokumentirovannye ocherk* (Moscow: "Nauka," 1970); "Blucher's 'Grand Plan' of 1926," trans. J. J. Solecki, *China Quarterly,* no. 35 (1968), pp. 18–39.

Powers in a tone of truculence comparable to that of the Russian Communist Government in its most unregenerate days, but boasted openly of their holding the whip hand through their ability to direct mob violence against foreigners and their interests. In the face of this arrogant and uncompromising ill will, the interested foreign governments seemed prone to "wishful thinking" about the situation, and each of their diplomatic representatives was harassed with a sense of futility in the effort to make his home government realize that only disillusionment could result from living in a fool's paradise—that the situation of foreign interests, already bad, must become disastrous if the interested Powers went on competitively holding out hopes of yielding indefinitely to the demands made upon them by those who only wanted to drive them into the sea. Not only did the foreign governments (and particularly the American and British) seek to bend to the storm; they seemed each zealous to show themselves more supple in doing so than the others.

What those on the spot had foreseen and dreaded happened at Nanking toward the end of March 1927.[29] As Chiang's armies triumphantly entered Nanking in the course of spreading down into the Lower Yangtsze valley, certain units of the troops, operating systematically under command, took possession of all foreign properties and attacked such foreign residents as they encountered, wounding some and killing six. The American Consul and his family, with various other foreigners who had joined them, were driven out of the Consulate and hunted through the outskirts of the city to a house on a hill above the river, from which they were rescued only by

---

[29]*Nanking toward the end of March:* On March 24, 1927, Kuomintang forces reached Nanking. The troops, originally concerned to defeat the Fengt'ien troops there, quickly turned on foreigners, 52 of whom took refuge at the Standard Oil property, called Socony Hill, while others were caught at the university. The Japanese and British Consulates were raided, and foreign houses were looted. The building at Socony Hill was invaded by a small group of Kuomintang soldiers who threatened to kill everyone; eventually John K. Davis, the American Consul, called upon two U.S. ships to lay down a curtain of gunfire, which enabled the foreigners to escape. Further naval gunfire cleared the streets and put an end to disorder by the afternoon. One American, three English, one French priest, and one Italian priest were killed. The incident brought the Powers up short on their policy of conciliation with the Kuomintang; indeed, that could have been the purpose of extremists within the party, who may have created the incident in order to weaken Chiang. How to deal with the incident immediately became a contentious diplomatic problem. *References:* Borg, *America and the Chinese Revolution,* pp. 290–317; Hung-Ting Ku, "The U.S.A. versus China: The Nanking Incident in 1927," *Tunghai Journal* 25 (1984), pp. 95–110.

means of a barrage from the American and British gunboats which dispersed their attackers.

The shock produced by this outrage brought about some realization that the Chinese Nationalist movement was not merely a striving for idealistic principles, but that incidentally to its agitation it had created a dangerous demoralization and an attitude of hatred against foreigners, such as its leaders could not and perhaps would not control. And so there began a series of developments by which the interested governments placed themselves upon the defensive against possible outbursts of violence. The American Legation, with the approval of the Department, not only sent away the women and children of its own establishment, as even the northern area seethed with unrest, but advised Americans to evacuate those regions occupied by the Nationalists or in their line of march, and urged that they take refuge either in Shanghai or in Tientsin, where it would be possible to afford them armed protection. The guards of the principal Legations at Peking were strengthened, and the American, British, French and Japanese forces stationed at Tientsin under the Boxer Protocol were heavily reinforced (we for our part sending a brigade of Marines). Considerable forces of American Marines and of British troops were likewise sent to Shanghai in addition to the available landing forces of the warships concentrated there. The Japanese also dispatched a large force to Tsinan.[30]

The incident at Nanking had excited a mob spirit even among those

---

[30]*Tsinan:* Japan made two interventions in Tsinan (Chi-nan), Shantung. The first began at the end of May 1927 and was designed to protect the Japanese residents of Tsinan from any incident as the Nationalist armies moved north; withdrawal of troops was envisioned as soon as "the fear of menace" against the Japanese residents was removed. (It was also probably prompted by Prime Minister Tanaka's need to show that his policy differed from that of Shidehara.) The second came in April 1928. Again the Nationalists were moving north, having overcome the splits and military defeats that had stymied them in the previous year. The Japanese commander, General Hikosuke Fukuda, advanced from Tsingtao (Ch'ing-tao) to Tsinan without instructions, a "fatal decision" that brought him into direct confrontation with the Nationalists who had entered the city, perhaps in defiance of Chiang Kaishek's orders. Agreement was reached for a Japanese withdrawal, however, and order seemed to be assured. But fighting did eventually break out. Both sides attempted to bring about a cease-fire, with little success. On May 7, the Japanese commanders presented an ultimatum to the Chinese "which should serve as a pretext for resuming hostilities." Fighting resumed on May 8, and the Chinese were finally driven from the city on May 11. "Until the end of the Japanese rule in early 1929, the Chinese lived under a reign of terror. The incident poisoned fatally any incipient Chinese-Japanese reconciliation." *Reference:* Iriye, *After Imperialism,* pp. 146–47, 198–204, 218–19.

Chinese who had been least responsive to Nationalist agitation. There was throughout the country an ominous tension—a feeling that violence might break out anywhere, at any time. And through the remainder of 1927, missionaries reluctantly abandoned their work in the interior, merchants gave up the attempt to carry on business in the outports, and to a large extent the foreigners in China either gave up and went home or concentrated in Tientsin or Shanghai to wait until the storm had blown over.

The governments whose nationals had been killed or abused at Nanking, and whose consulates had been seized, promptly took common action in demanding that appropriate amends be made. The reaction of our own Government was clear and definite. Following a conference with the White House, the Department instructed the Legation at Peking (by a telegram of April 2) that it should take steps to

> inform Chiang Kai-shek, Commander in Chief of the troops, that we hold his organization fully responsible for these acts, that we protest against these actions and demand reparations and full satisfaction for the insults offered the American Government and its flag and officials and for all damage done to American citizens, their persons and property and require guaranties for the protection of our citizens for the future. We think the note should conclude by reserving the right to take such action as shall be considered necessary in the light of his reply and the actual measures taken by him. This Government does not desire that note should contain anything in the nature of an ultimatum with a time limit.

In the chaotic political conditions that had come to prevail in the Nationalist movement there was some difficulty in determining the method by which representations might be made in behalf of the Powers; but it was decided that identic notes in behalf of the five Powers concerned (the United States, France, Great Britain, Italy, and Japan) should be presented both to the Nationalist Administration at Hankow, which still professed to have authority to act as the "Nationalist Government of China," and to General Chiang, who alone seemed actually to possess the capacity to act. The notes, presented on April 11, demanded adequate punishment of the commanders of the troops responsible for the outrages, a written apology from the Commander in Chief (General Chiang) and "an express written undertaking to refrain from all forms of violence and agitation against foreign lives and property," and reparations for personal injuries and material damages; and it concluded:

> Unless the Nationalist authorities demonstrate to the satisfaction of the interested governments their intention to comply promptly with these

terms the said governments will find themselves compelled to take such measures as they consider appropriate.

To this note the Hankow authorities replied wholly unsatisfactorily, rather derisively suggesting a joint inquiry which should also be charged with investigating "the circumstances of the bombardment of the unfortified city of Nanking," maintaining that the fundamental trouble was the maintenance of the "unequal treaties," and proposing negotiations for treaty revision. General Chiang made no reply at all, avoided contacts with any foreign representatives, and permitted his troops to continue the occupation and looting of the consulates and other foreign properties at Nanking.

But when, in view of the ignoring of their demands, the Powers sought to concert means of pressure by which to validate them, it appeared that our Government was not prepared to join in any coercive measures to that end. This decision was doubtless within our rights, but in view of our having collaborated with the other Powers in the identic notes which by inescapable implication threatened action to force the Chinese to meet the demands, our withdrawal from such cooperation paralyzed their action and left them in a false position.

From then on, the brunt of the effort to bring about a settlement fell upon the British Minister, who eventually formed contacts with the Nanking authorities who had superseded the Hankow group in the control of the Nationalist Administration. His negotiations almost reached the point of concluding an agreement in the spring of 1928; but his Government, at the last moment, found the proposed settlement unsatisfactory. He went aboard a British naval vessel, to sail back to Tientsin the following morning, and with remarkable generosity he spent most of the night in preparing for his American colleague, who was to arrive in Shanghai the next day, a full memorandum of his negotiations. This enabled the American Minister to conduct his own negotiations with a knowledge of the pitfalls likely to be encountered, and of the views and prepossessions of the Chinese with whom he was dealing, and made possible his concluding an agreement along very much the same lines that Sir Miles Lampson had worked out. It was not a satisfactory settlement of the case, although doubtless the best that was obtainable in view of the fact that the original demands had been allowed to lapse by default. The other Powers had shortly to effect similar settlements.

Even though the outcome had been thus favorable to the Nationalists, they delayed through many months to put our Nanking Consulate into habitable condition again, and backed and filled on the question of appropriate ceremonies to acknowledge the return of our flag to their capital; and at last, as though feeling ourselves under some compulsion to heal the estrangement, we hurriedly sent a staff to reoccupy our Consulate even before the necessary repairs were finished. The whole handling of the Nanking affair, doing more credit to the benevolence of our intentions than to the realism of our understanding of the situation and of Chinese psychology, lent itself to the assumption of the Nationalists that their resort to violence had justified itself by intimidating and humiliating the "imperialistic Powers."

While the Nationalist party was consolidating itself in the Yangtsze, with incidental fighting and intrigue among the Chinese factions, and with frequent acts of violence against foreigners and their interests, the Northern faction, still pretending to the functions of government, had been carrying on, by methods scarcely less arbitrary, the contest against the legal position of the Treaty Powers.

In the autumn of 1926, the Belgian Treaty of 1865 came to one of the decennial periods at which, by its formally unilateral terms, the Belgian Government might request negotiations for its revision: and the faction in control of Peking arrogated to itself the right to utilize that occasion to abrogate the treaty outright, even though the Belgian Government had, in the course of preliminary discussions, offered unreservedly to negotiate a new treaty and meanwhile to regard the old one as no longer in force, provided only that there should be arranged a satisfactory *modus vivendi* placing Belgium in the meanwhile on a basis of equality with the other Treaty Powers.[31] When (in August 1926) the Belgians first brought the

---

[31]*Placing Belgium on a basis of equality with the other Treaty Powers:* The Belgian Treaty of 1866 was the first of its type to be repudiated by the Chinese. The negotiations fell into three stages: first, an attempt to reach a *modus vivendi* that would maintain relations until a new treaty was agreed on (April 1926–November 1926); second, a period of delay during which Belgium took its case to the Permanent Court of International Justice at The Hague (November 1926–January 1927); and finally, after the Court had proposed measures not to Belgium's liking, a period of prolonged negotiation, first with Peking and then with Nanking, that led to the eventual, entirely new treaty (January 1927–November 1928). The case, as MacMurray stresses, would serve as an important precedent. But it is also interesting because of Belgium's status. A weak country, Belgium could not exert any pressure on China. Furthermore, during most of the negotiations, the foreign minister was Emile Vandervelde (1866–1938), a Socialist and a strong advocate of Chinese rights, who later wrote *A travers la révolution Chinoise: Soviets et Kuomintang* (Paris: Alcan, 1931). The Belgian representative in Peking, Baron Leon Le Maire de Warzée d'Hermalle (1877–1931), while an old-school diplomat by comparison with his foreign minister, was nevertheless a champion of "a policy of concession and abandonment of

discussions to the attention of the other Powers signatory to the Washington Treaty, it was for the purpose of asking their support in persuading the Chinese to consent to a satisfactory *modus vivendi* for that purpose. To this appeal for cooperation, the American and British Governments both replied sympathetically with the Belgian case, but pointed out that insistence upon the terms of the *modus vivendi* (the suggestion of which the Chinese had

---

privilege." Belgian business was more strongly in favor of immediate agreement to Chinese demands than even the foreign minister. In the Belgian case, in other words, the only obstacles to Chinese demands were the legal technicalities of treaty revision, and the complications created by one Power's moving in a situation in which many have interests. The treaty in question had been concluded on November 2, 1865, and ratified the following year. On April 26, 1926, Peking informed the Belgians that as of October 27 the treaty would be terminated. Peking's action immediately raised the question whether such action was legal: Article 46, which governed the renewal of the treaty, assigned the right to request revision to Belgium unilaterally. Of course, if China chose to repudiate the treaty there was little Belgium could do, but, like a declaration of default, such an action could not avoid having broad repercussions. Vandervelde felt the dilemma; he was sure the agreement over matters of substance could be reached, but procedures were also important. On May 27, he told de Warzée that separate negotiations would mean reneging on Washington Conference agreements. Furthermore, Belgium's security depended on the Powers, and Belgium was reluctant to set the pattern for revision of treaties with far more important countries. So, leaving the question of the validity of the repudiation in abeyance, the Belgians sought a *modus vivendi*—something that would provide a temporary framework for relations while negotiations continued. These talks failed when the Chinese insisted on a time limit, at the expiration of which, in the absence of agreement, the Belgians would lose all rights. This Brussels would not accept; for China to insist would force them to argue at The Hague the vexed question of the validity of repudiation, which could otherwise be avoided by concluding a new treaty. With great reluctance Brussels finally decided to do what de Warzée and MacMurray, among others, felt was their only alternative. They asked the Permanent Court of International Justice to examine the legality of China's actions, and to propose interim measures to safeguard Belgians during the litigation. Although both China and Belgium recognized the Court, China maintained the matter was a political dispute, outside the Court's jurisdiction. Thus Belgium's appeal was unilateral. Belgium was seeking to acquire negotiating leverage, but the Court's first measure, on January 8, 1927, which called for the application of interim policies outlined in a Chinese Presidential Mandate repudiating the treaties on November 6, 1926, was not what it had expected. This setback to Belgium, and the growing threat to Peking from the South, got negotiations under way again. At the first meeting of the new series of negotiations, on October 17, 1927, de Warzée announced a measure long considered in Belgium: the retrocession of the Tientsin Concession. Such a move was of symbolic significance but little practical conse-

already seized upon as constituting an admission of their right to denounce the treaty) seemed tactically inadvisable as tending to compromise the clear-cut issue of Belgium's right to insist that the old treaty was legally in force until replaced by a new one. The Belgians then proposed to the Chinese to submit that question by a *compromis* to The Hague Court for decision; but the Chinese refused to do so, maintaining that the only question at issue was the political and non-justiciable one of China's right to freedom from the "unequal treaties." Our Legation in Peking telegraphed (on November 12, 1926) its view that

> Denunciation of the Belgian Treaty was a studied effort to determine the extent of the complaisance of the treaty powers toward a repudiation of China's treaty obligations. . . . This action brings us to the juncture . . . at which those professing to control the foreign affairs of China find it to their personal advantage to espouse doctrine of repudiation. We are now confronted with a state of fact in which an organization purporting to represent China internationally though actually but a derelict of a former *régime* enjoying foreign recognition has by its action in the case of Belgium given notice to all the treaty Powers of its disregard of the binding force of treaties. . . .
>
> In view alike of our own interests and of our real sympathy with the international development of China on a basis of fair dealing and understanding we should take occasion to intimate informally that our Government has no sympathy with the Chinese in the doctrine of international irresponsibility which has stood in the way of our recognition of the Russian *régime*. I respectfully beg to suggest that an informal intimation to

---

quence. Acquired only in 1902, the Concession had never been developed; in 1926, it had a population of 2,000 Chinese and no foreigners. Good will was generated by the Belgian action but quickly dissipated by Chinese insistence that Belgium withdraw its case at The Hague. The fact of civil war meant that Belgium was increasingly reluctant to treat with Peking. Official Belgian sympathies were with the Nationalists, and Brussels sought to carry out a tandem negotiation, in which terms agreed in Peking were tacitly cleared with Hankow as well. The idea was that when the Nationalists won, Belgium would be ahead of the game. Indeed, Brussels expended much energy in opening a channel of communication to Eugene Ch'en and the Hankow Government, a task triumphantly completed the day before Wuhan expelled Chiang Kai-shek, who set up the new government in Nanking. With the Nationalist victory, negotiations were restarted, and a preliminary agreement was signed on November 22, 1928. *References:* Text in China, Imperial Maritime Customs, *Treaties, Conventions, etc. between China and Foreign States* (Shanghai: Inspectorate General of Customs, 1908), 2:758–59; John Patrick Martin, "Politics of Delay: Belgium's Treaty Negotiations with China, 1926–1929" (Ph.D. dissertation, St. John's University, 1980).

that effect from the Secretary in person would have great influence in
deterring the Chinese from pursuing course of conduct which I gravely
apprehend would lay a basis for a new war in the Far East in a future not
very distant. . . .

The Department replied, however (in a telegram of November 15), that
it did not "understand the purpose of the suggestion . . . to the effect that
the Secretary intimate that this Government has no sympathy with the
Chinese in the doctrine of international irresponsibility that had stood in
the way of our recognition of the Russian *régime*"; and notwithstanding the
earlier assurance that we sympathized with Belgium's case and would have
supported it as requested by the Belgian Government but for a question
whether the particular form of cooperation then envisaged would not have
tended to defeat the purpose in view, the Department's instruction added
(in reference to the Legation's inquiry regarding the basis of a Reuter report)
that the Secretary had, on November 8, stated to the press correspondents
that he "did not know of any reason why this Government should support
the Belgian Government in any protest against the denunciation by China
of its treaty with Belgium."

Although the matter at issue was that of the binding force of one of the
typical treaties establishing the basis of the relations of the Powers with
China, and therefore manifestly could not be considered apart from the
nexus of rights and obligations with regard to which the Washington
Conference had recognized the necessity of cooperation, our Government
so far disinterested itself in the case that the Belgian Ambassador here, in
private communications to American friends, expressed himself as resigned
to the fact that our Administration did not welcome any suggestions for
cooperative action—that it was set upon giving China her head, regardless
of any question of common interest.

Left to fight the issue not only without support but in spite of the
publicly declared indifference of the Government that so recently had
sponsored and achieved adherence to the policy of cooperation, Belgium
took the case to the Permanent Court at The Hague, to determine whether
China's abrogation of the treaty was legally valid. But the Chinese (setting
a new precedent) disdained to respond in the proceedings: and Belgium at
last yielded, not only abandoning her defense of her treaty position, but (in
order to obtain even a doubtful unilateral assurance that Belgians would as
a matter of favor be treated as though they still had the status of nationals
of a treaty Power) throwing in as a makeweight in the negotiations the
retrocession of their Concession at Tientsin. It was while this humiliating
surrender was under contemplation that our Embassy in Brussels reported
(in a telegram of January 20, 1927)

. . . I have gathered that even should Belgium's action in retroceding the Concession to China unfavorably affect other nations she will, nevertheless, proceed with her plan since it is hoped that such a gesture of friendship and good will may have a fortunate effect on the treaty negotiations. As I have reported to the Department . . . the Government considers that European [i.e., foreign] solidarity in China belongs to the past and that now each nation, particularly Belgium, must make the best of a bad situation and must follow whatever course may appear to be most to its advantage. . . .

This statement marks the degree to which, within five years of the close of the Washington Conference, the ideal of cooperation in the Far East had been nullified by our Government's permitting itself to be diverted from the pursuit of the traditional policy for which it had so recently succeeded in winning international support.

And (to anticipate other developments in order to treat of an analogous but more fundamental case) with regard to the Chinese abrogation of the Japanese treaties of 1896 and 1903, we similarly washed our hands of all concern in the matter. These treaties constituted the basis of the whole treaty relationship between China and Japan.[32] The earlier of them made

---

[32] *The whole treaty relationship between China and Japan:* The Treaty of Commerce and Navigation between Japan and the Ch'ing was concluded at Peking on July 21, 1896. The ten-year clause, which provided for revisions, fell due in October 1926. On October 20, the Peking Government of Wellington Koo proposed negotiations on the subject. Yoshizawa advised that Shidehara state his sympathy with the Chinese demands, and his willingness to begin informal discussions. The Chinese note, however, had suggested that the treaties might be denounced if negotiations were not completed within six months. Shidehara tried to have this "veiled threat" removed, but without success. On November 10, he sent a note to Peking agreeing to begin negotiations. These began on January 1, 1927. The Japanese were aware of the growing strength of the Kuomintang and therefore did not wish to commit themselves to a definite stand concerning the Peking *régime*. The Northern Government, however, would be strengthened if it could wrest real concessions from Japan and therefore grew increasingly committed to the negotiations. The initial request from the Chinese side had been made only ten days after the Kuomintang had captured Wuhan on October 10, 1926. Not surprisingly, the talks rapidly became deadlocked. The Peking Foreign Ministry "had carefully studied tariff autonomy, extraterritoriality, inland navigation, and other issues connected with treaty revision, and had apparently drawn up a rough draft of a new treaty of commerce and navigation." Japan had already accepted the principle of tariff autonomy at the Peking Tariff Conference. Peking insisted that explicit recognition of this principle must precede any discussion of a reciprocal tariff agreement. Wellington Koo would not budge from these positions. The Japanese position was likewise lacking in

provision for the possible decennial revision of the stipulated tariffs and of the commercial articles; and the Chinese availed themselves of the occurrence of one of these decennial periods, in the autumn of 1926, to demand a fundamental revision of both the treaties, to be effected within six months—failing which, they would be regarded as terminated. The Japa-

---

flexibility. Shidehara would make a general concession only if he received specific guarantees that would undo much of what would otherwise have been the effect. When Yoshizawa requested that Shidehara declare Japan's willingness to restore tariff autonomy the foreign minister refused; that would be done only if "adequate temporary adjustments," that is, reciprocal tariff agreements, were arrived at. The Chinese political scene was cloudy; the Japanese were inclined to delay the negotiations, hoping it might sort itself out. Koo, by contrast, kept extending the negotiations, hoping that in the end his tight conditions would be accepted. The problem of the treaties came up again and again as the Nationalists, now victorious in the civil war, consolidated their position. The campaign, and Tanaka's intervention in it, had created a host of problems that ultimately came to be negotiated; the revision of the 1896 and 1903 treaties was by no means the most important of them. Affecting all of them was the grave situation Japan faced in Manchuria. After an insubordinate Japanese officer arranged the killing of Chang Tso-lin on June 4, 1928, Tokyo had lacked a reliable associate there. The success of the Northern Expedition was being felt north of the passes, and the Old Marshal's son, Chang Hsüeh-liang, was influenced by it. Certainly the new Nationalist Foreign Ministry seemed to envision the gradual repudiation of the treaties of 1905, 1915, and other years, which established Japan's position in Manchuria; that much was implicit in the July 7 declaration of the Government's wish to revise all unexpired "unequal treaties." The announcement on July 19, 1928, by Wang Cheng-t'ing, that the 1895 and 1903 treaties would be repudiated was simply the first shot. Tanaka initially adopted a hard line. But Tanaka's policy choices were limited, and ultimately he was forced to compromise. Yoshizawa, who had returned to Japan for the coronation in the autumn of 1928, proposed a policy similar in conception to that the British had adopted in the South. It envisioned major concessions in China proper in return for substantive guarantees for Manchuria. The military opposed such a policy. Tanaka, however, ultimately accepted it, and Yoshizawa initiated negotiations with C. T. Wang on April 26, 1929. Discussion of the treaty was only a part of the discussions, which treated Shantung and other outstanding problems. In June, Tokyo recognized Nanking. When Yoshizawa returned to Japan, his deputy, Mamoru Shigemitsu (1897–1957), continued the talks, and on May 6, 1930, a new treaty was concluded at Nanking, restoring tariff autonomy to China. The real culmination of the process, though, was the recognition of the National Government by Japan on June 3, 1929. *References:* Text in John Van Antwerp MacMurray, *Treaties and Agreements with and concerning China* (New York: Carnegie Endowment, 1921), 1: 68–74; Robert T. Pollard, *China's Foreign Relations, 1917–1931* (New York: Macmillan, 1933), pp. 322–24; Iriye, *After Imperialism,* pp. 116–17, 359.

nese, while taking exception to this assumption and in effect reserving their rights, nevertheless consented to negotiate; and with various extensions of time necessitated largely by the confusion and absence of authority in China, they carried on negotiations, with conciliatory patience and moderation, first with the Peking group, and later with the Nationalist group at Shanghai and Nanking, for well over a year. In the summer of 1928, however, the Nanking authorities rather abruptly declared that, since the revision had not been effected within the time specified, the treaties were to be considered as having terminated. The Japanese refused to accept this ouster from their treaty rights, and the Chinese were not in a position to enforce it against them; but there was created a bitter issue in which the Japanese quite naturally and strongly felt that justice was on their side. With the case of Belgium before them, they did not appeal to the Washington Conference Powers, but first sounded out the attitude of the United States. For that purpose they made use of Count Uchida, a member of the Privy Council, who had been Minister for Foreign Affairs at the time of the Washington Conference. He visited Washington in September 1928, on his return from the ceremony of signature of the Kellogg-Briand pact in Paris. But he brought his wares to a bad market: he found our Government suspicious, aloof, and unresponsive to his presentation of the Japanese case. The American Government seemed, in fact, to be definitely out of conceit with the Japanese by reason of certain events indicating a disposition to take in China a line of action more drastic than American opinion approved.

There had come into power in Japan a reactionary Ministry headed by General Tanaka,[33] who had long been the leader of the military group

---

[33]*General Tanaka:* MacMurray's characterization of Gichii Tanaka's Ministry (April 1927–July 1929) as "reactionary," and of General Tanaka himself as "the leader of the military group urging the doctrine of Japanese hegemony in eastern Asia and demanding a 'positive policy' to that end in China" corresponds with the common idea that Tanaka's foreign policy was dramatically different from Shidehara's. Ironically, though, cooperation with foreign Powers ultimately became far more critical to the maintenance of Japan's position under Tanaka than it had ever been under Shidehara. Giichi Tanaka (1864–1929) was a protégé of Aritomo Yamagata and Masataka Terauchi, in the Chōshū clique, and served as a major in the Sino-Japanese War. In 1898 he was sent to Russia, where he learned the language and familiarized himself with the nation's military position. In 1902, returning to Japan after visits to Germany, France, and Italy, he became head of the Russian Section in the General Staff. He served in Manchuria again during the Russo-Japanese War. In 1910, he became major general; in 1911, director of the Military Affairs Bureau for the Ministry of the Army. He also served as army minister in the Hara cabinet. In 1920 he was made baron; in 1921 he was promoted to general. On his retirement it

urging the doctrine of Japanese hegemony in eastern Asia and demanding a "positive policy" to that end in China. There has been much futile debate as to the genuineness of a document which was published through Chinese sources, stated to be a secret memorandum in which General Tanaka, as Chief of Staff of the Japanese Army, had laid before the highest authorities of his Government a philosophy and a program of action for Japan's

---

was natural for him to enter politics. In April 1925, Tanaka became leader of the Seiyukai. After Hara's assassination, the party had lacked leadership. Korekiyo Takahashi, who had succeeded, "had little taste for party leadership, and the party elders sought a successor." Tanaka was their choice, and in the summer of 1925 he and the Seiyukai withdrew from the Katō cabinet, hoping to bring it down and thereby make Tanaka prime minister. But with Prince Saionji's support, Katō led a minority government. After his death in January 1926, Reijirō Wakatsuki continued. The crisis that made Tanaka prime minister involved China policy only incidentally. Spring 1927 saw an economic crisis in Japan coincide with problems in China. The immediate problem was the looming insolvency of the Bank of Taiwan. At the critical Privy Council meeting of April 17, 1927, Miyoji Itō (1857–1934) linked the financial straits of the bank, and the difficulties Japanese firms were having owing to boycotts and disorder in China, to the policy of Shidehara. "China policy was therefore at the root of the crisis." This approach had already been made clear in a Seiyukai campaign; spring 1927 had seen concerted attacks in the Diet and in the press on Shidehara's policies. The Seiyukai China experts—Kaku Mori (1883–1932), Jōtarō Yamamoto (1867–1936), and Yōsuke Matsuoka (1880–1946)—made a fact-finding trip to China. Tanaka did not believe that the Chinese would be able to re-create a sound political order; rather, he feared that without an active Japanese role, "Soviet national power, with communism in the background, would carry the day." Shidehara had disagreed, and army intelligence had initially shared his appraisal of Chiang. But a week before the crisis, on April 8, Kazushige Ugaki (1868–1956) had recommended intervention to prevent a Soviet victory. Even in this crisis the government need not have fallen; but Wakatsuki was not the man for a fight to the finish, and he decided on a general resignation of the cabinet. On April 19 Tanaka received the order to form a new government. Because China policy was so affected, it is important to keep in mind that although politicking about China had played a role in the political crisis, the decision to call Tanaka had nothing to do with it. The people had faulted the Wakatsuki cabinet's leadership, wrote *The Economist* (Japan), and furthermore approved "as right and natural the passing of power to the opposition political party." Indeed, despite the appearance of great disagreement, there was much in common in the China policies of Shidehara and Tanaka. Both agreed on the pivotal importance of mainland Asia, though Shidehara disagreed that some form of autonomy for Manchuria and Mongolia could be envisioned, preferring to secure Japan's interests in a united China. Furthermore, Shidehara had proved very successful at providing the kind of toleration of Chiang Kai-shek that enabled him ultimately to end his dependence on

assumption of a dominant position in the East: even though the purported memorandum may have been entirely spurious, it nevertheless did set forth views and purposes such as subsequent developments have shown to be substantially the same as those which have in reality actuated the military leaders who had received their inspiration from General Tanaka.[34] It had, moreover, such a degree of inherent plausibility, even before such confir-

---

the left; that was the real significance of Shidehara's inaction over the problems at Nanking and Hankow. Furthermore, Tanaka's hopes for Chiang were virtually the same as Shidehara's, though he proved less able to realize them. But the evidence of Shidehara's success in dealing with Chiang "came too late to influence domestic political development." Criticism of China policy had already become crucial in the political assault on the Kenseikai cabinet. Certainly no great discontinuity was evident at first between Tanaka's and Shidehara's policies. Tanaka's first official statement about China, on April 22, some four days after Chiang Kai-shek had established his government at Nanking, "said that the new cabinet would treat the wishes of the Chinese People sympathetically" and probably reflected "cautious optimism in Tokyo." Indeed, Tanaka fostered Chiang's preeminence—despite statements to the contrary—by keeping Chang Tso-lin from interfering, for factional reasons, in the anti-Communist campaign. As it turned out, though, policy in Manchuria proved the undoing of Tanaka's program. Tanaka "was disposed to support the unity of China proper under a non-Communist government led by Chiang Kai-shek, but he was determined to retain Japan's special position in Manchuria and Mongolia, if warranted, by assisting Chang Tso-lin." This was a reasonable policy, although it was rather different from that of the other Powers. This scheme, however, was ultimately scuttled by Japan's own moves, not in Manchuria, but in Shantung. The intervention in Shantung in the spring of 1928, and the bloodshed that followed, led to the resignation of Huang Fu (1880–1936) as foreign minister, and his replacement by Wang Cheng-t'ing. The new foreign minister favored using the Americans and the British against Japan, and the kinds of compromises Huang might have agreed to moved out of reach. The same spring saw the assassination of Chang Tso-lin. On hearing of it, and understanding its grave implications, Tanaka is alleged to have said, "my life's work is ruined." Without Chang, plans to build an autonomous, pro-Japanese Manchuria were bound to fail. Tanaka resigned on June 28, 1929, as a result of the emperor's apparent displeasure with him for compromising with the army over the punishment of Chang's assassins. Although MacMurray and others perceived Tanaka's policies as differing substantially from Shidehara's, arguably neither ends nor means were different; what differed were circumstances in China, and an indefinable quantity, the skill at implementation. Shidehara did not shy from using gunboats, nor was he forthcoming about the binding force of treaties, or Japan's position in Manchuria. But he managed not to undermine Chiang Kai-shek despite extreme provocations. Tanaka, by contrast, allowed the Shantung expeditions to sidetrack the broader goals of his policy, and rather than opening a way for compromise with the

mation, that his assumption of the Prime Ministership, accompanied by attacks upon the "spineless" China policy pursued by the liberal cabinet that he displaced, was ominous and disquieting.

The merits of what thereupon occurred are as debatable as the authenticity of the Tanaka memorandum, and perhaps quite as academic. The Tanaka Ministry did what it had, in opposition, been unable to force the

---

Nationalists, closed it off. Of course, Shidehara and Tanaka could scarcely have been more different in background, values, and personal style. But it is a comment on the essential unanimity about certain Japanese policy goals that one can really say only that Tanaka was inept, not that he was reactionary. *References: NGJ,* pp. 520–21; William Fitch Morton, *Tanaka Giichi and Japan's China Policy* (Folkestone, Eng.: Wm. Dawson & Sons, 1980), pp. 56–57, 66, 76, 80, 83, 86, 90, 132; Bamba, *Japanese Diplomacy in a Dilemma;* Kitaoka, "China Experts in the Army."

[34] *The Tanaka memorandum:* The Tanaka memorandum, or more properly memorial, as it was alleged to have been presented to the Japanese emperor on July 25, 1927, is a spurious document of more than 13,000 words outlining a plan of Japanese world conquest. Its origins are cloudy, but its influence, even up to the present, cannot be doubted. The document was apparently first presented at a meeting of the Institute of Pacific Relations held at Nara and Kyoto, October 23–November 9, 1929. The Japanese Legation in Peking wired Tokyo on September 16, 1929, that Ch'en Li-ting, the secretary of the Chinese delegation, would make the document public at the meeting in order to arouse world opinion. In fact, though, no mention of the document occurs in the published proceedings. This suggests a desire to avoid a confrontation. It probably reflects, as well, the doubts some Chinese harbored about the authenticity of the document, and the effectiveness of Japanese rebuttal. The most baffling problem with the memorandum is that no Japanese original is known. The first published version appeared in the Nanking Chinese-language journal *Shih-shih yüeh-pao* in December 1929. Chinese and English pamphlet versions appeared at about the same time, and a retranslated Japanese version put out by the Sino-Japanese Club appeared in Japan in June 1930. After its publication in Nanking, the Japanese Foreign Ministry denied the authenticity of the document, and Mamoru Shigemitsu, acting (in Yoshizawa's absence) minister to China, protested about the harm pamphlets were doing to Sino-Japanese relations. Wang Cheng-t'ing, though he promised to give proper public notice to the Japanese protest, in fact did nothing, and in his memoirs he refers to the document as if to suggest it was genuine. The appearance of the first version of the document in Chinese, and the persistence with which the Chinese still continue to assert its authenticity, suggest that they had reason, more than the simple political usefulness that might have commended it to Wang, to believe in its genuineness. The document probably had been obtained clandestinely from a Japanese source. General Kazushige Ugaki stated after the war that he believed that certain individuals in the Minseito had concocted the memorandum and sold it as a state secret to Chinese intelligence agents. Certain aspects of the outline clearly reflected the ideas of some in Japan. Shortly before the Eastern

preceding cabinet to do a year before—it sent a large Japanese Army contingent to protect Tsinan, where there were very large Japanese interests, and which incidentally was the principal railway junction on the line that the Kuomintang forces were following on their expedition to conquer Peking and the North. However much of pretext and provocation may have been mingled in with it, there was at least a very substantial Japanese interest to justify this precautionary measure. The Japanese, unlike the Americans and the British, had given no advice to their people to withdraw from the line of march of the Nationalist armies: they had stuck to the letter of their rights and decided that, at least in that area which was as important for them as Shanghai or Tientsin for us, they would not allow their people to be harried out. That decision was variously interpreted. To the representatives of other Powers in China, it was a matter of envy that the Japanese should be in a position to do what they themselves could not do and hold off the elated Nationalist armies which in their march had been confiscating the properties of foreign missionary institutions and showing themselves wanton and regardless of foreign lives. To the Chinese, however, the Japanese defense force at Tsinan was a mere subterfuge—a means of picking a quarrel and holding the railways so as to obstruct the victorious northern march of the Nationalists.

The worst possibility came to pass: the advance guard of General Chiang's troops came into conflict with the Japanese; there were several days of bloody though small-scale fighting; the Japanese ended in control

---

Conference (a meeting convened by Tanaka in 1927 to discuss China policy), Kaku Mori and Teiichi Suzuki met with Shigeru Yoshida (1878–1967) and Ambassador to the United States Hiroshi Saitō (1886–1939) to discuss a plan for separating Manchuria and Mongolia from China proper. The plan would clearly be unacceptable to the United States and to certain members of the Tanaka cabinet, so Saitō "converted it into a harmless, and ambiguous plan for laying the diplomatic groundwork so Japan could fulfill its tasks in Manchuria-Mongolia without opposition from the United States." Some version of this scheme may have gotten into the hands of agents of Chiang Kai-shek, perhaps through the agency of Minseitō members. Firm Japanese denials had appeared to have discredited the memorandum until the Manchurian incident. In the midst of that crisis, *The China Critic* in Shanghai published the text in English. Thereafter it became better and better known, and it is still cited erroneously in some general histories. *References:* Text in *The Tanaka Memorial: An Outline Presented to the Japanese Emperor on July 25, 1927 by Premier Tanaka for the Japanese Conquest of China and Other Nations, Also a Prediction of a Japanese-American War* (San Francisco: Chinese National Salvation Publicity Bureau, 1937); also *NGJ*, p. 521; W. F. Morton, *Tanaka Giichi and Japan's China Policy*, pp. 205–14; John J. Stephan, "The Tanaka Memorial (1927): Authentic or Spurious?" *Modern Asia Studies* 7 (1973), pp. 733–45.

of the local situation, and the Nationalists had to modify their strategy and find their way around Tsinan to utilize a branch line which connected them with the only other railway to the North. They were successful in that and soon forced their way to Peking and made themselves masters of North China. But they felt bitterly and made vehement outcry against what they considered a hostile intervention on the part of the Japanese. Chinese feeling was in fact greatly aroused, and the principal onus of antiforeign feeling was shifted from the British to the Japanese. Throughout the country there began to be carried out an anti-Japanese boycott far more effectively organized and more damaging than any of the half-dozen or so previous boycotts. Japanese trade was seriously dislocated, and Japanese subjects and their interests were in jeopardy.

Although what happened to them in the course of affording legitimate protection to their nationals at Tsinan was no different from what, but for the grace of Providence, might have happened to us at Shanghai or at Tientsin, the fact that an incident did occur with them put them on the defensive as having contrived it all in order to block the Nationalist conquest of North China. Perhaps they did, or perhaps not—doubtless the inner verity of that incident, like many another of the sort, will never be known. Those foreign representatives nearest to the event (including our own exceptionally able Consul in Tsinan)[35] were disposed to the belief that the Japanese forces had in good faith done only what had been forced upon them to do in fulfillment of their mission to protect the lives and property of their nationals. But Japan had "a bad press" about it all, particularly in this country. And the record seems to show that our own Department of State inclined toward the view that Japan had deliberately provoked the Tsinan affair by way of an interposition to circumscribe the Nationalist movement. From the viewpoint of an American official policy that had, so to speak, placed its bet on China as against Japan, what occurred at Tsinan was therefore not a merely debatable question of local responsibilities and provocations on the one side or the other, but an evidence of antagonism toward the Nationalists, whom American public opinion continued to favor as though they were the champions of our own ideals.

This partisanship of American official and popular opinion for the Nationalist cause had been accentuated, before Count Uchida came to America, by the conclusion of our Customs Treaty of July 25, 1928,[36] and

---

[35]Ernest B. Price (1890–1973).

[36]*Customs Treaty of July 25, 1928:* Concluded by MacMurray with exceptional speed, the Customs Treaty marked the abandonment by the United States of the detached and multilateral approach that the minister had recommended, and its substitution

its interpretation as constituting a formal recognition of the Nationalist *régime* as the Government of China. Of the circumstances under which that treaty was concluded, more will be said hereafter; but for immediate purposes it is to be noted that it gave the occasion for our Government, pressed as it was by popular opinion into the espousal of a "pro-Chinese" policy of hastening our renunciation of rights under the "unequal treaties," to acclaim the Nationalists there and then as being a responsible sovereign government such as we had been eager to deal with; and the attitude of the Japanese seemed to be in opposition to our effectuating that purpose.

It was under such circumstances that, on September 29, Count Uchida called at the Department of State and read to the Secretary a memorandum setting forth clearly and moderately the Japanese Government's viewpoint on several current problems, and particularly on the matter of China's abrogation of the treaties.[37] The memorandum recalled the difficulties that

---

by measures to establish relations immediately with the Nationalist Government. This reflected political pressure at home, where Secretary Kellogg was determined to stay ahead of the China issue, and the changing situation in China, where even as they secured military control, the Nationalists adopted the negotiating tactics of the Northern Government they had displaced, pushing forward with the step-by-step abrogation of foreign treaties. MacMurray was less sanguine about the Nationalists than was the secretary of state, and likewise far more concerned about the repercussions unilateral American action would have on cooperation among the Powers. Nevertheless, once Kellogg and Coolidge had set policy, MacMurray worked with T. V. Soong (1894–1971) to conclude the treaty. Conclusion of the treaty indicated at least *de facto* American recognition of the new Chinese *régime*. It also greatly strengthened China's hand in dealing with other Powers, notably Japan. *References:* Text in *FRUS* 1928, 2:475–77; Borg, *America and the Chinese Revolution*, pp. 386–417.

[37]*China's abrogation of the treaties:* The signing of the Kellogg-Briand pact in Paris (August 27, 1928), to which Count Yasuya Uchida (1865–1936), a former foreign minister and ambassador to Washington, was sent as the Japanese representative, provided an opportunity for the new cabinet of Giichi Tanaka to sound out the attitudes of the United States and the United Kingdom in light of the new situation developing in China. Tanaka had come to power with the intention of reversing the "weak-kneed" China diplomacy of Shidehara. Ironically, though, for a number of reasons, Tanaka quickly found himself in as much need of foreign cooperation as had been his predecessor as foreign minister. One reason for this was Chiang Kai-shek's successful conquest of the North. Tanaka's attempt to interfere by landing troops in Shantung (April 20, 1928) had not stopped Chiang; rather, it had worsened relations and put Tanaka in a position from which there was no graceful exit. Furthermore, Manchuria threatened to come unstuck. The only way that Japan could avoid single-handed intervention in such a situation was cooperation with the

Japan had encountered in endeavoring to bring the negotiations to a satisfactory conclusion, and stated,

---

other Powers. But the other Powers had, in the meantime, been moving away from cooperation with Japan. Both the British and the Americans had made major concessions to the Nationalists. These in turn had strengthened foreign minister C. T. Wang, and increased the incentive for the Powers to deal unilaterally with the new government. The Japanese minister in Peking, Kenkichi Yoshizawa, was irritated by the "popularity-courting policy" of the United States and felt that certain American actions amounted to a unilateral abrogation of the Washington Treaties. Yoshizawa was a professional diplomat, and initially at least he did not work closely with Tanaka. But politicians and professional diplomats alike agreed about the basic question of Manchuria. Tanaka's action in sending Uchida followed Yoshizawa's reasoning. Japan had three alternatives: She could move to guarantee her position in Manchuria unilaterally; she could seek rapprochement with China; or she could seek understanding with the other Powers. The preparation of this third alternative was Count Uchida's mission. Uchida had been instructed to propose to London that periodic meetings be held "to evolve common policies on such questions as recognition of the Nanking Government, tariff, and the salt and customs administrations." London, where he met the acting foreign secretary on September 8, 1928, was aware that the two countries had different views on a number of questions and all "London would do for Japan was to agree in principle to a constant exchange of views of each other's policies in China." In Paris, Uchida saw Poincaré and Aristide Briand, who assured him that "they well understood Japan's peculiar position in China as well as the need for international cooperation." In Washington, Uchida, accompanied by Setsuzō Sawada (1884–1976), saw Kellogg on September 29. Sawada, the chargé d'affaires, had graduated from Tokyo Imperial University in 1909, entered the diplomatic service in 1909, served in China (1909–1910), England (1911–1918), and the United States (1924–1930); from 1930 to 1933 he would be Japanese minister to the League of Nations. During their meeting, Kellogg did not mention Manchuria, though it was the matter of greatest concern to Japan, but rather expressed the optimistic belief that "the present Nationalist Government appeared to be making every effort to build a stable and ordered government in China." Clearly he neither desired, nor entertained the possibility of, closer relations with Japan. Uchida, who served several times as foreign minister (1911–1912; 1918–1923; 1932–1933) as well as ambassador to the United States (1909–1911) and other important posts, was one of the architects of the Washington Conference. His shift from support for internationalism to unilateralism may be connected with his experiences during this trip, which convinced him of the Western Powers' lack of concern for Japan's position. *References: FRUS* 1928, 2:425–30; Japan, Gaimushō, comp. *Nihon Gaikō Nempyō Narabini Shuyō Bunsho* (Tokyo: Nihon kokusai rengō kyōkai, 1955) 1:117–19; *NGJ,* p. 71; Iriye, *After Imperialism,* pp. 182, 243, 327; Uchida Kōsai denki hensan iinkai, *Uchida Kōsai* (Tokyo: Kajima Heiwa Kenkyūjo, 1969), pp. 284–89.

In entire disregard . . . of these circumstances, and in defiance of the explicit provisions of the Treaty, the Nationalist Government sent to Japan some time ago the abrupt notice that the Commercial Treaty between China and Japan would be abrogated and that, pending conclusion of a new treaty, the Japanese nationals and commerce in China would be governed by provisional regulations unilaterally adopted by China.

Independent of the question of the sanctity of treaties, Japan is deeply concerned that if this kind of procedure is ever concurred in, it may lead to the subversion of all the rights and interests legitimately secured by Japan under treaties or agreements.

Having then declared the Japanese Government's continuing readiness to negotiate for treaty revision "as soon as the policy of the Nationalist Government makes it possible for them to do so," and having further stated a willingness "to cooperate with the other governments concerned in the completion of tasks started at the time of the Tariff Conference at Peking and by the Commission on Extraterritoriality[38] if only the demands of China are fair and reasonable," the memorandum concluded,

---

[38] *The Commission on Extraterritoriality:* The Commission on Extraterritoriality, which had been provided for by the Washington Treaties, opened in Peking on January 12, 1926, with thirteen nations represented and Wang Ch'ung-hui (1881–1958) as the purely ceremonial honorary president. Silas H. Strawn (1866–1946), the American delegate at the Tariff Conference, was the chairman. The commission convened when most were agreed that the extraterritorial system was an anachronism. While so-called die-hards in the treaty ports might view abolition with horror, missionary opinion was, by and large, favorable. As for the diplomats, they were of course aware of the recent precedents for abolition of extraterritoriality elsewhere in Asia. The first of the treaties that ended extraterritoriality in Japan had been signed in 1894; in Siam, Britain had given it up in 1909; and the United States and Japan, in 1920. Given the civil war in China, however, it seemed unlikely that the system there could be abolished immediately. In their early sessions the delegates examined the new Chinese law code, which had been translated by the Commission on Extraterritoriality established by the Chinese Government in 1920. Subsequently, a subcommittee undertook a tour of inspection, covering more than 4,200 miles, and visiting courts, prisons, and the like. The commission concluded unanimously that extraterritorial rights could not be yielded until the judiciary of China was effectively protected against governmental or military interference; measures of amelioration were nevertheless proposed. But the Chinese, for political reasons, wanted faster steps. When the Kuomintang consolidated its power, a mandate was issued abolishing extraterritoriality as of January 1, 1930; this led to negotiations over 1930 and 1931, which were bedeviled by the rivalry of the new Canton Government of Wang Ching-wei (1884–1944) and the consequent need for Nanking not to be outdone in its insistence on Chinese rights. The Manchurian incident,

It is believed that the attitude of the Japanese Government toward China as above enunciated is not incompatible with the policy of the United States Government now being pursued in that country. Hopeful as it is, the present situation in China is still pregnant with difficulties of various nature and the best way for the Powers to follow in dealing with such a situation is to act in the spirit of cooperation. In this conviction it is most sincerely desired that guided always by this spirit the countries having deep interest in China, particularly those signatory to the Washington Treaty of 1922, would exchange their views frankly from time to time in regard to questions affecting their common interests and act in conjunction as far as possible with a view to each making its contribution to the stabilization of the political situation and the durable establishment of peace in China.

In the comments which the Secretary offered when the memorandum had been read to him, he made no reference to the question of Japan's treaty difficulties beyond stating that our case was different in that our basic treaty ran to 1934, and that in the meanwhile we had already signed a treaty forgoing restrictions upon China as to tariffs, and were eager to hasten arrangements for giving up extraterritoriality. The Japanese Chargé d'Affaires, who accompanied Count Uchida, then asked whether the memorandum's concluding statement, quoted above, concerning cooperation, was acceptable to the United States. The Secretary replied that

> . . . it was his feeling and the feeling of the United States that all the Powers should cooperate to strengthen the efforts of the present government of China insofar as it was possible to the end that a stable government might be built up there. It was our feeling that this might be done by going as far as each country could go, considering its own interests, toward solving these questions of the treaties, and that it was our desire to cooperate with the other Powers to that end. He repeated once more that he hoped to ascertain what the views of the Japanese Government would be on the subject of treaty revision. . . .
>
> The interview here ended.

---

which created a need for Nanking to get on well with foreigners, led to suspension of the discussions. Talks were renewed after the United States entered the Pacific war, and on January 11, 1943, Britain and the United States both signed treaties in which extraterritorial rights were relinquished. *References: Report of the Commission on Extraterritoriality in China* (Washington, D.C.: U.S. Government Printing Office, 1926); Wesley R. Fishel, *The End of Extraterritoriality in China* (Berkeley: University of California Press, 1952); Peter B. Oblas, "Treaty Revision and the Role of the American Foreign Affairs Adviser, 1909–1915," *Journal of the Siam Society* 60.1 (1972), pp. 171–86.

This statement by the Secretary, although impeccable as a formulation of current American opinion, must have seemed to Count Uchida somewhat unresponsive, if not indeed irrelevant, to the question which his memorandum implied.

A newly arrived Japanese Ambassador nevertheless reverted to the same theme three months later.[39] The American Government had meanwhile

---

[39]*A newly arrived Japanese Ambassador:* Katsuji Debuchi (1878–1947), a distinguished diplomat of moderate views, saw service in China and Washington as well as in Tokyo, where he opposed the Twenty-one Demands. Later, Debuchi was a member of the Japanese delegation to the Washington Conference, chief of the Asia Bureau in the Foreign Ministry, and ambassador in Washington from 1928 to 1934. He visited Nelson T. Johnson on December 29, 1928, and presented him with a copy of the *aide-mémoire* which he had just given to the secretary of state, Mr. Kellogg. The *aide-mémoire* reflected both Japanese concerns about the direction American China policy was taking and willingness to accommodate as much as possible. It indicated that Japan was prepared to make large concessions to the Chinese Nationalists, provided that these took place "gradually and through proper methods." Tariff autonomy would be recognized if the arrangements would prevent "too violent changes being caused in the existing economic relations between Japan and China," and the abolition of consular jurisdiction could be discussed "on the basis of the recommendations of the Committee on Extraterritoriality of 1926." But unlike the United States, Japan was not willing simply to make unilateral concessions. In a sense, the Japanese were asking Washington if it still stood by the Washington Treaties. The Japanese wished, as the ambassador pointed out, to assure themselves on certain points. The first was a point of law. The Treaty of Commerce and Navigation of July 21, 1896, between Japan and China provided that "either of the High Contracting Parties may demand a revision of the Tariffs and of the Commercial Articles of this Treaty at the end of ten years from the date of exchange of the ratification; but if no such demand be made on either side and no such revision be effected, within six months after the end of the first ten years then the Treaty and Tariffs, in their present form, shall remain in force for ten years more . . . [and] so it shall be at the end of each successive period of ten years." China had insisted "on repudiating unilaterally the treaty," something not permitted by the text; to this Japan could "never assent." Provided China yielded on that point, though, the Japanese were willing to discuss a whole range of issues. The second point had to do with the fulfillment of existing treaties, a more general statement of the principle made specifically in the first point. The Japanese were worried by "the tendency of the Chinese to insist upon attaining their objects while neglecting the fulfillment of the promises which they have on previous occasions given." The Japanese placed great importance on the insistence by the Powers that "China should not entirely disregard actual conditions within her own territories and commitments made to other powers." Johnson accepted the Japanese description of Chinese behavior, explaining it by noting that "under duress" the Chinese had made promises that

asked the views of the various interested governments regarding a request on the part of the Nationalist Government for treaty revision, with particular reference to the problem of extraterritoriality. In replying to that inquiry (in an *aide-mémoire* of December 29), Ambassador Debuchi wrote:

> . . . The Japanese Government, who heartily cooperated in all these international efforts [i.e., "to promote the attainment by China of her national aspirations"], would be animated by the same spirit in the coming negotiations on the subject of treaty revision. The recent tendency, however, of the Chinese Government to persist only in their zealous endeavors to attain their desired objects while neglecting the fulfillment of the promises which they have on various occasions given in the past will not have escaped the notice of the Powers who have the main interest in China. The Japanese Government cannot but express the hope that the nations concerned, in lending assistance to China for the realization of her aspirations, may not neglect that fact and will endeavor to secure that in her attempt at liquidating her foreign relations, China does not entirely disregard actual conditions and commitments.
>
> The Japanese Government, who are greatly interested in China and who hope for the sound and genuine development of this neighboring country, attach great importance to this last point and are confident that the American Government will find themselves in agreement with them in this respect.

The Ambassador, when presenting this *aide-mémoire,* took occasion to call upon the Assistant Secretary in charge of Far Eastern matters,[40] in order

---

they "never intended to fulfill." Indeed, he provided a good example of it, "entirely off the record": "I recited somewhat the history of the question on *likin,* pointing out that although China had on various occasions promised to abolish *likin,* it was known to everyone that there was no established feeling of opposition to *likin* current among the Chinese and that therefore it was almost impossible for the Chinese to fulfill any promise to give up this matter." But Johnson deflected the Japanese request for joint action to enforce treaty provisions. While not disagreeing with Debuchi's characterization that he "would be opposed to any concerted action on the part of the powers against China," he wished to qualify that to allow for "concerted action in constructive measures." In concluding what was, from the Japanese point of view, a rather unsatisfactory interview, Debuchi stated that "if the Secretary or [Johnson] could find an opportunity to make some frank comments officially either orally or in writing, upon the Japanese Government's statement of their position, they would be very happy." Johnson said he would see if he could arrange it. *References: NGJ,* pp. 585–86; *FRUS,* 1928, 2:445–49.

[40] *The Assistant Secretary in charge of Far Eastern matters:* Nelson T. Johnson (1887–

to emphasize certain points, including that made in the passage quoted above. The conversation (as recorded in a memorandum by the Assistant Secretary on December 29) took the following course with regard to that subject:

> The second important point in the *aide-mémoire*, the Ambassador said, was to be found in the next to the last paragraph where the Japanese Government mentioned the tendency of the Chinese to insist upon attaining their objects while neglecting the fulfillment of the promises which they have on various occasions given. The Ambassador said that his Government placed great importance upon the hope that the nations should concert themselves while lending assistance to China for the realization of her aspirations in insisting on the other hand that China should not entirely disregard actual conditions within her own territories and commitments made to other powers.
>
> I said to the Ambassador that I realized the importance of this matter. I said that personally, and entirely off the record, I would like to say with regard to China's promises in the past that I was of the opinion that frequently China had made promises under duress or in the hope of

---

1954) was born in Washington, D.C., and raised in Oklahoma. He entered the Foreign Service in 1907 as a student interpreter. After two years of language study in Peking, he served as vice consul in Mukden and Harbin, then in Hankow, and in Shanghai as deputy consul general and assessor attached to the Mixed Court. He served as consul in Chungking and Changsha, then returned to the Division of Far Eastern Affairs in Washington. After two years as consul-general-at-large in China, he succeeded MacMurray as chief of the Far Eastern Division in 1925. He served as assistant secretary of state from 1927 until the end of 1929, when he succeeded MacMurray as minister, and served in China until 1941, the Legation being raised to an embassy in 1935. In 1941 he was sent to Australia, where he served as ambassador until 1946. Although MacMurray and Johnson differed more in style than in substance—one an Ivy League professional diplomat, the second a relaxed Westerner who worked his way up—they did place different emphases on their diplomacy. MacMurray's deep concern with international law was not shared by Johnson, who, superficially at least, was far more willing to accommodate Chinese demands than was MacMurray. *References:* Russell T. Buhite, *Nelson T. Johnson and American Policy toward China, 1925–1941* (East Lansing: Michigan State University Press, 1968); Herbert J. Wood, "Nelson Trusler Johnson: The Diplomacy of Benevolent Pragmatism," in *Diplomats in Crisis: United States–Chinese–Japanese Relations, 1919–1941,* ed. Richard Dean Burns and Edward M. Bennett (Santa Barbara: Clio Books, 1974), pp. 7–26; Daniel P. Starr, "Nelson Trusler Johnson: The United States and the Rise of Nationalist China, 1925–1937" (Ph.D. dissertation, Rutgers University, 1967).

obtaining some benefit thereby, promises which the Chinese people and
the Chinese officials who made the promises never intended to fulfill. . . .

The Ambassador said that he would understand from what I said that I
would be opposed to any concerted action on the part of the powers against
China and I said that I would like to qualify that statement a little, that I
felt there were certain things upon which the Powers could agree to take
action alike. At least we could take concerted action in constructive
measures, or in the line of moderation, but unfortunately in the past the
Powers had only considered it necessary to concert themselves when one
or more of them were in the position of the defensive and it seemed to me
that that fact reduced our action to one of mutual interest in our defense
but individual interest in all other matters. I was somewhat doubtful as to
the benefits when action was limited in this way.

Whatever doubt underlay this personal statement, it was officially
resolved when, on February 19, 1929, the Department replied to the
Ambassador's *aide-mémoire* on the subject of treaty revision, in an *aide-
mémoire* reciting at length the American viewpoints as to China problems.[41]
In the course of the document occurs the following general comment upon
the policy of cooperation based upon the acts of the Washington
Conference:

---

[41]*An* aide-mémoire *reciting the American viewpoints:* The reply to Debuchi's request
of November 1928 was finally made on February 19 of the following year. In it the
abundant ambiguities of American policy are clear. The Washington principles are
upheld, though limited implicitly to joint "constructive" actions. Consultation
among the Powers is important, but should not be binding: "There is . . . no
provision in any of the agreements which requires that in all particulars and at all
times each of the Powers shall refrain from independent action." The requirement
that the revision of treaties should be orderly was recognized. There were "juridical
and administrative reforms which must *of necessity* [emphasis added] accompany any
steps taken toward abolishing extraterritoriality in order that there may be assurance
of adequate protection for the lives and property of foreign nationals in China." But
no procedure, other than "frank conversations between the representatives of the
other Powers and the representatives of China," was envisioned to promote this
end. On the key question of Chinese fulfillment of treaty obligations, the Americans
provided only the classic bit of policy double-talk quoted by MacMurray: "With
regard to treatment to be accorded by the National Government of China in
fulfilling China's commitments to foreign governments and obligations to nationals
of foreign countries, the United States, believing that the National Government
desires to conform its practices to the best standards of international practice, hopes
that the National Government's acts will demonstrate that such is its intention."
References: FRUS 1929, 2:549–54.

The provisions of those treaties and resolutions clearly indicate that the Powers, including China, were convinced of the desirability of cooperative effort for certain purposes. There is, it should be noted, no provision in any of the agreements which requires that in all particulars and at all times each of the Powers shall refrain from independent action or that in every situation there shall be international consultation. Nevertheless, in the opinion of the American Government, where interests common to all or to several Powers are involved, it is desirable that each of the Powers be solicitous not alone with regard to its own interests but also with regard to the interests of the others. In relation to certain situations it has been agreed that there shall be consultation. In relation both to these and to other matters, frequent and frank consultation may well be regarded as in order. Wherever cooperative or concurrent action may be expected usefully to serve a legitimate purpose, it would seem that due consideration should be given to that possibility. In accordance with this conception, when new situations arise and new problems are presented, no Power should hesitate to make or be unwilling to receive suggestions. When, however, there is proposed some new form of joint action not envisaged in the agreements, each Power, though ready to give the proposal consideration, must be free to make its own decision. And in situations where cooperative or concurrent action has not been agreed upon or has been attempted but has failed, each Power must have the right, limited only by the spirit and the letter of its outstanding commitments, to act independently.

But to the specific point on which Count Uchida and Ambassador Debuchi had not only written but taken occasion orally to urge its fundamental importance from the viewpoint of Japan—the question whether the policy of cooperation contemplated that the other Powers should concert to get China to "play the game" and desist from treaty violations which made all-round cooperation impossible—there was no reference beyond the following meager paragraph:

> With regard to treatment to be accorded by the National Government of China in fulfilling China's commitments to foreign governments and obligations to nationals of foreign countries, the Government of the United States, believing that the National Government desires to conform its practices to the best standards of international practice, hopes that the National Government's acts will demonstrate that such is its intention.

That answer to the Japanese inquiries, unless it be construed broadly as voicing a hope of better international behavior on the part of the Nationalist Government, could mean only that we refused to entertain Japan's claim that that Government, in abrogating the Japanese treaties, had acted otherwise than in conformity with "the best standards of international practice."

Count Uchida had been delegated by his Government to state its understanding of the Chinese situation and to seek enlightenment on this thesis: That Japan, by geographical necessity, is more dependent upon China, economically and *ergo* politically, than any of the other Powers; that she had in the past yielded to the temptation to smash through all obstacles and impose her will on China; that the Washington Conference had then given reason and occasion for her to realize that her own best interest would be served by the policy of live-and-let-live which the American Government has postulated; that in the faith of a whole-hearted execution of a policy of international cooperation on that basis, she had not only given up various claims, but had forgone a good deal of the prestige or "face" that counts so much in the East; that she had loyally and scrupulously lived up to the American conception that such cooperation should include all adherents to the Washington Treaties; that China, nevertheless, had eschewed the promised cooperation, and established a policy of antagonism and of irresponsibility with regard to her co-signatories, and particularly with regard to Japan; that if China refused and resented the promised cooperation for purposes incidentally beneficial to Chinese interests, and insisted upon defying and repudiating all established relations with the supposedly cooperating Powers, they must at least concert among themselves as to the means by which they could best achieve the purposes to which China had given a welcome consent at a less agitated time; and that the Japanese Government, recognizing the American Government as the sponsor of the idea of cooperation with regard to Chinese problems, wished to know whether or not we would throw our undoubted influence toward bringing the Chinese back into the scheme of cooperation. The Japanese wanted indeed to know whether the moral influence we had so effectively asserted at the Washington Conference was, in practice, to prove discerning and just, or whether it was to prove vacuous and (as they would consider it) hypocritical in that it curried favor with the Chinese by encouraging their obduracy against everybody but ourselves.

Count Uchida could have carried away no impression but that we Americans were "pro-Chinese" to the extent that we wanted to advance our own interests by siding with the Chinese in their national aspirations, regardless of the effects upon the interests of our collaborators.

The indefinite reply made to his inquiries, and the more baldly negative response to the further insistence of Ambassador Debuchi, could scarcely have seemed anything but disquieting to the Government of the nation which is most intimately and vitally and inescapably concerned with Chinese affairs. Whatever may have been the reasons or intentions of our Government, the effect upon the Japanese was that of a rebuff: to them it signified that, in the essential issue of treaty observance which the Chinese had forced with them, the American Government had taken a position in favor of China and against Japan. To the Japanese, this attitude on our part meant not merely a disappointment of their hopes for at least our moral support: they realized that, in conjunction with our solicitously active efforts to promote negotiations with a view to satisfying Chinese demands for treaty revision, the effect of our attitude would be to condone the high-handed behavior of the Chinese and encourage them to a course of further recalcitrancy.

They were, moreover, acutely conscious that our recent conclusion of the Customs Treaty, however legitimate and proper, had nevertheless increased their already great difficulties in arriving at an agreement upon such tariff arrangements as they felt to be necessary for their commerce. That treaty had not, indeed, been concluded without notice of our intentions to the Japanese and other nationalities interested. When the American Minister was in Washington for consultation in the autumn of 1927, approval had been given to his endeavoring to conclude an agreement relinquishing our treaty restrictions upon the Chinese tariffs, in view of the fact that at the Peking Tariff Conference we and other governments had so far committed ourselves to a moral (even though not a legal) obligation to grant tariff autonomy, that the implementation of that commitment seemed necessary as a manifestation of good faith. Since the proposed grant was a mere relinquishment or quittance on our part, the making of it need not be dependent upon the existence in China of a really sovereign government such as would be capable of living up to new obligations; and it was therefore contemplated that an agreement to that end might, in the absence of such a government, be concluded by means of some very informal understanding with the leaders of the principal factions. This proposal was explained informally by our Minister, upon his return to Peking, late in 1927, to his Japanese and other interested colleagues—who took note of it, and at any rate made no remonstrance. It was then broached to the "Acting Minister for Foreign Affairs" of the Peking *régime* on the occasion of a conversation in which he urged treaty revision; but he showed no interest in the suggestion. Shortly afterward, in the course of the negotiations for the settlement of the Nanking affair, the so-called Minister of Foreign Affairs of the Nationalist *régime* made a strong appeal for treaty revision, particularly as regarded the tariffs, but likewise completely ignored the same suggestion.

During the following July, at a time when the Nationalist Government had fairly widely consolidated its power in the country, and when its revolutionary temper had been somewhat sobered by responsibility and perhaps chastened by the sharp repulse of its impetus by the Japanese at Tsinan, our Government decided to make a pronouncement on the tariff question; and while the terms of that statement were still under discussion, by telegraph, between the Department and the Legation, the Nanking Minister of Finance arrived in Peking, raised the question of treaty revision, was informed of our proposal, and at once undertook to negotiate such an agreement on the basis suggested. The whole transaction required only a few days during which arrangements had to be made for the full powers and other necessary formalities. Meanwhile, the Department had thought it inadvisable to give any notice to the other Powers of what was in progress. The actual conclusion of the treaty, on July 25, 1928, therefore came as a complete surprise to the other interested governments; and although they were presumably on notice that something of the sort was in contemplation, the press and the public in the countries most interested (particularly in Japan) were taken unawares and predisposed to assume that we had stolen a march on them.

The treaty was very far-reaching in its effects: it was not only a concession, by one of the most interested and influential of the Powers, of Chinese tariff autonomy, but it was construed as a recognition of the Nanking (Nationalist) organization as the Government of China, and in practical effect that *fait accompli* put a strong compulsion upon the other interested Powers to give the same recognition and to make the like concession. One by one, the representatives of the other Powers had to go to Nanking, establish formal relations, and sign similar treaties.

They found difficulties, it is true. For the Chinese, having regained tariff autonomy subject only to the obligations of granting unconditional most-favored-nation treatment in all tariff matters, then sought to limit the scope of application of most-favored-nation treatment. They obstinately maintained against us, and quoted in their negotiations with the other Powers, a strained and prejudicially restricted interpretation of our treaty; and they conceded its full effect only when, after months of negotiation, our Government threatened to withhold its ratification.

When the tariff question had thus been disposed of, the Chinese next turned their attention to the other most important aspect of the "unequal treaties," namely, extraterritoriality, looking not to gradual evolutionary discontinuance of the system by such steps as the Extraterritoriality Commission had recommended, but to its outright abolition. They asked for negotiations, but in so doing they made it clear that they would accept no terms except absolute relinquishment of extraterritorial rights. The Minister of Justice (Dr. Wang Chung-hui),[42] who had himself signed as the

---

[42] *The Minister of Justice:* Wang Ch'ung-hui (1881–1958) was a distinguished jurist, educated in Hong Kong, China, the United States, and Europe, and an associate

Chinese representative the report of the Extraterritoriality Commission, went so far as to convey (in a private conversation with the American Minister) the threat that, so long as extraterritoriality was retained, American plaintiffs in the Chinese courts might expect to meet with denial of justice.

This drive for getting rid of extraterritoriality was pressed throughout the summer. The Powers were reluctant to abandon the safeguards recommended by the Commission, but they found it impossible to take any firm united stand on that ground—one element of their difficulty being that our own Government postponed its decision, and throughout the most acute stage of the controversy gave no reply to the requests of the Peking Legation for instructions as to the position it should take. The Chinese, conscious of the advantage accruing to them through the disunity of the Treaty Powers, undertook to cut the Gordian knot by simply declaring on December 29, 1929, that the extraterritorial provisions of the treaties would be void as from January 1, 1930. Later, indeed, they receded from this sweeping challenge to the treaty system sufficiently to postpone the date, and to enter into negotiations: and these discussions were still in progress, with very considerable concessions to the Chinese demands, when they were interrupted by the Manchurian incident of 1931.[43] They have not since then been resumed since the Chinese, hoping for a maximum of support against the

---

from boyhood of Dr. Sun Yat-sen. In 1921, he served as a delegate to the Washington Conference, and in February 1922, he was named deputy judge on the Permanent Court of International Justice at The Hague. In late 1922 he became acting premier in Peking and formed the so-called cabinet of able men. He and his cabinet resigned late in 1922, and in 1923 Wang left for The Hague. He returned to Peking in 1925 and served as delegate to the Special Conference on the Customs Tariff and as chairman of the Commission on Extraterritoriality. In 1927, he joined Chiang Kai-shek's Government as minister of justice. He subsequently served as president of the Judicial Yüan (1928–1930; 1948–1957), as foreign minister (1937–1940), and in other posts in law and diplomacy. *References: Biographical Dictionary of Republican China,* 3:376–78.

[43] *The Manchurian incident:* Beginning on September 18, 1931, Japanese troops took control of Manchuria. Their pretext was an explosion on the tracks of the South Manchurian Railway, blamed on the Chinese but caused by a bomb placed for that purpose by the Japanese themselves. If the incident does not quite mark the beginning of full war between China and Japan, it certainly marks the end of the period that had begun with the Washington Conference, when at least the possibility of multilateral diplomatic solutions seemed to exist. The complex reactions that it elicited from the various Powers seemed inexorably to set the course toward total war. *References: NGJ,* pp. 903–8; *Concise Dictionary of Modern Japanese History,* pp. 120–21; Iriye, *After Imperialism,* pp. 293–99.

encroachments of Japan, have found it advisable for the time being not to create antagonisms by an insistence upon doing away with a jurisdictional system which the Powers still consider it premature to dispense with.

Another important episode in Chinese foreign relations took place in the autumn of 1929—the attempt of the semi-autonomous Manchurian Administration to oust the Soviet interests from their share in the Chinese Eastern Railway. That line, after a fateful history beginning in 1896, had been recognized as a joint Soviet-Chinese commercial enterprise, on a basis of equality, by treaties concluded in 1924; but the Russians had managed to get into their own hands the key posts and consequently the predominance in the control of the road. In 1929, however, apparently without consultation with higher authorities, the Manchurian Director of Railways, by a sudden *coup,* took forcible possession of various physical properties of the line, and arrested and removed from their functions most of the Russian staff on the railway. This dubious action was at first acquiesced in rather half-heartedly by the Manchurian Administration, and even more luke-warmly by the Nationalist Government; but the Chinese attitude soon stiffened into united resistance against what were mistakenly assumed to be impotent protests on the part of the Russians. The Soviet Government, however, was determined not to be victimized, and took steps to assert its rights by military force. The Chinese then took a more reasonable tone, and were about to conclude a satisfactory settlement with the Russians, when an appeal under the Kellogg-Briand pact emboldened them to be intransigent again. After several repetitions of the cycle of Chinese temerity, Russian pressure, Chinese timidity, neutral appeal to the Kellogg pact, and again Chinese temerity, the Russians at last forced a settlement that was substantially in accord with the existing treaty arrangement.[44]

---

[44] *The Manchurian railways:* The Chinese Eastern Railway, which connected Russian Siberia to the Russian maritime province by a short route passing through Manchuria, was built by Russia in the wake of the Sino-Japanese War of 1894–95, under treaties similar to those guaranteeing the positions of other Powers. Although ostensibly a Sino-Russian venture, the railroad, whose headquarters were in the city of Harbin, was completely under Russian control, and in 1917 became caught up in Russian politics. It was a base of resistance to the Bolsheviks, and the anti-Communists kept control of it even after the Soviet victory elsewhere. But to maintain their position, these Russians had to make local concessions to the increasingly nationalistic Chinese. The Soviets, however, rejected such moves, paradoxically insisting on the validity of tsarist treaties that gave them uncontested control of the railway, though expressing willingness to sell it to the Chinese. Establishment of diplomatic relations between Peking and Moscow in 1924 saw tacit Chinese acknowledgment of the Russian position, but since Chang Tso-lin con-

In this affair with Soviet Russia the Manchurian Administration manifestly overreached itself, to an extent that brought the matter to international notice, in a course of procedure that Marshal Chang Tso-lin had more circumspectly followed for many years, and which his son strove to emulate when he succeeded to the Old Marshal's power in 1928. Old Chang, ruling as a personal domain the Manchurian territories in which Japan had a stake so vital to her interests, had for years followed astutely the policy of yielding with apparent good grace and friendliness whenever obduracy would have created too much antagonism, and then finding surreptitious means of nullifying the advantages he had conceded. This policy was not of merely abstract or theoretical application; it was severely practical. He himself, in the days when he ruled North China from Peking, used to boast rather genially of the craftiness that he had learned in his days as a brigand. And his lieutenants would quite complacently narrate, to their friends in the foreign Legations, instances of the Old Marshal's cleverness in "double-crossing" the Japanese—cases such as that of a mining concession which had been granted to certain Japanese interests, upon fixed terms as to royalties, etc., which later appeared to be less than the traffic would bear; demands for higher royalties being made and refused; then bandits beginning to appear in the neighborhood and so harassing the operation of the mines as to bring it to a standstill; whereupon the Japanese concessionaires, grasping the situation, volunteered to pay much higher royalties, and a new contract to that end was concluded with manifestations of great cordiality on both sides; after which, the bandits disappeared.

On the testimony of the Chinese themselves, Japanese interests in Manchuria were always in the position of having to fix things, without even the satisfaction of assurance that things would stay fixed. But they understood and matched wits with Chang, and preferred him to the westernized nationalistic type of leader such as Kuo Sung-ling, whose revolt the Japanese

---

trolled the territory, substantive moves were up to him. These facts, plus the complex Soviet role in Chinese internal politics, led to repeated conflict between the Soviets and Chinese representatives in Manchuria, culminating in the bold attempt by Chang Hsüeh-liang to take the railroad by force in 1929. The Soviets responded with immediate military action, in which the Chinese took heavy casualties and Chang was forced to back down. This result weakened him in his rivalry with Chiang Kai-shek; it also both gratified and worried the Japanese, who were pleased to see the Chinese taught a lesson but disturbed that the USSR should have the capacity to do so. Thereafter they identified Moscow as a primary threat to their own position. *Reference:* George Alexander Lensen, *The Damned Inheritance: The Soviet Union and the Manchurian Crises, 1924–1935* (Tallahassee: Diplomatic Press, 1974), pp. 1–82.

assisted Chang to suppress in 1926.[45] That was comprehensible; what is not clear is that it was apparently certain Japanese—whether the military group or individuals of the irresponsible "China *rōnin*" class—who brought about Chang's assassination in 1928. For his inevitable successor was his son, Chang Hsueh-liang—a weakling of the dangerously egoistic type, semi-westernized, and falling between two stools because of a confusion between vague liberal ideas and ruthless methods such as he had learned from his father—an undependable and unsettling factor in the situation.[46] The rela-

---

[45]*Revolt of Kuo Sung-ling:* Kuo Sung-ling (1883–1925), a trusted member of Chang Tso-lin's army, led a revolt against Chang that probably would have succeeded had not the Japanese intervened. Kuo was an able military man, and perhaps a secret Kuomintang member, who was introduced to the inner circle of the Fengt'ien group by Chang Hsüeh-liang. The year 1925 found Chang Tso-lin's forces overextended, deployed as far south as Shanghai, and therefore vulnerable in the north. Feng Yü-hsiang, who had already joined a conspiracy against Chang that called for him to oppose Kuo, then the commander of the strongest Fengt'ien forces, made a secret agreement to cooperate with him in an attack on the Old Marshal. According to this agreement, probably reached on November 12, Chang would be forced to retire, leaving Manchuria to Kuo, and Chihli and the region of the Peking-Hankow railway to Feng. But Kuo's revolt, when declared, failed to win the expected support within the Fengt'ien forces. Nevertheless, the situation in Manchuria was chaotic, and Kuo might have succeeded had not the Japanese, after toying with him briefly, decided that Chang Tso-lin was indispensable for their purposes. Kuo was planning a two-pronged assault on Mukden (Shen-yang), with part of the army passing through Chin-chou, another portion through Ying-k'ou to the south. Japanese forces intervened to stop Kuo at Ying-k'ou, which would otherwise have been captured, and Japanese armies in Manchuria were strengthened. The decisive battle came at Hsin-min, some twenty miles or so from Mukden, beginning December 21. Kuo's forces were finally cut off by a cavalry attack from behind, led, apparently, by a Japanese officer. Kuo's forces then collapsed, and Kuo fled with his wife. Both were discovered and shot on December 24. *References:* McCormack, *Chang Tso-lin,* pp. 146–87; Kitaoka, "China Experts in the Army," p. 362.

[46]*Chang Hsüeh-liang:* Chang Hsüeh-liang (1898–), the son of Chang Tso-lin, is probably best known for his role in the kidnapping of Chiang Kai-shek in 1936, the "Sian incident." He took over control of Manchuria after the death of his father, with whom he had been on bad terms since the rebellion of Kuo Sung-ling, and consolidated his own control by having his chief rivals shot. At the same time he kept the Japanese at arm's length. But their worst fears were realized in December 1928, when he raised the Nationalist flag at Mukden, indicating the union of Manchuria and China proper. Despite the symbolic union, Chang sought to keep all real power in his own hands. He probably precipitated the confrontation with the Soviet Union in 1929 that MacMurray mentions in the memorandum. Wellington Koo, in his memoirs, suggests that the Nationalists, wanting to cut Chang

tions of the Japanese with the father had never been wholly satisfactory, but never impossible; whereas with young Chang the situation may well have seemed to them unendurable. And it can easily be understood how, when he gave his allegiance to the Kuomintang, they conceived of him as a spearhead of Chinese revolutionary attack upon their vested rights and interests in Manchuria.

This situation underlay the developments in Japan which made possible the successful assertion by the military clique of a "positive policy" in Manchuria, as against the moderate policy that the Japanese Government had been following since the Washington Conference: it was the setting for the incident of September 18, 1931, which set in motion the expanding wave of Japanese encroachments upon Manchuria and other Chinese territories, and led to the growth among the Japanese people of a changed conception of their opportunity, their mission, or their destiny in China and in the Far East generally—a conception not new to the military leaders or to certain groups of rabidly nationalistic intellectuals, but hitherto alien to the thinking of the vast majority of hard-worked and overtaxed peasants.

Although we may not sympathize with, or condone, the harshly aggressive course that Japan has followed in Manchuria and seems bent on following elsewhere in China, we must, if we are to comprehend the motives actuating Japan, understand that it was in large measure the result of the challenge that the Nationalist Government offered—that China, in effect, had "asked for it." The Chinese, in their resurgence of racial feeling, had been willful in their scorn of their legal obligations, reckless in their resort to violence for the accomplishment of their ends, and provocative in their methods; though timid when there was any prospect that the force to which they resorted would be met by force, they were alert to take a hectoring attitude at any sign of weakness in their opponents, and cynically inclined to construe as weakness any yielding to their demands. Those who sought to deal fairly with them were reviled as niggardly in not going further to satisfy them, and were subjected to difficulties in the hope of forcing them to grant more; so that a policy of appeasement and reconciliation, such as that with which our own Government attempted to soothe the hysteria of their elated racial self-esteem, brought only disillusionments.

Those foreign representatives who felt most congenial with the Chinese people, and most sympathetic with their desire to be rid of the irksome restraints to which their country had been compelled to submit because of

---

down to size, may have urged him on. *References: Biographical Dictionary of Republican China,* vol. 1, pp. 61–68; Wellington Koo, *Memoirs,* microfilm of typescript available in rare books and manuscripts room, Columbia University Library, 3:298–300.

its arrogance in refusing, a couple of generations ago, to conform to reasonable standards of equality and responsibility in international relations, used to plead with their Chinese friends to avoid repeating the error of their grandfathers, at a time when they had so favorable an opportunity to redeem themselves; and such friends of the Chinese would urge that persistence in a course of antagonism and bad faith toward foreign nations must sooner or later drive one Power or another to assert itself against an intolerable situation. Of those who offered such counsel, doubtless none specified Japan; but in their own minds it was nevertheless clear that Japanese interests were at least relatively the most impaired and menaced by China's course of action, and that Japan's temper was the most likely to be detonated by it. But it was characteristic of the mood of overweening pride with which the Chinese were possessed, and of the political immaturity which limited their understanding of the actual situation, that such friendly pleas and warnings seem scarcely ever to have aroused any response except that China must follow up her successes in ridding herself of the imperialistic oppression of the Powers.

Nemesis came perhaps sooner, and in more drastic form, than had been foreseen by those who predicted it. Nationalist China has been not only humbled but partitioned, and appears to be destined in the end to some form of subjugation to Japan. The policy of cooperation, which might well have averted the catastrophe, or might even yet have served to mitigate it, is no longer available: it was wounded in the house of its friends—scorned by the Chinese and ignored by the British and ourselves, until it became a hissing and a byword with a Japanese nation persuaded to the belief that it could depend on only its own strong arm to vindicate its rightful position in eastern Asia.

IV. The Present Situation

The primary fact of the present situation in the Far East is that China is now under the shadow of Japanese domination; and China herself is helpless against it. There are those who even yet believe that the Chinese, with all their faults, possess certain fundamental traits of strength which will in the end make them prevail over the Japanese. But even the proponents of that belief acknowledge that it is a matter not of years but of generations. And while that belief has so much basis that realistic international politics should allow for it as a possibility, it is nevertheless a possibility so remote in time and so speculative that it cannot be reckoned as more than a contingency. For the foreseeable future, certainly, it is not to be anticipated that China will be able to bear her own part. Nor is it to be expected that other nations, either severally or collectively, will undertake the burden of her defense.

The developments consequent upon the Manchurian crisis not only confirmed the breakdown of the Washington Conference plan of international cooperation among its signatories but demonstrated the unreadiness of the League of Nations to assume major responsibilities in the Far East.

There is, of course, more than a possibility that Russia might contest with Japan the domination of eastern Asia, but to the extent that Russia might be successful in that, the result would doubtless be not a restoration of China's independence but her subordination to the Soviet Union rather than to Japan—a result which would create a new situation and give rise to new problems. Otherwise, the only obstacle to Japan's domination over China would seem to be some inherent flaw in the economic or political or social system of Japan herself. It may well be that Japan will overreach herself—that in the attempt to conquer and hold too much territory, and develop it to the point of profitable exploitation, against the steady passive resistance of the Chinese people, Japan's material or human resources either may prove insufficient and be constrained to withdraw, or may break down and thereby set up internal strains which would disrupt the whole economy and social fabric of the Empire. The latter and more dangerous of these contingencies is perhaps the more likely and would itself involve a new catastrophe if it were to lead Japan into the way of revolution and make her a rabid pariah in the Far Eastern world.

What seems so far the more probable course of events—so much so as to appear the safest theorem to assume for the purpose of practical guidance—is that Japan will continue indefinitely her gradual encroachment upon the integrity of China, bringing more and more territory under such direct control as she now exercises in "Manchukuo," gaining a greater ascendancy over the administration of the remaining territories of China, building up for herself a monopolistic system of control over the trade of China and (the more intensively as she encounters increasing difficulties in digesting her conquests) jealously opposing rival national interests and forcing the issue in all cases where other interests than her own may seek to establish any independent relationship with the Chinese.

In such circumstances, the application of American policies to the particular situation in the Far East has been confronted with three possible alternatives—(1) to oppose the Japanese domination of China and actively take all available means and occasions to frustrate it and assert the contrary position; (2) to acquiesce in it approvingly, and indeed to participate in it, publicly and whole-heartedly withdrawing all objections or reservations or qualifications; or (3) to take a passive attitude, conceding nothing from the liberal principles that have traditionally underlain our policy not only in the Far East but throughout the world, but avoiding all positive action, or even the appearance of active concern, at least so long as the occasion is unpropitious.

The first of these alternatives seems scarcely worth argument. It would, if pursued consistently and determinedly, almost inevitably mean war with Japan. And, even apart from humanitarian or sentimental reasons, such a war would be a major misfortune for us, even assuming our victory, as well as for Japan and the Far East and the world in general. We should have, for our purposes, to fight it on the farther side of the Pacific Ocean, without any adequate base beyond Pearl Harbor, in waters where geographical conditions would give Japan every strategic, tactical and logistic advantage against us. The Washington and London Naval Treaties[47] were predicated upon the theory of ratios such as would make it impracticable for either side to operate successfully against the other across the vast expanse of the Pacific, and we have in fact allowed our construction to fall far behind our ratios—so far, indeed, that even our present spurt to rectify the deficiency gives almost the impression of a challenge.

In case of need we could and doubtless would outbuild Japan to the extent that we could successfully attack her navy even within the protecting ring of islands that make the western Pacific almost a Japanese lake. But it would be a hideously long and costly process, at the best; and there would be the danger, always, that the American people, in their eagerness and impatience for results, would force the Administration of the moment to press the attack before the completion of the toilsome business of construct-ing a fleet so overpowering as to be sure of overcoming the formidable disadvantages of the situation: so that there might even be a large-scale disaster before eventual victory was achieved. And no steps to redress our disadvantage are possible, in the circumstances that have been created, without giving a new provocation to the war that we want to avoid; even if (as now seems possible) at the end of next year the termination of the Washington Naval Treaty relieves us from the renunciation of our right to build naval bases west of the Hawaiian Islands, we could not make adequate

---

[47] *The Washington and London Naval Treaties:* The London Naval Conference met from January 21 to April 22, 1930, and led to a treaty limiting naval forces that was accepted by Japan only with very great reluctance. Opposition in Tokyo led indirectly to the wounding, by an assassin, of Prime Minister Hamaguchi (Novem-ber 4, 1930) and his death six months later, a clear indication of the increasing political infeasibility of the multilateral diplomacy begun a decade earlier. *References:* Thomas F. Mayer-Oakes, *Fragile Victory: Prince Saionji and the 1930 London Treaty Issue* (Detroit: Wayne State University Press, 1968); Raymond G. O'Connor, *Perilous Equilibrium: The United States and the London Disarmament Conference of 1930* (Law-rence: University of Kansas Press, 1962).

preparations in the Aleutian Islands or in Guam without its appearing a direct challenge to Japan, and since granting the independence of the Philippine Islands, we should find it an even more challenging action to establish a naval base in their waters. With no mitigation of our naval situation possible in the meanwhile, we should have to make a bad best of such a war. It would almost certainly be inconclusive, but even winning it, at great costs and sacrifices, we should find ourselves advantaged not at all.

The defeat of Japan would not mean her elimination from the problem of the Far East. It might mean the destruction of her present feudal and militaristic organization and her reversion to a period of upheaval and political and social disorganization—perhaps bolshevization; but the examples of the USSR and of Germany are clamant reminders that a virile people (and the Japanese are such) are not made tractable by defeat and national humiliation; they tend, rather, to reassert themselves with a passionate impulse of self-esteem, by methods which may well give them a destructive influence—a "nuisance value"—scarcely if at all less potent than the force which they exerted in their prime of imperial power. But even the elimination of Japan, if it were possible, would be no blessing to the Far East or to the world. It would merely create a new set of stresses, and substitute for Japan the USSR as the successor of Imperial Russia as a contestant (and at least an equally unscrupulous and dangerous one) for the mastery of the East. Nobody except perhaps Russia would gain from our victory in such a war.

There may be pacifists and idealists who foresee that our victory over Japan would remove her as a disturbing factor in the East and so open a readier opportunity for closer understanding and collaboration, along liberal lines, between the United States and China. That is a delusive hope. The Chinese always did, do, and will, regard foreign nations as barbarian enemies, to be dealt with by playing them off against each other. The most successful of them might be respected, but would nevertheless be regarded as the one to be next put down—just as the tangled history of recent Chinese internal politics can be summed up in the formula that every combination to put a particular leader into power splits up into a loyal minority and a majority intent upon some new combination to put him down, before he became too powerful, and substitute someone else. If we were to "save" China from Japan and become the "Number One" nation in the eyes of her people, we should thereby become not the most favored but the most distrusted of the nations. It is no reproach to the Chinese to acknowledge that we should have established no claim upon their gratitude: nations and races collectively do not seem in general to be susceptible to that sentiment. And our experience with the Washington Conference, the Peking Tariff Conference and our Customs Treaty do not encourage any belief that the Chinese would feel beholden to us for having redeemed them from bondage to Japan. They would thank us for nothing, and give us no credit for unselfish intentions, but set themselves to formulating resistance to us in the exercise of the responsibilities we would have assumed.

Since, at the best, a war with Japan would gain us no benefits and would in any case entail great sacrifices and risks, we must recognize that the avoidance of such a war must itself be a major objective. It cannot be a merely incidental consideration in our course of action in the Far East, because the temper of the Japanese people has become so fanatically and belligerently jealous of Western influence in their determined field of action that any positive opposition to it might very probably lead them to make even a desperate attack upon any nation seeking to thwart them: and for years their people have been taught by militaristic propaganda to feel that the United States is a dog in the manger—the enemy that stands across their way and that must be beaten if Japan is to realize her high destiny. We have therefore to reckon with a hypersensitive and quarrelsome tendency that might force us into a war we do not want, unless we walk circumspectly. Japan, in her present temper, might indeed create a situation which our sense of national self-respect and dignity could not tolerate. But short of that, and from the viewpoint of mere dollars-and-cents advantage, the China trade (which in fact has not in modern times been anywhere near so profitable to us as our Japan trade) could scarcely conceivably be worth the risk of a war with Japan. It would therefore seem clear that we could not afford to maintain a policy of positive opposition.

It does not follow, however, that we should go to the other extreme, disavow our traditional principles, and adopt an apologetic tone toward Japan. To begin with, our universal principles (which in their application to the particular case at issue have come to be known as the policies of the open door and of the integrity of China) cannot so lightly be surrendered. Even though we may not be in a position to champion them, we cannot renounce them without self-stultification and falsity to our own fundamental conceptions of the proper relations among nations.

It must also be borne in mind that, although the present situation and prospects in the Far East are such as justify our adoption of a working hypothesis that we should forgo our expectations of great things in China and take a minor part in order to avoid a clash with Japan, there can be no certainty that that situation will be permanent. We can at most foresee only the most obviously probable developments of the future: the interplay of human forces is so complex and so various that it would be an arrogant intellectual presumption to assume that the current of events might not form a pattern that we have not even imagined. And so it may be that what comes to pass in the Far East will reverse what today seems almost sure:

and conceivably China, now a rapidly dwindling star in our firmament, may again outshine Japan in importance to us. If our policy is to take long views and be as capable of application to an unforeseen future as to the present moment, it should at least take account of such unanticipated contingencies. With such consideration in view, we could not "withdraw from the Far East," and publicly recant our advocacy of the open door and Chinese integrity, as is now being urged in certain quarters, without embarrassing or precluding ourselves from taking such a course as might eventually prove to be the wise and prudent one for us to follow.

There is, however, a more immediate and positive reason for not making any such surrender of our convictions. It is a fact constantly manifested in human relations that the appearance of fear or weakness suggests and encourages attack—as a dog will give chase to another that is on the run. Those who have had experience in dealing with Orientals are aware that in their mentality there is an especially strong tendency to grow elated, and become unreasonable and harsh in their demands, at the first sign of an opponent's wavering. To swallow our pride and make a forthright surrender of our position in regard to China would buy us no reconciliation with the Japanese, gain us no respect, and ease none of our difficulties; rather, it would stimulate them to press home their attack—so vigorously, it may be feared, that they would drive us beyond what our self-respect would find endurable; and what we had sought to avoid would have been made inevitable.

The remaining alternative would seem to be obviously the wisest—to yield nothing of our principles and refrain from trifling with our own convictions, even though we do not find it prudent to go crusading in furtherance of them. We can and should go on believing that the principles of the integrity of China and the open door are particular applications of a "good neighbor policy" that is too axiomatically right to be disputed, and that the formulations of those doctrines, in the Washington Treaties concerning China and the Pacific Islands, are valid acknowledgments of concurrence on the part of all the nations concerned. There is no more reason why they should be repealed, because there have been recent developments inconsistent with them, than why the Decalogue should be repealed because there is a crime wave. But while believing these things are right, we need not necessarily make ourselves leaders of any forlorn hope for the purpose of vindicating them in the Far East, any more than we do in Europe or in Africa. We can keep to our own faith and moderately profess it without raucous scolding of the backsliders; and while there is no reason for us to humble ourselves because we have been true to our own instincts, we can prudently avoid raising issues that are unprofitable and dangerous and that we are not in a position to resolve as we should wish.

But we should, in our own minds, be clear as to what we are doing, and not just drift, or shirk from difficulties regardless of whether they may be worth encountering; we should at any rate have a working theory of the relative importance of the various objectives in our Far Eastern policy. And first it should be recognized that we have in the Far East no policies, no interests, and no responsibilities of an order fundamentally different from what we have in the rest of the world; if, in other circumstances, they appeared to be different in essence, it was merely because of our having made an especial preoccupation of applying our general principles to the circumstances of a singularly complex situation. There, as elsewhere, we have no alliances or other involvements conditioning our freedom to act according to our own conception of our interests, whether those interests be direct and concrete and material (as, for instance, in maintaining our commercial rights), or more indirect and abstract and ideal (as in endeavoring to preserve peace). The one possible qualification of our freedom of action was the understanding that we would endeavor to work in cooperation with the other signatories of the Washington Treaties. That understanding has, largely through our own attitude, fallen into desuetude: but there would seem to be little doubt that, in the new circumstances that have arisen, it must as a practical working system be restored at least to the extent of free consultation and mutual consideration among those Powers which have a common interest of their own in trying to keep China a member of the world community rather than a field for monopolistic exploitation by Japan. But we have no mission to undertake any duties or responsibilities on behalf of China.

It should be recognized, also, that China is for us no longer the primary factor in the Far East. Although it may still be a land of opportunity, we must reconcile ourselves to the realization that very little of that opportunity is likely to be available to us. The present value of the China trade is relatively small: and the expected increment would now seem destined to accrue in preponderant degree to Japan's benefit, if only for reasons of economic geography, quite apart from the circumstances of political and military pressure. Little as we may relish admitting to ourselves the necessity of discarding a rather romantic conception of what the development of China has in store for the world, we must face the fact (or the probability so overwhelming that we must accept it as the basis of a working theory) that China has become, from our viewpoint, an almost negligible factor.

In contrast, Japan has come to be one of paramount interest to us in the Far East. It is an uncomfortable relationship, in which we feel (unquestionably with reason, but perhaps with not quite enough of judicial clemency in view of the extenuating circumstances) that Japan has broken faith with us and has ousted us from our place of importance with respect to China;

and Japan (likewise with some degree of justification) feels that we have stood across her path no less when she tried to reach a peaceful settlement with China than when she took to the law of self-help. On both sides there is some bitterness of feeling. But we, who live in a large country with natural resources that make us relatively self-sufficient and between oceans that give us ready access to the markets of all the world and at the same time form a barrier against invasion, can scarcely realize how much more the Japanese are concerned about us than we are about them. They live huddled upon small islands of meager natural resources, much farther away from all markets except those of eastern Asia, and just across narrow waters from two nations—China and Russia—that have menaced them in the past and that they must always regard as potential threats to their very existence. For them, the access to China's raw materials and to China's markets constitutes the indispensable means of maintaining in their country the industrial system by which alone its population can get a livelihood. Discounting all the dramatization of this situation by propaganda, there is a real problem such as we often fail to comprehend and which at least explains their sensitiveness and jealousy and querulousness in regard to their position in Asia, and their resentful preoccupation with what the bulk of the Japanese people (however mistakenly) have come to consider a gratuitous meddling on the part of the United States in an effort to keep Japan down. It is a tragic misunderstanding that has been foisted upon them largely for reasons of unscrupulous domestic politics: but the passionate sentiment it has aroused is none the less real and none the less dangerous. For the Japanese, in spite of a superficial stolidity, are a people capable of deeply cherished resentments and of quick, ungovernable accesses of anger: there is perhaps no people in the world more prone to "go off the deep end" when not restrained by their disciplined loyalty to those whom they recognize as their real leaders. And it would now seem that leadership has passed to those who cannot be relied on to be prudent in restraining the berserker rages of the masses. So Japanese opinion is in a perilously inflammable state, in which a chance spark might well cause an explosion.

We have in the past spoken, in regard to China, with a voice of some authority, not only by virtue of a certain moral leadership, but also on the basis of our material stake in the country. Although our investments are relatively small as compared with those of either Great Britain or Japan, our share in the trade of China has been roughly equal to that of each of them. Not only have we been accustomed to protect energetically our citizens and their interests, but in keeping with the importance of our position, we have made a point of participating in all questions of international import concerning China, and manifesting our possession of the means by which to bear our part in any necessary common protective measures. For that purpose we have generally maintained in China armed forces—the Legation Guard at Peking, and the Infantry Regiment at Tientsin under the Boxer Protocol, considerable Marine Expeditionary Forces at Shanghai and (at one recent period) at Tientsin—at least equal to those of any other Power;* and our Asiatic Fleet, based upon Manila, has in fact been principally occupied in Chinese waters, and consists in large part of vessels scarcely suitable for any other service. We have consciously supported our interests, and our position of moral leadership, by keeping up our prestige as a great power.

In the changed situation since 1931, China has ceased to be, for us, a field of unlimited opportunity, and seems in the way of becoming a waste area. Japan, on the other hand, has become a jealous and irascible and dangerous claimant to the estate. So it may well be questioned whether, in the absence of any present prospect for substantial advancement of our material interests in China, we should not make up our own minds to write off our claims to leadership, forgo the attempt to assume initiatives or otherwise take a decisive part in current problems relating to China, discontinue the effort to afford our citizens there a degree of support and protection superior to what we attempt to give our nationals in other parts of the world, and desist from the manifestations of material forces for which the necessity has virtually disappeared and which is therefore a mere play at "prestige politics" such as cannot impress anybody but serves only as an irritant and a challenge to Japan. It is a hard decision for us to make— the more so because it means an abatement of our interest in developments in which we have heretofore borne an honorable part in which we take just pride. But it is plain common sense to stop rowing when a falling tide has grounded our boat in the shallows.

But while self-interest seems patently to dictate that, in the circumstances now apparent, we should divest ourselves of any such especial concern as we have in the past shown with regard to Chinese affairs, we obviously cannot prudently disinterest ourselves and merely consider ourselves quit of the whole business. Remembering the possibility that even yet the situation may eventually change in ways that we cannot now foresee, we should take no measures that would irrevocably sever our connections with the Far East and terminate our chances of advantaging ourselves or others. And having in mind, also, the natural tendency of others to harass those in manifest retreat, we should avoid any overt and palpable acknow-

---

*It should be noted, however, that one reason for our maintenance of relatively large forces in China has been our remoteness, making reserve forces less readily available in case of emergency [MacMurray's note].

ledgment of defeat and proceed only cautiously and inconspicuously to minimize our involvements and liabilities.

We might, in our own minds, abate somewhat the rather exaggerated zeal with which we have been accustomed to afford "protection" to citizens whom we are no longer actually in a position to protect. We might let the other most interested Powers carry the heavy end of the log in meeting new situations, go along with them as best we may, and take no marked initiative of our own either in devising solutions or in holding out against such solutions as they may agree on. While having it in mind to take our superfluous military forces out of China, we might let them dwindle by attrition, until there comes a time at which to remove them without antagonizing others or breaking too obtrusively with our own practice. And our Asiatic Fleet might similarly be reduced ship by ship, kept more and more away from Chinese waters and perhaps indeed (now that the Philippines are entering upon a phase of qualified independence) withdrawn practically *in toto* from the Far East, where it cannot be anything but a hostage to Japan. There will of course continue to arise difficult questions of expediency and of tactical method in making such a strategic retreat, but the drawing in of our outposts and retirement in good order to a safe defensive position would seem to be clearly imposed upon us as a principle of action in China for such future as we can now foresee.

Perhaps even more difficult problems confront us in applying with respect to Japan a similarly negative course of action. We want, above everything else in our Far Eastern policy, to escape becoming involved in hostilities with her. But in avoiding any antagonism or offense such as might be an occasion or pretext for quarrel, we must (if only because it is expedient for the end in view) be meticulously careful not to lose the wholesome respect with which the Japanese at heart regard us, by any attempts to ingratiate ourselves with them by compromising our own national power or dignity or principles. We cannot make them love us or feel at ease with us as neighbors across the Pacific: but we can avoid bringing ourselves into low esteem in the eyes of a people who whole-heartedly respect force and the qualities of resoluteness and fidelity to principles. We can deal with them fairly and honorably and in a friendly spirit, and we can dispel some of their groundless suspicions—since China is no longer a game worth the candle for us, we can so deal with that situation as to remove all apparent ground for the jealous fear that we are secretly inciting the Chinese against them; and we can similarly let our conduct make it evident to them that we are not intriguing to egg Russia on against them. We can be careful not to omit any occasion for those little international amenities which (like social courtesies in individual relationships) may create a feeling of sympathy more than commensurate with their intrinsic

importance, and the neglect of which may give rise to a wholly dispropor-
tionate feeling of irritation. We may indeed find further occasions to act in
a magnanimous spirit of good will. But we must be on our guard lest an
excess of our desire for friendly relations should mislead us into attitudes
or actions which they would construe and despise as truckling self-abase-
ment; by being less than true to ourselves, we should gain not their good
will but their contempt. It would be dangerous to the peace we are trying
to preserve, if we were to propose the cancellation of the Washington
Treaties concerning China, or disclaim the principle of the open door, or
retract our refusal to recognize the puppet state of "Manchukuo."

The abruptness with which our whole traditional system of policy with
regard to China was brought to bankruptcy by a few years of experimen-
tation with the policy of "playing up to" the Chinese might well serve as a
warning against heeding the advice of those well-meaning citizens who are
now urging that we "set ourselves right with Japan." Both Chinese and
Japanese are Asiatics; and while Asiatics are of the same human flesh and
blood as ourselves and respond to the same emotional impulses and are
nowise so alien or inscrutable as popular conceptions make them out, it is
nevertheless the fact that they have a wholly different history and cultural
background which has strongly conditioned their characteristic intellectual
and emotional reactions and in some respects differentiated them from the
characteristic reactions of us Westerners. Like us, they understand and
respect intellectual and moral integrity, firmness of purpose, and the spirit
of just dealing. But they normally attach to force a degree of reverence that
most Western peoples do not, and they are far quicker to sense a weakness
and not merely to exploit it but let themselves be tempted into reckless and
unscrupulous browbeating of anyone who has thus lost their respect and
esteem.

Our problem in the Far East, in the difficult years that are to come,
will be to husband our strength while making no challenging display of it;
to write down our interest in China to its present depreciated value; to deal
with Japan fairly and sympathetically, without either provocations or
subserviencies; and to be guided by our own interests as conceived in an
enlightened and generous spirit, with no wandering into false trails of "pro-
Chinese" or "anti-Chinese" or "pro-Japanese" or "anti-Japanese" sentiment. Above all, we must for our own part be faithful to the principles and
ideals of conduct that we profess and that others, even while dissenting,
respect us for maintaining with dignity and integrity.

J. V. A. MacMurray

JVMacM:MBS:SS

Chronology

1898	*December*	Cession of the Philippines
1916	*August*	Right of Philippine independence conceded
1917	*August*	China enters the war; Allies defer Boxer indemnity payments
1919	*September*	Shidehara named ambassador to Washington
1921	*February*	Federal Telegraph Company contract with China
	November	Washington Conference opens
1922	*February*	Washington Conference ends
	July	France, Italy, and Belgium insist on payment in gold when Boxer indemnity payments are resumed
	December	Shidehara replaced as ambassador to Washington
1923	*May*	Sun Yat-sen threatens to seize Canton Customs; dissuaded by naval demonstration
1924	*June*	Shidehara becomes Japanese foreign minister
	September–October	Second Chihli-Fengt'ien war
	October	Feng Yü-hsiang's *coup;* Huang Fu administration with C. T. Wang as foreign minister
	November	Tuan Ch'i-jui cabinet
1925	*March*	Death of Sun Yat-sen
	April	MacMurray appointed minister to China
		Agreement reached on gold franc
	May	Disorder in Shanghai; eleven Chinese killed by police
	July	Nationalist Government proclaimed at Canton

		Hong Kong seamen's strike
		Firing at Shameen (Canton)
	August	Kato forms minority cabinet
	October	Special Conference on Customs Tariff opens in Peking
	November	Revolt of Kuo Sung-ling
1926	January	Commission on Extraterritoriality opens in Peking
	March	Taku incident
	April	Tuan Ch'i-jui Government falls; Powers will not recognize the Regency cabinet of Chang Tso-lin and Wu P'ei-fu
		Beginning of Belgian Treaty negotiations
	July	Special Conference on Customs Tariff adjourned
		Northern Expedition launched
	September	Kuomintang reaches Hankow
		Lampson replaces Macleay as British minister
		Commission on Extraterritoriality closes in Peking
	October	Kuomintang announces plan to take over Canton Customs
		Peking proposes negotiations over Japanese Treaty of Commerce and Navigation
	November	Belgian case taken to Court of International Justice
	December	MacMurray proposes granting customs concessions within the Washington structure
		Northern army, the *Ankuochün*, formed
		New British policy announced
		Chang Tso-lin announces new customs levies
1927	January	Porter Resolution
		Kellogg statement
		Sino-Japanese treaty negotiations begin
		Hornbeck takes over Far Eastern Division
	February	Agreement reached on retrocession of British Concessions in Hankow and Kiukiang

	March	Nanking incident
	April	Chiang establishes government in Nanking
		Tanaka cabinet; Shidehara out as foreign minister
	May	First Tsinan incident
1928	April	Second Tsinan incident
		Nationalists arrive in Peking
	June	Assassination of Chang Tso-lin
	July	C. T. Wang announces repudiation of Japanese Treaties of 1895 and 1903
		U.S.-Chinese Customs Treaty; effective recognition of Nationalists
	August	Kellogg-Briand pact signed; Count Uchida investigates foreign attitudes to China
	November	New Belgian Treaty concluded
	December	Debuchi meets Kellogg and Nelson Johnson
1929	February	U.S. *aide-mémoire* on policy
	April	Sino-Japanese negotiations begin
	June	Japan recognizes Nationalist Government
	July	End of Tanaka ministry
	Autumn	Tanaka memorandum first circulated
	October	MacMurray resigns
1930	January–April	London Naval Conference
1931	September	Japanese occupation of Manchuria
1932	January	Japanese attack on Shanghai begins
	March	State of Manchukuo proclaimed
	May	Cease-fire in Shanghai
1934	March	Philippine independence set for 1946
1937	July	Sino-Japanese War begins
1938	October	Fall of Wuhan
1941	December	Japan attacks Pearl Harbor; United States enters war

Bibliography

Manuscript Materials

Joseph C. Grew Papers, Houghton Library, Harvard University.

Stanley K. Hornbeck Papers, Hoover Institution, Stanford University.

George F. Kennan Papers, Seeley Mudd Library, Princeton University.

John Van Antwerp MacMurray Papers, Seeley Mudd Library, Princeton University.

Jay Pierrepont Moffat Papers, Houghton Library, Harvard University.

William Phillips Papers, Houghton Library, Harvard University.

Franklin D. Roosevelt Papers, Franklin D. Roosevelt Library, Hyde Park, N.Y.

State Department Decimal File: China, National Archives, Washington, D.C.

Foreign Office General Correspondence, Far Eastern Department (F.O. 371), Public Record Office, London.

Published Materials

Abend, Hallett. *My Life in China, 1926–1941.* New York: Harcourt, Brace, 1943.

Adshead, S.A.M. *The Modernization of the Chinese Salt Administration, 1900–1920.* Cambridge, Mass.: Harvard University Press, 1970.

Asada, Sadao. "Japan's 'Special Interests' and the Washington Conference, 1921–1922," *American Historical Review* 56 (1961), pp. 62–70.

———. "Japan and the United States, 1921–1925." Ph.D. dissertation, Yale University, 1963.

———. *Japan and the World, 1853–1952: A Bibliographic Guide to Japanese Scholarship in Foreign Relations.* New York: Columbia University Press, 1989.

Bamba, Nobuya. *Japanese Diplomacy in a Dilemma: New Light on Japan's China Policy, 1924–1929.* Kyoto: Minerva Press, 1977.

Beal, Edwin George. *The Origin of Likin (1853–1864).* Cambridge, Mass.: Chinese Economic and Political Studies, Harvard University, 1958.

Beasley, William G. *Japanese Imperialism, 1894–1945.* Oxford: Clarendon Press, 1987.

Bennett, Edward M. "Joseph C. Grew: The Diplomacy of Pacification," in Burns and Bennett, eds., *Diplomats in Crisis,* pp. 65–90.

Bergère, Marie-Claire. *L'Âge d'Or de la Bourgeoisie Chinoise, 1911–1937.* Paris: Flammarion, 1986.

Binns, Christopher C. "John Van Antwerp MacMurray: An Old China Hand in the New China—1925–1928." B.A. thesis, Princeton University, 1969.

Bland, J.O.P. *China: The Pity of It.* London: William Heinemann, 1932.

Blum, Robert M. *Drawing the Line: The Origin of the American Containment Policy in East Asia.* New York, London, W. W. Norton, 1982.

Boorman, Howard L., ed. *Biographical Dictionary of Republican China.* New York: Columbia University Press, 1967.

Borg, Dorothy. *American Policy and the Chinese Revolution, 1925–1928.* New York: American Institute of Pacific Relations, 1947; reprint edition, with new introduction by the author, New York: Octagon Books, 1968.

———. *The United States and the Far Eastern Crisis of 1933–1938.* Cambridge, Mass.: Harvard University Press, 1964.

———, and Okamoto, Shumpei, eds. *Pearl Harbor as History: Japanese-American Relations, 1931–1941.* New York: Columbia University Press, 1973.

Brooks, Barbara J. "China Experts in the Gaimushō, 1895–1937," in *The Japanese Informal Empire in China, 1895–1937,* pp. 369–94, ed. Peter Duus, Ramon H. Myers, and Mark R. Peattie. Princeton: Princeton University Press, 1989.

Brown, Sidney DeVere. "Shidehara Kijūrō: The Diplomacy of the Yen," in Burns and Bennett, eds., *Diplomats in Crisis,* pp. 201–26.

Buckley, Thomas H. "John Van Antwerp MacMurray: The Diplomacy of an American Mandarin," in Burns and Bennett, eds., *Diplomats in Crisis,* pp. 27–48.

———. *The United States and the Washington Conference, 1921–1922.* Knoxville: University of Tennessee Press, 1970.

Buhite, Russell T. *Nelson T. Johnson and American Policy toward China, 1925–1941.* East Lansing: Michigan State University Press, 1968.

Burns, Elinor. *British Imperialism in China.* London: Labour Research Department, 1926.

Burns, Richard Dean. "Stanley K. Hornbeck: The Diplomacy of the Open Door," in Burns and Bennett, eds., *Diplomats in Crisis,* pp. 91–118.

———, and Bennett, Edward M., eds. *Diplomats in Crisis: United States–Chinese-Japanese Relations, 1919–1941.* Santa Barbara: Clio Books, 1974.

Campbell, Charles S. *Special Business Interests and the Open Door Policy.* New Haven, Conn.: Yale University Press, 1951.

Chan, F. Gilbert, and Etzold, Thomas H., eds. *China in the 1920s: Nationalism and Revolution.* New York: New Viewpoints, 1976.

Chan, K. C. "The Abrogation of British Extraterritoriality in China, 1942–43; A Study of Anglo-American-Chinese Relations," *Modern Asian Studies* 11 (1977), pp. 257–91.

Chapman, Nancy E. "Zhou Zuoren and Japan." Ph.D. dissertation, Princeton University, 1990.

Ch'en, Fang-chih. "Mei-kuo ti-kuo chu-yi tsai Hua-sheng-tun hui-yi-chung tsai-ko Chung-kuo di yin-mo," *Pei-ching ta-hsüeh hsüeh-pao,* no. 2 (1955), pp. 75–77.

Ch'en Ts'un-kung. *Lieh-ch'iang tui chün-huo chin-yün.* Taipei: Chung-yang yen-chiu-yüan, 1983.

Chi, Madeleine, *China Diplomacy, 1914–1918.* Harvard East Asian Monographs, no. 31. Cambridge, Mass.: East Asian Research Center, Harvard University, 1970.

———. "China and the Unequal Treaties at the Paris Peace Conference of 1919," *Asian Profile* 1 (1973), pp. 49–61.

China, Imperial Maritime Customs. *Treaties, Conventions, etc. between China and Foreign States.* Shanghai: Inspectorate General of Customs, 1908.

China, Wai-chiao-pu tang-an-tzu-liao-ch'u, ed. *Chung-kuo chu-wai ko ta kung shih-kuan-kuan li-jen kuan-chang hsien-ming nien-piao.* Taipei: Taiwan Shang-wu, 1969.

The China Year Book (annual). Edited by H.G.W. Woodhead. Peking and Tientsin: Tientsin Press.

Christie, Clive John. "The Problem of China in British Foreign Policy, 1917–1921." Ph.D. dissertation, Cambridge University, 1971.

Chu, Pao-chin. "V. K. Wellington Koo: The Diplomacy of Nationalism," in Burns and Bennett, eds., *Diplomats in Crisis,* pp. 125–52.

Clifford, Nicholas R. *Shanghai, 1925: Urban Nationalism and the Defense of Foreign Privilege.* Michigan Papers in Chinese Studies, no. 36. Ann Arbor: University of Michigan, 1979.

Clymer, Kenton J. *John Hay: The Gentleman as Diplomat.* Ann Arbor: University of Michigan Press, 1975.

Coates, P. D. *The China Consuls.* New York: Oxford University Press, 1988.

Cohen, Warren I. "America and the May Fourth Movement: The Response to Chinese Nationalism, 1917–1921," *Pacific Historical Review* 35 (1966), pp. 83–100.

———. *The Chinese Connection.* New York: Columbia University Press, 1978.

———. "Ambassador Philip D. Sprouse on the Question of Recognition of the People's Republic of China in 1949 and 1950," *Diplomatic History* 2 (1978), pp. 213–17.

———. *America's Response to China: An Interpretative History of Sino-American Relations,* 2d ed. New York: Knopf, 1980.

———, ed. *New Frontiers in American-East Asian Relations: Essays Presented to Dorothy Borg.* New York: Columbia University Press, 1983.

Collester, Janet Sue. "J.V.A. MacMurray, American Minister to China, 1925–1929: The Failure of a Mission." Ph.D. dissertation, Indiana University, 1977.

Conference on the Limitation of Armament, Washington, November 12, 1921–February 6, 1922. Washington, D.C.: Government Printing Office, 1922.

Coons, Arthur Gardiner. *The Foreign Public Debt of China.* Philadelphia: University of Pennsylvania Press, 1930.

Coox, Alvin D. "Shigemitsu Mamoru: The Diplomacy of Crisis," in Burns and Bennett, eds., *Diplomats in Crisis,* pp. 251–74.

———, and Conroy, Hilary, eds. *China and Japan: Search for Balance since World War I.* Santa Barbara: ABC-Clio, 1978.

Crowley, James B. *Japan's Quest for Autonomy: National Security and Foreign Policy, 1930–38.* Princeton: Princeton University Press, 1966.

D'Auxion de Ruffé, R., trans. R. T. Peyton-Griffin. *Is China Mad?* Shanghai: Kelly and Walsh, 1928.

Dayer, Roberta Allbert. "The British War Debts to the United States and the Anglo-Japanese Alliance, 1920–1923," *Pacific Historical Review* 45 (1976), pp. 569–95.

———. *Bankers and Diplomats in China, 1917–1925: The Anglo-American Relationship.* London: Frank Cass, 1981.

DeAngelis, Richard Clarke. "Jacob Gould Schurmann and American Policy Toward China, 1921–1925." Ph.D. dissertation, St. John's University, 1975.

De Martel, D., and De Hoyer, L., trans. D. De Warzee. *Silhouettes of Peking.* Peking: China Booksellers, 1926.

Dennett, Tyler. *John Hay: From Poetry to Politics.* New York: Dodd, Mead and Co., 1933.

Doenecke, Justus D., comp. *The Diplomacy of Frustration: The Manchurian Crisis of 1931–1933 as Revealed in the Papers of Stanley K. Hornbeck.* Stanford: Hoover Institution Press, 1981.

Dolsen, James H. *The Awakening of China.* Chicago: Daily Worker, 1926.

Dower, John. *Empire and Aftermath: Yoshida Shigeru and the Japanese Experience.* Cambridge, Mass.: Harvard University Press, 1979.

Duus, Peter. *Party Rivalry and Political Change in Taishō Japan.* Cambridge, Mass.: Harvard University Press, 1968.

———, Myers, Ramon H., and Peattie, Mark R., eds. *The Japanese Informal Empire in China, 1895–1937.* Princeton: Princeton University Press, 1989.

Eiler, Keith E., ed. *Wedemeyer on War and Peace.* Stanford: Hoover Institution Press, 1987.

Ellis, L. Ethan. *Frank B. Kellogg and American Foreign Relations, 1925–1929.* New Brunswick: Rutgers University Press, 1961.

Embree, Ainslie T., ed. *Encyclopedia of Asian History.* New York: Scribner's, 1988.

Esthus, Raymond A. "The Changing Concept of the Open Door, 1899–1910," *Mississippi Valley Historical Review* 46 (1959), pp. 435–54.

Etō, Shinkichi. "China's International Relations, 1911–1931," in *The Cambridge History of China,* vol. 13, *Republican China, 1912–1949, Part II,* pp. 74–116, ed. John K. Fairbank. Cambridge, Mass.: Cambridge University Press, 1986.

Etzold, Thomas H. "In Search of Sovereignty: The Unequal Treaties in Sino-American Relations, 1925–1930," in Chan and Etzold, eds., *China in the 1920s,* pp. 176–96.

Farnsworth, Lee. "Hirota Kōki: The Diplomacy of Expansionism," in Burns and Bennett, eds., *Diplomats in Crisis,* pp. 227–50.

Field, Frederick V. *American Participation in the China Consortiums*. Chicago: University of Chicago Press, 1931.

Fifield, Russell H. *Woodrow Wilson and the Far East: The Diplomacy of the Shantung Question*. New York: Crowell, 1952.

Fishel, Wesley R. *The End of Extraterritoriality in China*. Berkeley: University of California Press, 1952.

Fogel, Joshua, ed. and trans. *Life Along the South Manchurian Railway: The Memoirs of Itō Takeo*. Armonk, N.Y.: Sharpe, 1988.

Foreign Relations of the United States (annual). Washington, D.C.: Government Printing Office.

Fung, Edmund S. K. "Anti-Imperialism and the Left Guomindang," *Modern China* 11 (1985), pp. 39–76.

Garon, Sheldon. "Katō Takaaki," in Embree, ed., *Encyclopedia of Asian History*, 2:283.

George, Brian T. "The State Department and Sun Yat-sen: American Policy and the Revolutionary Disintegration of China, 1920–1924," *Pacific Historical Review* 46 (1977), pp. 387–408.

Gilbert, Rodney. *What's Wrong with China*. London: John Murray, 1926.

Gillin, Donald G., and Myers, Ramon H., eds. *Last Chance in Manchuria: The Diary of Chang Kia-ngau*. Stanford: Hoover Institution Press, 1989.

Goodnow, Frank J. *China: An Analysis*. Baltimore: Johns Hopkins University Press, 1926.

Granat, Stanley J. "Chinese Participation at the Washington Conference, 1921–1922." Ph.D. dissertation, Indiana University, 1969.

Grant, Natalie. "The Russian Section, a Window on the Soviet Union," *Diplomatic History* 2 (1978), pp. 107–15.

Hata, Ikuhiko, ed. *Senzenki Nihon Kanryōsei no seido, soshiki, jinji*. Tokyo: Tokyo University Press, 1981.

Heinrichs, Waldo. *American Ambassador: Joseph C. Grew and the Development of the United States Diplomatic Tradition*. Boston: Little, Brown, 1966.

———. "The Middle Years, 1900–1945, and the Question of a Large U.S. Policy for East Asia," in *New Frontiers in American-East Asian Relations*, pp. 77–106, ed. Warren I. Cohen. New York: Columbia University Press, 1983.

Holubnychy, Lydia. *Michael Borodin and the Chinese Revolution, 1923–1925*. New York: University Microfilms for East Asian Institute, Columbia University, 1979.

Hornbeck, Stanley K. *The Situation in China*. New York: China Society of America, 1927.

———. *The United States and the Far East: Certain Fundamentals of Policy*. Boston: World Peace Foundation, 1942.

Hosoya, Chihiro, "Britain and the United States in Japan's View of the International System, 1919–1937," in *Anglo-Japanese Alienation, 1919–1952*, pp. 3–26, ed. Ian Nish. Cambridge: Cambridge University Press, 1982.

Hoyt, Frederick B. "The Open Door Viewed as a Chinese Dynasty," *Australian Journal of Politics and History* 22 (1976), pp. 21–35.

Hu, Shih. "Kuo-chi-chung de Chung-kuo" [1922], in *Hu Shih Tso-p'in-chi*, 9:89–95. Taipei: Yüan-liu, 1986.

Huang, Chinliang Lawrence. "Japan's China Policy under Premier Tanaka, 1927–1929." Ph.D. dissertation, New York University, 1968.

Huang, T. Young. *The Doctrine of Rebus Sic Stantibus in International Law*, Foreword by V. K. Wellington Koo. Shanghai: Comacrib Press, 1935.

Hunt, Michael H. "Americans and the China Market: Economic Opportunities and Economic Nationalism, 1890–1931," *Business History Review* 51 (1977), pp. 276–307.

———. *The Making of a Special Relationship: The United States and China to 1914*. New York: Columbia University Press, 1983.

———. *Ideology and U.S. Foreign Policy*. New Haven: Yale University Press, 1987.

Hunter, Janet E., comp. *Concise Dictionary of Japanese History*. Berkeley: University of California Press, 1984.

Ikei, Masaru. "Dainiji Hōchoku sensō to Nihon," in *Tai-Manmō seisakushi no ichimen: Nichi-Ro sengo yori Taishōki ni itaru*, pp. 193–225, ed. Ken Kurihara. Tokyo: Hara Shobō, 1966.

———. "Ugaki Kazushige's View of China and His China Policy, 1915–1930," in *The Chinese and the Japanese*, pp. 199–219, ed. Akira Iriye. Princeton: Princeton University Press, 1980.

Iriye, Akira. *After Imperialism: The Search for a New Order in the Far East, 1921–1931*. Cambridge, Mass.: Harvard University Press, 1965.

———. *Across the Pacific: An Inner History of American–East Asian Relations*. New York: Harcourt Brace Jovanovich, 1967.

———. "The Failure of Military Expansionism," in *Dilemmas of Growth in Prewar Japan*, pp. 107–39, ed. James Morley. Princeton: Princeton University Press, 1971.

———. "The Failure of Economic Expansionism: 1918–1931," in *Japan in Crisis: Essays on Taishō Democracy*, pp. 237–69, ed. Bernard S. Silberman and H. D. Harootunian. Princeton: Princeton University Press, 1974.

Jacobs, Dan N. *Borodin: Stalin's Man in China*. Cambridge, Mass.: Harvard University Press, 1981.

Jansen, Marius B. *The Japanese and Sun Yat-sen*. Cambridge, Mass.: Harvard University Press, 1954.

The Japan Biographical Encyclopedia and Who's Who. Tokyo: Rengo Press, 1958.

Japan, Gaimushō, comp. *Nihon Gaikō Nempyō Narabini Shuyō Bunsho*. Tokyo: Nihon kokusai rengō kyōkai, 1955.

Japan, Gaimushō gaikō shiryōkan, comp. *Nihon gaikōshi jiten*. Tokyo: Okurashō, 1979.

Jeanneney, Jean-Nöel. "L'affaire de la Banque industrielle de la Chine (1921–1923)," *Revue Historique*, no. 514 (1975), pp. 377–416.

Jiang, Arnold Xiangze. *The United States and China*. Chicago: University of Chicago Press, 1988.

Jones, Francis Clifford. *Extraterritoriality in Japan and the Diplomatic Relations Resulting in Its Abolition, 1853–1895*. New Haven: Yale University Press, 1931.

Jordan, Donald A. *The Northern Expedition: China's Revolution of 1926–1928*. Honolulu: University Press of Hawaii, 1976.

Josephson, Harold. "Outlawing War: Internationalism and the Pact of Paris," *Diplomatic History* 3 (1979), pp. 377–90.

Kane, Harold Edwin. "Sir Miles Lampson at the Peking Legation, 1926–1933." Ph.D. dissertation, University of London, 1975.

Kartunova, A. I. *V. K. Bliukher v Kitae, 1924–1927 gg.: dokumentirovannye ocherk*. Moscow: "Nauka," 1970.

Kedourie, Elie. *Nationalism*, 2d ed. London: Hutchinson University Library, 1985.

Kennan, George F. *American Diplomacy, 1900–1950*. Chicago: University of Chicago Press, 1951.

———. *Memoirs, 1925–1950*. Boston: Little, Brown, 1972.

King, Wunsz. *China at the Washington Conference, 1921–1922*. New York: St. John's University Press, 1963.

Kirwin, Harry W. "The Federal Telegraph Company: A Testing of the Open Door," *Pacific Historical Review* 22 (1953), pp. 271–86.

Kitaoka, Shin'ichi. *Nihon rikugun to tairiku seisaku 1906–1918*. Tokyo: Gannandō, 1978.

———. "China Experts in the Army," in *The Japanese Informal Empire in China, 1895–1937*, ed. Duus, Myers, and Peattie, pp. 330–68.

Klein, Ira. "Whitehall, Washington, and the Anglo-Japanese Alliance, 1919–1921," *Pacific Historical Review* 41 (1972), pp. 460–83.

Koo, Wellington (Ku Wei-chün). *Memoirs*, microfilm of typescript available in rare books and manuscripts room, Columbia University Library.

Ku, Hung-Ting. "The U.S.A. versus China: The Nanking Incident in 1927," *Tunghai Journal* 25 (1984), pp. 95–110.

Ku Wei-chün, *Ku Wei-chün hui-yi-lu*. Pei-ching: Chung-hua shu-chü, 1983.

Kurihara, Ken, ed. *Tai-Manmō seisakushi no ichimen: Nichi-Ro sengo yori Taishōki ni itaru*. Tokyo: Hara Shobō, 1966.

Lattimore, Owen. *Manchuria, Cradle of Conflict*. New York: Macmillan, 1932.

Lau, Kit-Ching. "Sir John Jordan and the Affairs of China, 1906–1916, with Special Reference to the 1911 Revolution and Yüan Shih-k'ai." Ph.D. dissertation, University of London, 1968.

Lensen, George Alexander. *The Damned Inheritance: The Soviet Union and the Manchurian Crises, 1924–1935*. Tallahassee: Diplomatic Press, 1974.

Liu, Ta Jen. *A History of Sino-American Diplomatic Relations, 1840–1974*. Taipei: China Academy, 1978.

Louis, William Roger. *British Strategy in the Far East, 1919–1939*. Oxford: Clarendon Press, 1971.

Lovett, R. M. "Siamese Precedent for China: Extraterritoriality and Tariff Autonomy," *New Republic* 46 (March 31, 1926), pp. 167–69.

McCormack, Gavan. *Chang Tso-lin in Northeast China, 1911–1928*. Folkestone, Kent, Eng.: Dawson, 1972.

Mackenzie-Grieve, Averil. *A Race of Green Ginger*. London: Putnam, 1959.

MacMurray, John Van Antwerp. *Treaties and Agreements with and Concerning China* (2 vols.). New York: Carnegie Endowment, 1921.

MacNair, Harley Farnsworth. *China's New Nationalism and Other Essays*. Shanghai: Commercial Press, 1926.

———. *China in Revolution: An Analysis of Politics and Militarism under the Republic*. Chicago: University of Chicago Press, 1931.

May, Ernest R., and Thomson, James C., Jr., eds. *American–East Asian Relations: A Survey*. Cambridge, Mass.: Harvard University Press, 1972.

Mayer-Oakes, Thomas F. *Fragile Victory: Prince Saionji and the 1930 London Treaty Issue*. Detroit: Wayne State University Press, 1968.

Martin, John Patrick. "Politics of Delay: Belgium's Treaty Negotiations with China, 1926–1929." Ph.D. dissertation, St. John's University, 1980.

Megginson, William James, III. "Britain's Response to Chinese Nationalism, 1925–1927: The Foreign Office Search for a New Policy." Ph.D. dissertation, George Washington University, 1973.

Millard, Thomas. *The End of Extraterritoriality in China*. Shanghai: A.B.C. Press, 1931.

Milne, R. S. *Politics in Ethnically Bipolar States: Guyana, Malaysia, Fiji*. Vancouver: University of British Columbia Press, 1981.

Miwa, Kimitada, "Shidehara Kijūrō," in Embree, ed., *Encyclopedia of Asian History*, 3:439.

Morley, James, ed. *Dilemmas of Growth in Prewar Japan*. Princeton: Princeton University Press, 1971.

———, ed. *Japan's Foreign Policy, 1868–1941: A Research Guide*. New York: Columbia University Press, 1974.

———, ed. *Japan Erupts: The London Naval Conference and the Manchurian Incident, 1928–1932: Selected Translations from Taiheiyō sensō e no michi: kaisen gaikō shi*. New York: Columbia University Press, 1984.

Morse, Hosea Ballou, and MacNair, Harley Farnsworth. *Far Eastern International Relations*. Cambridge, Mass.: Houghton Mifflin, 1931.

Morton, William Fitch. *Tanaka Giichi and Japan's China Policy*. Folkestone, Eng.: Wm. Dawson & Sons, 1980.

Myers, Ramon H., and Peattie, Mark, eds. *The Japanese Colonial Experience, 1895–1945*. Princeton: Princeton University Press, 1984.

Nish, Ian H. *The Anglo-Japanese Alliance: The Diplomacy of Two Island Empires, 1894–1907*. Westport: Greenwood Press, 1966.

————. *Alliance in Decline: A Study in Anglo-Japanese Relations, 1908–1923*. London: University of London Press, 1972.

————. *Japanese Foreign Policy, 1869–1942*. London: Routledge and Kegan Paul, 1977.

————, ed. *Anglo-Japanese Alienation, 1919–1952*. Cambridge: Cambridge University Press, 1982.

Oblas, Peter B. "Treaty Revision and the Role of the American Foreign Affairs Adviser, 1909–1925," *Journal of the Siam Society* 60.1 (1972), pp. 171–86.

O'Connor, Raymond G. *Perilous Equilibrium: The United States and the London Disarmament Conference of 1930*. Lawrence: University of Kansas Press, 1962.

Ogata, Sadako. *Defiance in Manchuria: The Making of Japanese Foreign Policy, 1931–32*. Berkeley: University of California Press, 1964.

Oudendyk, William. *Ways and By-Ways in Diplomacy*. London: Peter Davies, 1939.

Pelcovits, Nathan A. *Old China Hands and the Foreign Office*. New York: King's Crown Press, 1948.

Pollard, Robert T. *China's Foreign Relations, 1917–1931*. New York: Macmillan, 1933.

Pong, David. "The Ministry of Foreign Affairs during the Republican Period, 1912–1920," in *The Times Survey of Foreign Ministries of the World*, pp. 135–53, ed. Zara Steiner. London: Times Books, 1982.

Pugach, Noel H. "Embarrassed Monarchist: Frank J. Goodnow and Constitutional Development in China, 1913–1915," *Pacific Historical Review* 42 (1973), pp. 499–517.

————. "American Friendship for China and the Shantung Question at the Washington Conference," *Journal of American History* 44 (1977), pp. 67–86.

————. "Anglo-American Aircraft Competition and the China Arms Embargo, 1919–1921," *Diplomatic History* 2 (1978), pp. 351–71.

————. *Paul S. Reinsch: Open Door Diplomat in Action*. Millwood, N.J.: KTO, 1979.

Quint, Howard H., and Ferrell, Robert H., eds. *The Talkative President: Calvin Coolidge*. Amherst: University of Massachusetts Press, 1964.

Reinsch, Paul S. *An American Diplomat in China*. New York: Doubleday, 1922.

Report of the Commission of Extraterritoriality in China. Washington, D.C.: Government Printing Office, 1926.

Rigby, Richard W. *The May 30 Movement: Events and Themes*. Canberra: Australian National University Press, 1980.

Rockhill, William Woodville. *Treaties and Conventions with or concerning China and Korea, 1894–1904, Together with Various State Papers and Documents Affecting Foreign Interests*. Washington, D.C.: Department of State, 1904.

Rosenberg, David A. "Philippines," in Embree, ed., *Encyclopedia of Asian History*, 3:246–51.

Sheridan, James E. *Chinese Warlord: The Career of Feng Yü-hsiang*. Stanford: Stanford University Press, 1966.

Silberman, Bernard S., and Harootunian, H. D., eds. *Japan in Crisis: Essays on Taishō Democracy*. Princeton: Princeton University Press, 1974.

Solecki, J. J., trans. "Blucher's 'Grand Plan' of 1926," *China Quarterly*, no. 35 (1968), pp. 18–39.

The Special Conference on the Chinese Customs Tariff. Peking: n.p., 1928.

Stephan, John J. "The Tanaka Memorial (1927): Authentic or Spurious?" *Modern Asia Studies* 7 (1973), pp. 733–45.

Starkey, Lois MacMurray. "J.V.A. MacMurray: Diplomat and Photographer in China, 1913–1929." M.A. thesis, Harvard University, 1990.

Starr, Daniel P. "Nelson Trusler Johnson: The United States and the Rise of Nationalist China, 1925–1937," Ph.D. dissertation, Rutgers University, 1967.

Takemoto, Toru. *Failure of Liberalism in Japan: Shidehara Kijuro's Encounter with Anti-Liberals*. Washington, D.C.: University Press of America, 1978.

The Tanaka Memorial: An Outline Presented to the Japanese Emperor on July 25, 1927 by Premier Tanaka for the Japanese Conquest of China and Other Nations, Also a Prediction of a Japanese-American War. San Francisco: Chinese National Salvation Publicity Bureau, 1937.

Taylor, A.J.P. *English History, 1914–1945*. Reading: Pelican Books, 1970.

Takeuchi, Tetsuji. *War and Diplomacy in the Japanese Empire*. New York: Doubleday, Doran, 1935.

Teters, Barbara. "Matsuoka Yōsuke: The Diplomacy of Bluff and Gesture," in Burns and Bennett, eds., *Diplomats in Crisis*, pp. 275–96.

Thomson, James C., Jr.; Stanley, Peter W.; and Perry, John Curtis. *Sentimental Imperialists: The American Experience in East Asia*. New York: Harper and Row, 1981.

Thorne, Christopher. *The Limits of Foreign Policy: The West, the League and the Far Eastern Crisis of 1931–33*. New York: Putnam's, 1972.

Trani, Eugene P. "Woodrow Wilson, China, and the Missionaries, 1913–1921," *Journal of Presbyterian History* 49 (1971), pp. 328–51.

Uchida Kōsai denki hensan iinkai, ed. *Uchida Kōsai*. Tokyo: Kajima Heiwa Kenkyūjo, 1969.

United States, Department of State, Conference Series: Joint Preparatory Committee on Philippine Affairs. *Report of May 20, 1938*. Washington, D.C.: Government Printing Office, 1938.

Usui, Katsumi. *Nitchō gaikō: hokubatsu no jidai*. Tokyo: Hanawa shinso, 1971.

———. *Nihon to Chūgoku: Taishō jidai*. Tokyo: Hara Shobō, 1972.

———. "The Role of the Foreign Ministry," in *Pearl Harbor as History*, pp. 127–48, ed. Dorothy Borg and Shumpei Okamoto. New York: Columbia University Press, 1973.

Van Meter, Robert H., Jr. "The Washington Conference of 1921–1922: A New Look," *Pacific Historical Review* 46 (1977), pp. 603–24.

Van Slyke, Lyman P., ed. *The China White Paper, August 1949*. Stanford, Calif.: Stanford University Press, 1967.

Vandervelde, Emile. *A travers la révolution Chinoise: Soviets et Kuomintang.* Paris: Alcan, 1931.

Varè, Daniele. *The Maker of Heavenly Trousers.* New York: Doubleday, Doran, 1936.

———. *Laughing Diplomat.* New York: Doubleday, Doran, 1938.

Varg, Paul A. *Open Door Diplomat: The Life of W. W. Rockhill.* Urbana: University of Illinois Press, 1952.

———. *Missionaries, Chinese, and Diplomats: The American Protestant Missionary Movement in China, 1890–1952.* Princeton: Princeton University Press, 1958.

Vinson, John Chalmers. *The Parchment Peace: The United States Senate and the Washington Conference, 1921–1922.* Athens: University of Georgia Press, 1955.

Wang, Cheng-t'ing. "Looking Back and Looking Forward." Unedited typescript memoir available in microform at the Rare Books and Manuscripts Library, Columbia University.

Warburg, Gabriel. "Lampson's Ultimatum to Faruq, 4 February, 1942," *Middle Eastern Studies* 11 (1975), pp. 24–32.

"What's the Matter with China?" *China Weekly Review* 29.1 (June 7, 1924), pp. 3–4.

Wilbur, C. Martin. *Sun Yat-sen: Frustrated Patriot.* New York: Columbia University Press, 1976.

———. *The Nationalist Revolution in China, 1923–1928.* Cambridge: Cambridge University Press, 1983.

———, and How, Julie Lien-ying. *Missionaries of Revolution: Soviet Advisers and Nationalist China, 1920–1927.* Cambridge, Mass.: Harvard University Press, 1989.

Williams, E. T., and Nicholls, C. S., eds. *Dictionary of National Biography, 1961–1970.* Oxford: Oxford University Press, 1981.

Wilson, David A. "Principles and Profits: Standard Oil Responds to Chinese Nationalism, 1925–1926," *Pacific Historical Review* 46 (1977), pp. 625–48.

Winkler, Max. *Foreign Bonds: An Autopsy. A Study of Defaults and Repudiations of Government Obligations.* Philadelphia: Swain, 1933.

Wood, Herbert J. "Nelson Trusler Johnson: The Diplomacy of Benevolent Pragmatism," in Burns and Bennett, eds., *Diplomats in Crisis,* pp. 7–26.

Woodhead, H.G.W., ed. *The China Yearbook* (annual). Peking and Tientsin: Tientsin Press.

———. *A Visit to Manchukuo.* Shanghai: Mercury Press, 1932.

Wright, Stanley F. *China's Struggle for Tariff Autonomy.* Shanghai: Kelley & Walsh, 1938.

Yoshizawa, Kenkichi. *Gaikō rokujū nen.* Tokyo: Jiyū Ajiasha, 1959.

Young, C. Walter. *The International Relations of Manchuria.* Chicago: University of Chicago Press, 1929.

———. *Japan's Jurisdiction and International Legal Position in Manchuria.* Vol. 1, *Japan's Special Position in Manchuria.* Baltimore: Johns Hopkins University Press, 1931.

———. *Japan's Jurisdiction and International Legal Position in Manchuria.* Vol. 2, *The*

International Legal Status of the Kwantung Leased Territory. Baltimore: Johns Hopkins University Press, 1931.

————. *Japan's Jurisdiction and International Legal Position in Manchuria*. Vol. 3, *Japanese Jurisdiction in the South Manchuria Railway Areas*. Baltimore: Johns Hopkins University Press, 1931.

Young, Ernest P. *The Presidency of Yuan Shih-k'ai: Liberalism and Dictatorship in Early Republican China*. Ann Arbor: University of Michigan Press, 1977.

Index

162 *Index*

Powers (*continued*)
from cooperation with Japan, 109*n*–10*n*;
reaction to Chinese nationalism, 93–94;
relationships with Chinese factions, 85–
87; response to Manchurian crisis, 30; response to Tientsin affair, 107; surprised by
Britain's China proposals, 89*n*
Pravda, on Sun Yat-sen's testament, 69*n*
"The Present Situation," 34
*The Presidency of Yüan Shih-k'ai: Liberalism
and Dictatorship in Early Republican China*
(Young), 13*n*
Propaganda: of Cantonese armies, 92–93;
impact of Communist, 83; impact on Japanese view of U.S., 130, 133
Psychology of countries. *See* Cultural
differences
Pugach, Noel H., 14*n*

Quezon, 60*n*
Quint, Howard H., 9*n*

A Race of Green Ginger (Mackenzie-Grieve),
47*n*
"Realist" school, 7–8
Realpolitik, 2–3
Rebus sic stantibus, 18
Reinsch, Paul S., 14
*Report of the Commission of Extraterritoriality in
China*, 112*n*
"Research in Sino-American Relations in
People's Republic of China" (Luo and
Jiang), 42*n*
Riga mission, 28
Rigby, Richard W., 71*n*
"Rights recovery" movement, 68–69
Rockhill, William Woodville, 10–11, 17
Roosevelt Administration, 30, 33
Roosevelt, Franklin D., 28, 39
Root-Takahira Agreement of 1908, 19
Rosenberg, David A., 60*n*
Russian Empire, 11
"The Russian Section, a Window on the So-
viet Union" (Grant), 28*n*

Saburi, Sadao, 18, 36, 61*n*, 78–79
Sawada, Setsuzō, 110*n*
Schwartz, Bruno, 49*n*
"Security clause," Nine-Power Treaty, 19–20

Shameen, 70–71
*Shanghai, 1925: Urban Nationalism and the De-
fense of Foreign Privilege* (Clifford), 71*n*
Shanghai: bloodshed at, 70–71; Japanese 1932
occupation of, 1. *See also* May 30th
Movement
Shantung intervention, 19, 105*n*
Shen Jui-lin, 73*n*
Shidehara, Kijūrō: belief in Washington sys-
tem by, 29, 61*n*; diplomatic career of,
79*n*–80*n*; foreign policy compared to Tan-
aka's, 102*n*–3*n*; 105*n*–6*n*; inaction over
Nanking and Hankow, 104*n*–5*n*; policy to
maintain Japanese interests, 18; use of in-
ternational law, 52–53
"Shidehara Kijūrō: The Diplomacy of the
Yen" (Brown), 81*n*
Shidehara Kijūrō (Miwa), 81*n*
Shih Chao-chi. *See* Sao-ke Alfred Sze
Shih-shih yüeh-pao, 106
Siam. *See* Thailand
Sian incident, 124*n*
Silberman, Bernard S., 51*n*
Silhouettes of Peking (de Martel and De
Hoyer), 13*n*
Sino-Belgian treaty of 1865, 8
Sino-Belgian treaty of 1926, 49
"Sir John Jordan and the Affairs of China,
1906–1916, with Special Reference to the
1911 Revolution and Yüan Shih-k'ai" (Kit-
Ching Lau), 14*n*
*Sir Miles Lampson at the Peking Legation,
1926–1933* (Kane), 12*n*, 88*n*
Solecki, J.J., 92*n*
Soong Ch'ing-ling, 69*n*
Soong, T.V., 47, 109*n*
Soviet Union: as China's savior, 69–70; fills
power vacuum left by Japan, 7; as influ-
ence on China, 59; interest in Chinese
Eastern Railway, 122; as threat to Japan,
30, 123*n*; as threat to U.S., 127, 129; U.S.
estranged from, 5
*The Special Conference on the Chinese Customs
Tariff*, 73*n*
Special Relationship (Hunt), 42*n*
Special Tariff Conference (1925), 36–37, 72–
78
Sprouse, Philip, 6
Starkey, Lois MacMurray, 9*n*

About the Editor

ARTHUR WALDRON is a specialist in the diplomatic, political, and military history of modern China. Educated at Harvard University, he taught history and East Asian studies at Princeton University for six years. At present he is a professor at the U.S. Naval War College in Newport, Rhode Island.